For the Children?

For the Children?

Protecting Innocence in a Carceral State

Erica R. Meiners

University of Minnesota Press
Minneapolis
London

Published by the University of Minnesota Press
111 Third Avenue South, Suite 290
Minneapolis, MN 55401-2520
http://www.upress.umn.edu

Printed in the United States of America on acid-free paper

The University of Minnesota is an equal-opportunity educator and employer.

21 20 19 18 17 16   10 9 8 7 6 5 4 3 2 1

Library of Congress Cataloging-in-Publication Data
Names: Meiners, Erica R., author.
Title: For the children? : protecting innocence in a carceral state / Erica R. Meiners.
Description: Minneapolis : University of Minnesota Press, 2016. | Includes bibliographical references and index.
Identifiers: LCCN 2015036896| ISBN 978-0-8166-9275-0 (hc) |
ISBN 978-0-8166-9276-7 (pb)
Subjects: LCSH: Children—Effect of imprisonment on—United States. | Youth—Effect of imprisonment on—United States.
Classification: LCC HV9104 .M43 2016 | DDC 365/.420973—dc23 LC record available at http://lccn.loc.gov/2015036896

Contents

Introduction

Facing what news outlets proclaimed one of the worst fiscal crises in the history of Illinois, in 2011 the governor, Pat Quinn, targeted a number of prisons for closure. On the list to be shuttered was Illinois Youth Center (IYC) in Murphysboro. With a capacity to confine 156 people, in 2011, Murphysboro warehoused 75 detainees at an annual cost of $84,403 each (Illinois Department of Corrections Facilities Information 2011). A small and scrappy network of Chicago-based justice organizations supported these prison closures through community forums, e-mail blasts, and poster campaigns: *Educate, Not Incarcerate! School Counselors, Not Cops! Books, Not Bars! Schools, Not Jails!*

We were not the only child savers. More than two hundred local residents, including prison employees and their families, many sporting T-shirts emblazoned with "Save IYC Murphysboro," packed a public hearing to testify about how prison closure would harm their community. "We can't balance the budget on the backs of working families," said State Representative Brandon Phelps (Norris 2011). The "Save IYC Murphysboro" Facebook site included photos from rallies featuring families and children holding signs that said "Take MY Mom and Dad's Job and Where Does that Leave Me?" Closing the prison harms families, and a community needs jobs. A majority white town in southern Illinois, this prison offered unionized employment for some of the approximately eight thousand residents of Murphysboro. Families in Murphysboro and beyond imagine a thriving economic future where their sons are on the right side of the prison bars (or perhaps their daughters marry a unionized prison guard). Why not?

Murphysboro's response to the eventual closure of its prison is not unique. The United States has the world's largest prison population: At the end of 2014 over two million people were locked behind bars and 6,851,000 people under some form of correctional supervision (Glaze, Kaeble, Minton, Tsoutis 2015) This prison nation, to use a term from activist

1

scholar Beth Richie (2012), disproportionately targets communities of color. While many use the term *mass incarceration* to refer to the grotesque expansion of punishment in the United States, I prefer "targeted criminalization." Black adults are four times as likely as whites and almost two and a half times as likely as Latinos/as to be under correctional control, and close to 70 percent of incarcerated women are nonwhite. A growing percentage of people in prison are migrants, overwhelmingly from Mexico (Escobar 2010; Lopez and Light 2009; Pew Center on the States 2009; Glaze, Kaeble, Minton, Tsoutis 2015). This incarcerated population required a corresponding prison construction boom, the world's largest. Between 1984 and 2007, California built forty-three new prisons, largely in rural communities, a global record (Gilmore 2007). Despite evidence that newly built prisons fail to provide a sustainable boon to local economies (J. Fraser 2003; Gilmore 2007; Gottschalk 2015), communities like Murphysboro across the United States continue to push for immigrant detention centers and to hamper decarceration and prison closures, citing economic concerns and the impact on local families.

This theme of saving our children refracts across the criminal justice landscape. As Ruth Wilson Gilmore writes in *Golden Gulag*, an analysis of prison expansion in California: "In fact, people who organize against prisons invoke the same beneficiaries ('the kids') as those who organize for prisons" (2007, 177). Jobs, protection, and better lives for our children are cited in arguments for new prisons or against closures, and these themes also surface repeatedly in antiprison messaging: "Educate, Not Incarcerate." Invoking real or imagined children produces an irreproachable purity, a trump card. Speaking against the future of any child is almost unthinkable—tactically impossible, an intimate violation, a dead end. While I recognize significant differences between a six-year-old and a fifteen-year-old, I deliberately use *child, youth, minor,* and *juvenile* somewhat interchangeably, as these are constructed and dynamic categories with no clear borders.

While references to child saving are laced throughout campaigns both to keep open and to close prisons, each side invokes different conceptions of childhood. In the push to shut down Murphysboro, one group fought to have the (nonwhite) young people warehoused within the prison recognized as children painfully separated from families. Those fighting to keep the prison open used their (white) children—present and future—as proxies for the town's economic and political future. Neither group names and problematizes the fragile boundaries among or between adult, child, and juvenile in this political moment, including who might be eligible for the benefits associated with childhood. Notably, the core artifact associated with childhood, an a priori association with innocence, is buried, unacknowledged. In these child-saving struggles—the demand that black and brown youth count as children or the need to provide economically for white babies—innocence is brazen but imperceptible, never on the table.

Also masked is the cascade of effects associated with representations of children and childhood. For example, demanding that police view select youth as more childlike, therefore deserving of leniency or differential treatment, does not interrupt why so many adults are culpable, are not viewed as valued and do not merit rehabilitation, and are therefore unfree. If only a select few—the children—merit care, access to resources, or a future, what of the rest of us? As an influx artifact invoked in political work across the carceral landscape, *the child* can get us all into trouble, including those bodies that qualify as children. While a strategic tool in these struggles, the child also masks key social and political transactions.

Not a new phenomenon, child saving emerges in multiple social, political, and economic struggles. As the geographer Cindi Katz (2008) writes: "Childhood, as has been well realized in the literature of virtually every social science and humanities discipline, is a social construction of multiple dimensions—as a spatial life stage, as itself internally segregated, as a reservoir of memory and fantasy, and as always mobile—"becoming" defines its limits. As such, childhood and youth have proven to be readily available for mobilization around moral panics and the definition of social ills" (7). For the sake of the child, women (particularly poor, disabled, and/or nonwhite women) have been sterilized and continue to be denied reproductive and parenting rights (Garland-Thomson 2002; Silliman and Bhattacharjee 2002; Roberts 1997). Child welfare facilitated the development and implementation of judicial and criminal institutions and systems (Feld 1999), the expansion of policing and surveillance, and the restriction of First Amendment and privacy rights (E. Bernstein 2010). The need to protect girls has emerged as a powerful rationale to deny transgender and non-gender-conforming people gender-affirming bathroom access, particularly in schools (Steinmetz 2015). Child protection was also versatile enough to be invoked in campaigns to legalize and to challenge gay marriage (McCreery 2008).

In these struggles childhood, children, and the child operate as multiple and often intersecting (or as the literary theorist Kathryn Stockton writes, "braided") domains (2009). Childhood is understood as a biological and life-cycle development stage, an informal social class or grouping, a literary trope, a historic invention, and even a bona fide social science category. Perhaps most familiar is the development stage of childhood scaffolded and reinforced by contemporary research in psychology and neurology. Childhood, after infancy and before adolescence, is a popularly recognized and naturalized stage in the life cycle. Fewer people perhaps understand that childhood is a recent creation; Philippe Ariès (1962) argues that childhood emerged through social, economic, and political shifts over the previous three centuries. The child and childhood also function as malleable tropes, or the "child-as-idea," as Stockton writes (2009, 3), to represent a range of potentially contradictory ideas, including reproductive futures, purity, revolutionary potential, incompetence, incapacity, becoming, and also innocence.

Forefronting children —imagined and not—shields from view other transactions. While slogans such as "Education, not incarceration" aim to illustrate how many black or brown young people across the United States are denied the resources and privileges attached to childhood, this statement is also a claim, however diffuse, to claim access to innocence. The rallies to keep Murphysboro Prison open featured hard-working families—the children of prison employees held signs reading "Save Our Prison / Save Our Families." Yet masked are the kinship networks (overwhelmingly nonwhite) who are devastated by this prison. In these struggles we see families, particularly vulnerable children, not claims for or against racialized forms of innocence. The historian Robin Bernstein (2011) describes the "perfect alibi" of *the child*, or its ability to "retain racial meanings but hide them under claims of holy obliviousness" (8).

Conflicts over access to childhood and its attendant privileges are an old story in the United States. Within struggles against white supremacy and colonialism, images and associations with childhood have a particularly complex and flexible history. Take, for example, the figure of the child within movements to abolish and to defend chattel slavery. The historian Holly Brewer argues that the most popular argument in defense of the institution of slavery within a democratic republic in the early nineteenth century was that "blacks were children in terms of their inability to reason" (2005, 358). Yet, while enslaved black people were classified as childlike and in need of masters, attempting to associate enslaved people with children could also potentially make their vulnerability, particularly their pain and suffering, matter. Robin Bernstein (2011) outlines how a strand of white nineteenth-century abolitionism attempted to frame African Americans as childlike not to justify slavery but to secure "an increased appeal to pity and generosity" (25). As a future-oriented categorization, the figure of the child also held revolutionary potential—a child could become an adult, fully capable of consent and therefore self-governance. In revolutionary moments, the child could also represent, as the literary scholar Anna Mae Duane (2010) argues, "not an inevitable plea for pity, but an inalienable claim to liberty" (128).

Deployed simultaneously, these contradictory associations with childhood shored up diverse political ends. Anna Mae Duane (2010) and other historians document that white and nonwhite abolitionists and slave owners understood the malleable and often contradictory uses of these child associations. Thomas Jefferson rejected slavery "on the grounds that people were created equal and the necessity of consent," and yet "he began to compare enslaved adults to children in their reasoning abilities" (Brewer 2005, 355), therefore justifying slavery because enslaved people were "incapable as children of caring for themselves" (356). By invoking diminished capacity and associations with childhood, Brewer argues, Jefferson created new forms of white supremacy for emerging democratic forms of association and governance (356).

Our present moment continues this history. African American, Latino, and other nonwhite bodies continue to be denied access to childhood even as these communities are designated by laws and policies (that purport to be race- and gender-neutral) as not fully competent, not capable of self-governance or self-determination: childlike. These persistent associations with the child, a powerful and flexible artifact within our current carceral regime, are not arbitrary. "Skewed life chances, limited access to health and education, premature death, incarceration and impoverishment," are, as the historian Saidiya Hartman (2007) notes, part of the "afterlife of slavery"(6). The child became emblematic of modernity and chattel slavery through an inability to consent or to possess reason, and these same core relations of domination—who counts as fully human—echo throughout our prison nation.

Today everyone still wants to save the child. And, yes, of course, children matter. .Youth experience violence. Minors perpetuate harm. Juveniles are vulnerable. Children are dependent. Yet this status of precarity often translates into forms of protectionism enforced through criminalization that not only erase young people's agency, but this punitive matrix advanced to ensure safety, captures and harms many youth: *Truant, delinquent, incorrigible, runaway, promiscuous.* Meanings attached to childhood, and the institutions built to monitor and punish youth, impact everyone. It is never precisely clear who counts as a child or a youth, why benefits are attached to some childhoods and denied to others, and what the collateral consequences are when individuals and communities demand differential treatment either for or because of the children. Even when communities challenge the criminalization of young people, particularly young folks of color, a focus on the child reinforces key carceral logics. As Kathryn Stockton asks, "How does innocence, our default designation for children, cause its own violence?" (2009, 5). While child protection is invoked in organizing across the political spectrum, unacknowledged in these strategies are the meanings and associations embedded within, and consequently coproduced by, the child.

This book argues that the child is a critical artifact to understand in the struggle to dismantle our prison nation. The child—along with all institutions involved in shaping this figure, including schools, families, and juvenile justice systems—is a key technology of a shifting carceral regime. New forms of surveillance are invented to safeguard children, and new categories of crime are required to mold the child into an appropriate adult (or to indefinitely mark her as inalienable and less than fully human). This is an old story. Childhood has historically never been available to all. Yet the work to challenge or reform this carceral apparatus all too often naturalizes and invokes the very artifacts and technologies—in the form of the child—that reproduce and expand core carceral logics. As the United States begins to engage in rethinking facets of our prison nation, the child represents a significant and intimate thread, one that antiprison organizers, educational justice activists, and prison studies scholars must examine.

After "Educate, Not Incarcerate"

Movements against what has been called the school to prison pipeline (STPP) epitomize the complexities of organizing around the child within in our carceral state. A central facet of the carceral state, the public education system in the United States, has historically tracked nonwhite communities toward school push-out, non-living-wage work, participation in a permanent war economy, and/or incarceration (Anderson 1988; Lipman 2003; Oakes 1988; Sojoyner 2013; Vaught 2011; Watkins 2001). The development of the world's largest prison nation within the United States over the past three decades has strengthened policy and practice, forging new linkages between schools and prisons. Urban school districts employ some of the nation's largest police forces and place onsite police detachments in schools that lock down buildings for drug and weapons sweeps, naturalizing a seamless and interlocking relationship between public schools and juvenile justice.

In 2010, arrests of juveniles under eighteen years of age on Chicago public school property reached 5,574. Black youth accounted for 74 percent of school-based juvenile arrests in 2010; Latino youth represented 22.5 percent of arrests (Kaba and Edwards 2012). Removing students from an educational setting—the most dramatic educational sanction available—starts in preschool. A 2005 survey of forty states' prekindergarten programs found that boys were expelled at a rate more than 4.5 times that of girls. African Americans attending state-funded prekindergarten were about twice as likely to be expelled as Latino and Caucasian children and over five times as likely to be expelled as Asian American children (Gilliam 2005, 3). Students of color who are disabled have some of the highest rates of expulsion and suspension.

With police enmeshed in urban high-poverty schools, punishments for students of color often translate into a punch card on the train to prison. Once students are removed from school and marked by law enforcement agencies and school disciplinary personnel as disruptive, often for nonviolent behavior coded as disrespectful, their relationships to learning and schools are further corroded. Pushed out from schools that rarely reflected their life experiences, these young folks enter a well-worn track: no diploma, a shortage of jobs, hyperracialized and heterogendered police surveillance, nonlegal employment, and potential incarceration. Highlighting these relations that naturalize the movement of youth of color from our schools and communities into under- or unemployment and permanent detention, movements against the school to prison pipeline surged over the fifteen years (Advancement Project 2010; Duncan 2000; Browne 2003; Meiners 2007; Petteruti, Walsh, and Velázquez 2009; Simmons 2009; Schaffner 2006; Winn 2010; Laura 2014).

Interrupting this schoolhouse-to-jailhouse track is on the agenda of community groups across the United States. Youth-led projects including Chicago's Blocks Together, teacher-facilitated journals such as *Rethinking Schools,* and national grassroots conferences such as Education for Liberation's Free Minds Free People Conference have all provided leadership, analysis, and movement building around challenging discriminatory educational discipline policies at the local and state levels that track youth to prisons. High-profile meetings and institutes continue to be convened by community-based groups, networks, and institutions around the intersections of education, juvenile justice, and racialized systems of policing and imprisonment. Frequently called "Schools, Not Jails" or "Educate, Not Incarcerate," campaigns aim to push back against school policies and practices that suspend and expel black and brown students and against the economic strategy of allocating resources toward incarceration and not into education. Frequently initiated by young people, campaigns highlight how black and brown male youth are viewed as criminals, sanctioned as adults, and targeted for excessive and prison-like school disciplinary practices that function as pathways toward prison.

This research and organizing continues to identify significant and persistent racial inequities in school-based disciplinary sanctions, generally described as "disproportionate minority contact." In early 2014, the Obama administration issued a thirty-five-page report urging schools to use law enforcement as a "last resort" in school discipline. These federal nonbinding guidelines—a "Dear Colleague" letter outlining the problem, guiding principles for action steps, and a directory of federal resources—aimed to reduce the number of young men of color caught up in the criminal justice system through school-based interventions (Rich 2014). With no resources provided to train or hire needed personnel to implement viable alternatives to punitive school discipline policies, including counseling for students and restorative justice practices, or even to support transparent data collection to monitor racial disproportionality, this federal intervention is an unfunded mandate. And with a pressing silence around gender and sexuality, these guidelines reproduce persistent institutional ignorance around the experiences of young women and/or queer young people.[1] Queer youth are more likely than their straight peers to be punished by courts and schools, even though they are less likely to engage in serious acts of harm or crime, and "consensual same-sex acts more often trigger punishments than equivalent opposite sex behaviors" (Himmelstein and Bruckner 2011, 50).[2] Research clearly illustrates that nonwhite girls, specifically black girls, also experience disproportionately high rates of school disciplinary sanctions (Crenshaw 2015; Wun 2016). The 2014 federal intervention, in addition to being an inadequate diagnosis of the problem, reproduces the erasure of girls and/or queers from the equation: their harm does not register.

While the school to prison pipeline and the schoolhouse-to-jailhouse track are popular frameworks and have placed the question of the criminalization of U.S. youth in public schools on a global stage, these pipeline and railway images and metaphors increasingly obscure the wider and deeper analysis needed to build sustainable, dynamic, and stronger movements to end our nation's commitment to policing and punishment. The metaphor of the school to prison pipeline erases the historic and ongoing criminalization of many communities, suggests that the solution is more education or better discipline policies, and overwhelmingly misses the intertwined centrality of capitalism, heteropatriarchy, colonialism, ableism, and white supremacy to the work of public education.

The criminalization of select youth in schools is also tethered to the ongoing function of public education as a form of incapacitation or enclosure. I draw upon Damien Sojoyner's interpretation of the scholarship of Black Studies scholar Clyde Woods in his critique of the STPP framework:

> Enacted through various strategies such as forced removal, benign neglect, abandonment, and incapacitation, the goal of enclosures is to blur the social vision of Black communities. That is, rather than a school to prison pipeline, the structure of public education is just as and maybe even more so culpable in the enclosure of Black freedom, which in turn has informed the development of prisons. (Sojoyner 2013, 242)

Civil society necessitates mechanisms to restrict black freedom, particularly through public education. As Sojoyner's (2010) research illustrates, after de jure segregation was dismantled, cities such as Los Angeles used schools to explicitly enclose black (and brown) youth through the establishment of school-based police officers, the implementation of classes such as civics and government designed to rationalize a racialized "law and order" governance, and the focused eradication of any autonomous black spaces within schools.

One early component of the "schools, not jails" movement was a staunchly youth-led critique of the status quo of schooling—including calling out the persistence of test-driven, nonrelevant, racist curriculum and a sharp analysis of the limited public education available to urban youth (Acey 2000). This early movement is part of a long and ongoing history of mobilizations to demand and create quality and relevant public education for urban communities. Yet subsequent "education, not incarceration" interventions and analysis increasingly posited schooling as the antidote to carceral expansion. Narrowing the problem to bad schools or flawed policies—the responses offered by STPP research and organizing—often recirculates a liberal faith that, again, somehow fixing just the bad parts of schools or reforming a few bad policies will save children. As Sojoyner writes about most contemporary organizing against the STPP that centers on a demand for policy reform, "policy-based strategies have produced a set of conditions that reinforce anti-Black racism and simultaneously function to discipline Black movements for liberation" (2013, 242). A focus on unjust policies—such as school discipline—obscures and potentially reinforces the wider, and yet always contested, heteronormative racialized project of public education.

Struggles against the STPP also position schools and young people as outside of, and disconnected from, a wider carceral state. The 2014 federal disciplinary recommendations to end the school to prison pipeline were released as I was coteaching a college course on social movements for people locked inside Stateville Prison. A maximum-security prison about forty-five minutes from downtown Chicago, Stateville cages people the Illinois Department of Corrections considers among the "worst of the worst." For the approximately three and a half thousand people warehoused across Stateville Correctional Center, and serving very long sentences, not much happens. In 1955, the warden of Stateville stated, "Ninety-five per cent of all the men committed here are released some day" (Manly and Wright 1955). Today, many people in maximum-security prisons such as Stateville will die serving extraordinarily long prison terms. There are few GED and adult basic education classes offered, and many wait years to be admitted to these classes which students report as mainly consisting of worksheets. Long sentences often justify the prison's or the Department of Corrections' decision to not allocate any resources for people who will be "locked away for life." As we build a creative and rich college-level curriculum (currently with no credit) with related arts programs and recruit faculty to teach for no pay, the irony is inescapable. Almost free college courses for classes composed of 100 percent poor people of color taught by faculty from some of the whitest and most restrictive universities in the region in terms of their enrollment policies? Only at your local maximum-security prison!

Outside prison, these universities (and often associated faculty) have little interest in people who cannot pay tuition or meet their entrance requirements. The classes we offer at Stateville—Introduction to Marx, Social Movements—are also the kinds of college-level courses that are increasingly unavailable at public community colleges or four-year state universities, where the majority of poor people matriculate. As Chicago's community college offerings are increasingly dominated by job development programs, technical training certificates, and developmental (remedial) courses, the number of classes in the arts, humanities, and natural sciences contracts. A bitter pill: a prison is where poor people, particularly those who are black and brown, can access, for example, a course by a leading artist on digital animation.

In the midst of a discussion in my course about the limitations of the aforementioned K–12 disciplinary recommendations by the Obama administration that aimed to curb the flow of young people to prison, a student, Mr. Luna, asked, "Why is everything for the children?" He gestured around the room, to amplify his comment that none of the current educational, criminal, or immigration reforms would benefit the people there. He summarized a recent court decision to reevaluate those who received sentences of life without parole as juveniles and the federal government's current push to not deport youth who are living in the United States without legal immigration papers.[3] Mr. Luna's observation ricocheted around the room. None of us in the room disliked kids; in fact, many were parents. But the power of the child in current political reform movements was unmistakable and painful. Unsympathetic to policy makers, therefore undeserving of freedom or even full humanity, these students understood themselves to be left behind.

As understandings of the STPP gain traction and frame interventions, including changes in select educational policies and institutional discourses, movement assessment and reevaluation are required. How do discourses about the STPP help or hinder movements to end our nation's reliance on prisons and policing? How does the tactic of forefronting children harmed by forms of state violence assist in the work to achieve freedom for all? How are the ideologies central to policing and incarceration—white supremacy, heteropatriarchy, capitalism—displaced, masked, or made visible in institutional responses to the STPP? If movements against the STPP rely on conceptions of childhood that center innocence, does this enhance the vulnerability of all youth to negotiate sexuality? How do grassroots movements against the STPP dismantle or reinforce the crucial role of public schools to manage populations understood as superfluous to civil society yet integral to our expanding service economy and our prisons? How could a movement to end the STPP not include people like those inside Stateville Prison or those exiting prisons and jails who try to access quality public education in local universities, community colleges, and in high schools? People at Stateville Prison are not simply the end product of the STPP but instrumental to dismantling the punishing relationship between education and incarceration. While it might be child's play to name and protest linkages between schools and prisons, less visible and yet potentially more dangerous are the punishing and capricious conceptions of innocence and consent, embedded within and masked by the idea of the child, that naturalize jails and unfreedom, not learning or liberation, for too many.

"Ending Mass Incarceration?" / Abolition Futures

As this book goes to press, prison reform movements, particularly those that center on children or aim to protect childhood, such as the work against the school to prison pipeline, have moved into the mainstream. A wide array of political actors are unevenly but visibly organizing to support prison closure across the United States, to reform drug laws, to implement alternatives to incarceration (for some), and to raise the question why so many are locked up. In August 2013, then U.S. attorney general Eric Holder challenged federal sentencing guidelines for drug-related convictions (Savage 2013). Former president Bill Clinton, who ushered in the largest crime bill in U.S. history—the punitive 1994 Violent Crime Control and Law Enforcement Act, which funneled tax dollars to police and prisons—declared in 2014, "We just sent everybody to jail for too long" (Hunt 2014). Even earlier to the prison reform game, in 2011, Republican stalwart Newt Gingrich began to advocate for prison closure and criminal justice reform with the national organization Right on Crime: "The conservative case for reform: fighting crime, prioritizing victims, and protecting taxpayers." Other Republican and anti–big government actors are also speaking out in favor of the elimination of punitive mandatory minimum sentences, decarceration—or letting people out of prison—and moratoriums on the construction of new prisons (Gingrich and Nolan 2011). Right on Crime has been at the forefront of advocating for sentencing reforms, arguing against prison expansion, and supporting prison closures across the United States. Hardly a fringe organization, Right on Crime has made inroads in over two dozen states (and counting).

Carceral shifts are evident. In the past five years, many states have attempted, sometimes successfully, to decrease prison-related expenses through the expansion of parole, the implementation of early release programs, and prison depopulation, sometimes through prison closure. At end of 2014, as reported by the Bureau of Justice Statistics, the nation's population under correctional supervision continued to decline slightly: "About 1 in 36 adults (or 2.8% of adults in the United States) was under some form of correctional supervision at yearend 2014, the lowest rate since 1996" (Glaze, Kaeble, Minton, Tsoutis 2015, 1). A 2012 report by the Sentencing Project, *On the Chopping Block 2012: State Prison Closings*, highlights the cost-saving measures associated with prison closure: "In 2012, at least six states have closed 20 prison institutions or are contemplating doing so, potentially reducing prison capacity by over 14,100 beds and resulting in an estimated $337 million in savings. During 2012, Florida led the nation in prison closings with its closure of 10 correctional facilities; the state's estimated cost savings for prison closings totals [sic] over $65 million. This year's prison closures build on closures observed in 2011 when at least 13 states reported prison closures and reduced prison capacity by an estimated 15,500 beds" (Porter 2012, 1). These states are grappling with decarceration strategies, not because of an ethical recognition of the continuing harm of prisons, but rather because prisons and punishment consume budgets. Reforming the policies and laws that scaffold incarceration invariably avoids a rigorous and transparent analysis of the key investments that naturalized the buildup of the U.S. prison nation: white supremacy, colonialism, capitalism, and heteropatriarchy (Alexander 2010; Davis 2003; Gilmore 2007; K. Muhammad 2010; N. Smith and Stanley 2011).

Policies, laws, and associated rhetoric built our carceral state, including the "tough on crime" and "War on Drugs" frameworks typically associated with conservative policy makers. Administrative and procedural reforms advanced by liberals, particularly those that sought in part to reduce racial bias in policing and imprisonment, also contributed to the expansion of our carceral state, as scholar Naomi Murakawa outlines in *The First Civil Right: How Liberals Built Prison America* (2015). In the 1980s sentencing guidelines—one of the policies responsible for our bloated prison population—were pushed by a range of liberal policy makers, such as then Senator Edward Kennedy, supposedly to remove bias from the sentencing process. Our current moment of prison reform that focuses on the "non, non, nons" or the nonviolent, nonserious, and nonsexual offenders (Gottschalk 2015), and policing reform that seeks to further professionalize policing through the recruitment, training, or monitoring of officers, as Murakawa argues, is another opportunity for liberals to augment, rather than shrink, the racialized carceral state.

Many criminal justice reform campaigns over the past few decades have revolved around improving the lives of juveniles. Organizations have successfully argued that juveniles possess a unique status and, in some contexts, merit differential treatment from adults, including shorter sentences, better prison conditions, and exemption from the death penalty. To a limited degree, some of these reforms have also been extended to those who benefit from association with children: some women (particularly mothers), people with disabilities, and so on. These campaigns have achieved some protection and freedom for a number of people. This cannot be understated. Yet, arguing that children and juveniles are developmentally unique and merit differential treatment from adults fails to analyze who counts as a child or a juvenile in this political moment. Nor do these campaigns excavate the collateral consequences of this tactic, or that arguing for children's innocence seems to require that adults are developmentally static and therefore culpable. Also unaddressed is a key tension that arguing to be legally recognized as a child (and therefore potentially engendering protection) is also simultaneously a claim for legal incompetency. Despite these significant questions, as many across the United States rethink investments in the prison nation, children and juveniles continue to function as a particularly powerful weapon to advance limited criminal justice reform.

Of course, these political shifts toward criminal justice reform are neither universal nor uniform. While the 2008 recession created a willingness on the part of some budget-conscious state officials to reconsider facets of incarceration, not everyone is on board, including some labor unions, law enforcement agencies, and groups that identify themselves as representing victims' rights. Efforts to cut costs through criminal justice reform have inspired a range of reactions, including a backlash, summarized in the headline of a *New York Times* article by Monica Davey (2010): "Safety Is Issue as Budget Cuts Free Prisoners." According to Davey, in response to a proposed 2010 early release initiative in Oregon, "an anticrime group aired radio advertisements portraying the outcomes in alarming tones. 'A woman's asleep in her own apartment,' a narrator said. 'Suddenly, she's attacked by a registered sex offender and convicted burglar'" (2). Faced with criticism from police officers and labor unions and from "pro-prison" or "pro-policing" advocacy groups, politicians and state officials even moderately supportive of early release programs often become unwilling to be perceived as soft on crime or emotionally out of tune with victims' rights and can backpedal. As previously outlined, prisons are understood by surrounding communities to be economic engines. Politicians are reluctant to trade away the benefits affiliated with the patrician tough on crime stance, and communities, even those who experience high levels of violence by police, have been well schooled to understand public safety and to feel safe through the presence of police, prisons, and borders.

Child protection consistently emerges in the backlash to attempts to repeal or reform many criminal laws. Sex offender registries and community notification laws, public policies that have had no efficacy in reducing child sexual violence, persist and expand even in these moments of uneven but bipartisan commitments toward widespread criminal justice reform. In 2014, New York governor Andrew Cuomo's plan to offer a few incarcerated people access to degree-granting programs was rescinded because, as many critics highlighted, their own children were denied free education programs (Fay 2014). The statistically rare possibility of violent harm to children from strangers justifies and naturalizes a complex of surveillance apparatuses, including criminal background checks for an increasing number of workers and twenty-four-hour cameras in public places. Safeguarding select children from potential harm advances and legitimates expanded punishment and more intrusive forms of surveillance even in this moment of seemingly bipartisan commitment to rethinking our nation's addiction to incarceration.

Our public investments in punishment not only locked people up and built prisons and police forces, but diverted tax dollars from communities, particularly communities of color, and reshaped structures and systems seemingly unrelated to prisons. Organizers and academics popularized the term *prison-industrial complex* to refer to the creation of prisons and detention centers as a perceived growth sector in the economy during an era of deindustrialization and, as Angela Davis (2003) writes, "a set of symbiotic relationships among correctional communities, transnational corporations, media conglomerates, guards' unions and legislative and court agendas" (107). These interlocking economic and political relationships create social norms that require and legitimate prison and policing expansion and subsequently naturalize punishment and isolation as inevitable. I use the term *carceral state* somewhat interchangeably with prison-industrial complex to highlight the multiple and intersecting state agencies and institutions (including not-for-profit organizations) that have punishing functions and effectively police poor communities beyond the physical site of the prison: child and family services, welfare/workfare agencies, public education, immigration, health and human services agencies, and more (Beckett and Murakawa 2012; Gustafson 2011; Roberts 1997; Wacquant 2009).

Our carceral state has created "million-dollar blocks" (Gonnerman 2004), or neighborhoods with so many people locked up that the total cost of their incarceration exceeds $1 million. Research conducted in 2013 by Chicago's David Olsen and the *Chicago Reporter* determined that a disproportionate number of people in Illinois state prisons originate from Chicago's west side Austin neighborhood—a community that is almost 100 percent African American. Each person locked behind bars costs the state money, and just one block in the Austin neighborhood alone—Adams and Cicero—"is costing an estimated $4 million" annually (Caputo 2013, 12). The total price tag to lock up people from the neighborhood of Austin from 2000 to 2011 came to $644 million (12). These tax dollars were not available to support housing, health care, or education and instead built up the prison nation. Nationally, as Marie Gottschalk (2015) summarizes in *Caught: The Prison State and the Lockdown of American Politics*, the United States "spends over $100 billion on police and over $50 billion on the judiciary" and "one in eight state employees works in corrections" (32).

While nascent, these criminal justice reforms prompt some to herald the end of the prison nation. Natasha Frost, associate dean at Northeastern University's School of Criminology and Criminal Justice, stated, "This is the beginning of the end of mass incarceration" (Goode 2013, para. 3). A 2014 editorial in the *New York Times* proclaimed: "The American experiment in mass incarceration has been a moral, legal, social, and economic disaster. It cannot end soon enough" ("End Mass Incarceration Now" 2014). In April 2015, Hillary Clinton, then a newly minted Democratic presidential candidate, called for a national dialogue on public safety, stating, "It's time to end the era of mass incarceration" (Bump 2015). Antiprison activists have shouted these messages for decades. As Zundre Johnson stated in 2006 while locked inside a Californian prison, "We should not keep expanding the prisons when the current model is a failed venture" (as cited in Braz 2006, 88).

Some prison depopulation or potential closure is possible because other mechanisms are available to confine people. The population under formal state supervision is almost triple the number of people who are locked behind bars. (Glaze, Kaeble, Minton, Tsoutis 2015). Biometrics and electronic surveillance are increasingly deployed for surveillance and coercion. Since 2011 North Carolina has tripled its use of electronic monitors. In 2014 California placed seventy-five hundred people on GPS ankle bracelets as part of the state's "realignment" plan, theoretically aimed at reducing prison populations. Almost concurrently, in July 2014, SuperCom, an Israeli-based electronic monitor producer, announced a move into the U.S. market, estimating the development of a $6 billion a year global industry by 2018 (Kilgore 2014). Not only are new technologies and forms of surveillance available to confine bodies more cheaply (and to conscript the family, often mothers and sisters, into the role of guard or police), but a web of other state and state-like agencies and institutions police and regulate. Across the United States, those who seek food stamps are often subject to mandatory and/or random drug testing; postsecondary educational applicants looking for federal or state financial aid are required to disclose histories of arrests or convictions; and migrants face

Immigration and Customs Enforcement, the largest enforcement agency in the United States. Rethinking our prison nation is potentially palatable to mainstream audiences as other mechanisms emerge to enclose, monitor, and punish targeted communities.

Notably, many bipartisan prison reforms are motivated by the desire to curb spending. In New York, the 2009 Rockefeller drug reforms supported alternatives to incarceration and drug treatment programs in part because of the economics: an "overall net benefit of $5,144 per judicial diversion participant" (Waller et al. 2013, 48). States do not grapple with decarceration strategies and explore alternatives because of an ethical recognition of the continuing harm of prisons or an understanding of the intertwined histories of capitalism, white supremacy, and punishment in the United States, but rather because coffers are empty, and prisons and punishment consume ever-growing portions of shrinking revenues.

While still dismissed as utopic, outrageous, and even unthinkable by many, Angela Davis's question "Are prisons obsolete?" (the title of her 2003 book) is more timely that ever. Rather than tinkering around the edges of systems and institutions never designed to support people's liberation, why not invest in the question: Are prisons obsolete? Abolition—once the terrain of the so-called radical fringe—appears not only legitimate but, in some locations, imperative. The website of Critical Resistance, a national organization, defines PIC abolition as "a political vision with the goal of eliminating imprisonment, policing, and surveillance and creating lasting alternatives to punishment and imprisonment." "Both a practical organizing tool and a long-term goal," as Critical Resistance outlines, abolition recognizes that prisons are a plank in the "afterlife of slavery" (Hartman 2007, 6).

In a nation predicated on the humiliation and exclusion of too many, freedom is not simply the absence of laws that disenfranchise and dehumanize. The use of the term *abolition* by contemporary antiprison organizers is intentional. Angela Davis writes, "I choose the word 'abolitionist' deliberately. The 13th Amendment, when it abolished slavery, did so except for convicts. Through the prison system, the vestiges of slavery have persisted. It thus makes sense to use a word that has this historical resonance" (1996, 26). *Are Prisons Obsolete?* invites readers to consider the obsolescence of prison, but Davis also asks what else must be dismantled or transformed to reduce violence, support sustainable communities, and build forms of real public safety. What makes prisons and policing appear logical, necessary, and possible? Abolition involves the potentially more challenging work to build up networks, sites, and languages that facilitate self-determination and liberation. This necessitates moving away from the site of the prison to critically engage conceptions such as safety and justice, as well as the wider frames and artifacts that serve as their condition of possibility, including childhood and innocence.

Movement

Moments of transition are opportunities to anticipate and to resist new forms of capture. As select criminal laws and institutions are reformed, particularly those affecting young people, movement assessment is imperative. Historically, reforms that purported to improve the well-being of those caught in the criminal justice system often functioned to expand systems of control and punishment. As a few prisons close, as the discourse against the school to prison pipeline gains traction and galvanizes change, these reforms require scrutiny. As one infrastructure or institution breaks down, other structures—legal, medical, or educational—often take up the ideological work of dehumanization and disqualification.

As the contexts that produce and naturalize violence and inequities are dynamic, ongoing movement assessment keeps eyes on the prize. Movement assessment collectively asks: Where is the struggle to end our nation's overreliance on policing, occupation, punishment, detention, and borders? Where is an analysis of the core heteropatriarchal, racialized, capitalist regime that naturalizes our punishment economy? Responding requires deep engagement with the everyday work of site- or people-specific campaigns, as well as knowledge of the grinding daily work of survival within our prison nation. Responding also involves the ability to map local struggles against wider global changes in capital, state formation, and power. Responding also requires challenging boundaries between liberation struggles. Yet all responses are incomplete. Movement assessment is always partial and unfolding, limited and flawed.

Movements, like communities, are dynamic, and as Audre Lorde wrote in 1984, neither is monolithic or focused on single issues. *LGBTQ justice work is the struggle against police brutality. The work to end our nation's reliance on prisons is the work to dismantle white supremacy. Decolonization is gender and sexual self-determination. Fighting for access to educational opportunity is a part of a gender justice movement.* Stepping away from frontline work of any sort—service provision, direct action, organizing, political education—and engaging in reflection and analysis provide an opportunity to assess how a site- or campaign-specific initiative or movement is able to link and name ongoing and interrelated forms of oppression and liberation, and can ensure that in our labor and struggles no one is left behind. Yet, while some of the most prescient analysis and tools can emerge from those most directly engaged in resisting and/or surviving these punishing regimes, no course on feminist qualitative research methods, no memoir workshop, no text or reading group on decolonizing methodology provides enough tools to understand how to write—*How to write about something that harms people I love and myself? How to map movements and terrains that I have a stake in, with some semblance of humility, with rigor, and with the knowledge that my work is always situated, always partial?*

But beyond these reasons for movement assessment, the knowledge and experience from people in the center of the struggle for justice create theories of power that shape our world. Decolonialization, feminisms—people impacted by systemic forms of violence often produce the most useful tools to understand and dismantle oppression. Some of the most transformative analyses of punishment and policing come directly from those incarcerated, including writing by Assata Shakur, Linda Evans, Angela Davis, George Jackson, and Cece MacDonald. From Franz Fanon to Grace Lee Boggs, from bell hooks to Leslie Feinberg, lived justice mobilizations create tools, language, and frameworks to transform our world.

With an outrageous goal to speak with/against/across justice movements, this book includes stories from campaigns and projects. Some examples emerge directly from my ongoing labor and experience in Chicago. I offer these groundings not to create any romantic claims to authenticity but to illustrate the *how* and the *why* and the *where*—to situate this analysis. While one chapter (chapter 4, "Restorative Justice Is Not Enough") is collectively authored with comrades and while the analysis throughout this book comes from relationships with local and national organizations and ad hoc groups that do a range of work to resist our prison nation including the Chicago Teachers Union, Critical Resistance,

Gender JUST, Project NIA, the Prison + Neighborhood Arts Project, and the Sister Jean Hughes Adult High School. This book reflects my standpoints and therefore my limitations.

Chicago is a focal site for the analysis offered in this book. Recent mobilizations illustrate that people in Chicago are not waiting for justice. Often generating international attention, we are building another future, now. The 2012 Chicago Teachers Union strike, led by the Caucus of Rank and File Educators, built relationships with community organizations, parents, and other labor unions and pushed back on corporate-driven and privatizing educational reforms that fail communities. In 2015–2016, shaped by the collective leadership of youth-led organizations such as the Black Youth Project 100, direct action and analysis focused an international spotlight on the police killings of young black people, including the deaths of Laquan MacDonald and Rekia Boyd. In 2012 a coalition of faith and immigration justice groups, including the Moratorium on Deportations Campaign, halted the creation of a new private for profit immigration detention center outside of Chicago. While these, and many of the examples laced throughout this book, are locally grown, these movements are not confined to Chicago. Mobilizations to shrink the footprint of policing in schools and communities, to fund black futures, to build responses to harm outside of criminalization, to support gender and sexual self-determination for all, to resist deportations—are not Chicago specific. From Atlanta to Los Angeles, and from Montreal Canada to Brisbane Australia I have the privilege to learn about communities organizing in church basements and classrooms, and to join in street marches and vigils, where people refuse policing and imprisonment as the public safety solution. Across the world people are imagining and building other forms of community and accountability. While I argue against replication—or analysis and tactics produced in one context cannot necessarily be easily imported and used elsewhere—sharing and proliferating tools and engagements continues to be transformative.

Examples and testimony pulled from my practice and from this shifting carceral moment are threaded throughout this book. Although prisons are overwhelmingly public institutions that control people, many rely on the media to interpret them and other affiliated systems, including schools. Those locked up cannot freely communicate their experiences of being incarcerated to people outside. Mainstream media outlets communicate the realities and experiences of the criminal justice system, policing, and life inside through ongoing and often problematic representations. Television—the endless *Law and Order* and *CSI* franchises and the plethora of reality court and police shows—generates representations about harmed (white) girls, dangerous strangers, police-saviors, and violent criminals and convicts. The cluster of feelings produced from these cultural products often functions to solidify stereotypes and reinforce affective political investments in a carceral state. Less frequently, media representations challenge audiences to rethink common sense surrounding punishment. Consider the impact of *Orange Is the New Black*, a blockbuster of a television show that premiered in 2012 and chronicles the experience of an upper-middle-class white woman as she serves time in a federal prison for a drug-related conviction. While trafficking in many familiar racial stereotypes, *Orange Is the New Black* became a public vehicle for many audiences to think about the lives of women in prison. In particular, audiences accessed information about transgender people in prison through the character Sophia, played by the transgender actor Laverne Cox. While a flawed representation of "women in prison," this Netflix show started conversations.

Feelings and beliefs about public schools are also shaped through mainstream media narratives. Wisconsin governor Scott Walker (in 2001) and Chicago mayor Rahm Emanuel (in 2012) both tried, with mixed success, to weaken and break teachers' unions through invoking the story of the lazy (unionized female) public teacher who is negligent and harms children through undereducation. The many Hollywood depictions of public schooling, such as the 1995 film *Dangerous Minds* or the 2007 *Freedom Writers*, reproduce two of the most popular archetypes about urban schools: the White Bountiful Teacher (spoofed on the television show *Saturday Night Live* as the Nice White Lady Teacher) and her counterpoint, the Unruly/Dangerous/Misguided (Black) Male Student. While public schools are more accessible than prisons—the vast majority of people have personal experiences with the former—a surfeit of images and data does not ensure historical or contemporary accuracy. Yet narrative and representation matter, as evidenced during the 2012 strike when the members of the Chicago Teachers Union effectively framed their labor action as a fight for strong communities and not, as the mayor tried to characterize it, as greedy teachers asking for more. What story gets heard about the purpose of public education? About discipline? About safety? About justice? Who gets to tell the story?

This book faces another challenge: how to represent racialized violence to a wider, and probably predominantly white, audience. Toni Morrison writes that she lacked the ability in 1970, the original publication date of *The Bluest Eye*, to negotiate the novel's intersecting themes, which included slavery, white supremacy, and misogyny. She did not possess the "sophistication" to convey these complexities. Reflecting on *The Bluest Eye* in 1994, she noted: "One problem was [that] centering the weight of the novel's inquiry on so delicate and vulnerable a character could smash her and lead readers into the comfort of pitying her rather than into an interrogation of themselves for the smashing. My solution—break the narrative into parts that had to be reassembled by the reader—seemed to me a good idea, the execution of which does not satisfy me now. Besides, it didn't work: many readers remain touched but not moved" (211). In her assessment, a vulnerable child was an inadequate vehicle to convey to readers the interrelationships. Morrison wanted audiences to comprehend and be moved to another place, not simply be touched by the book.

While Morrison does not specify the race or gender of the reader who remains, in her assessment, unmoved, others explicitly investigate the struggle to have violence and trauma recognized by someone who is tacitly or viscerally complicit. Saidiya Hartman writes that asking white people to recognize the pain of slavery does more violence:

> The apologetic density of the plea for recognition is staggering. It assumes both the ignorance and the innocence of the white world. If only they knew the truth, they would act otherwise. I am reminded of the letter that James Baldwin wrote his nephew on the centennial anniversary of the Emancipation Proclamation, "The crime of which I accuse my country and my countrymen," he wrote, "and for which neither I nor time nor history will ever forgive them, that they have destroyed and are destroying hundreds of thousands of lives and do not know it and do not want to know it. . . . It is not permissible that the authors of devastation should also be innocent. It is the innocence which constitutes the crime." (2007, 169)

Some days, it feels unreasonable to expect that an academic text can work as a form of movement assessment or to support social and political change, including the redistribution of power. Perhaps nonfiction and the arts—literature, poetry, and film—are potentially much better suited to the work of politically engaging audiences than the staid tools of the academy.

While linkages to slavery and colonialism—including references to the work of Hartman and Morrison—for some readers may appear somewhat out of scale with the focus of this book, chattel slavery is deeply intertwined with our current systems of policing and imprisonment. Even the most cursory examination of who is locked in cages across the United States, Canada, Mexico, and Australia demonstrates that an analysis of punishment is unthinkable without the political context of the attempted genocide of Aboriginal peoples, black enslavement, the violence of heteropatriarchy, and the punishing practices of capitalism. Yet, as Julia Sudbury (2004) identifies in her introduction to *Global Lockdown*, the lives that testify to the failure of our prison nation to secure safety are precarious. It is a challenge for a book to represent these realities and lives in ways that do not pathologize, do not let the state—often the most violent actor—off the hook, and do not traffic further in dehumanization or distancing. How should one write about harm to illustrate the too often invisible hand of the state to shape *this bruise, this premature death, this child seized, this scar, this addiction?*

Analysis of the carceral state also circulates within the relentless focus on violence as spectacle. Catastrophic phenomena—earthquakes, wars, white girl-child kidnappings, (recognized) torture, or a school shooting—tend to obscure the daily, mundane engagements of people to survive the punishing every day as the scholar Lauren Berlant writes in *Cruel Optimism* (2011). Even within social justice domains, particular examples of violence surface and gain momentum: the 2013 murder of Trayvon Martin, an unarmed young black man, in Florida by George Zimmerman, and of Troy Davis, in 2011, by the state of Georgia; the 2013 placement of Assata Shakur as the "most wanted" woman on the FBI's terrorist list; Kemba Smith's twenty-four-and-a-half-year prison sentence (commuted by President Bill Clinton in 2000) for dating an abusive man who sold drugs; the case of CeCe MacDonald, a transgender woman who was locked up in 2012 for defending herself against racist transphobic violence. These are cases of interpersonal and state violence that have penetrated mainstream media and garnered some critical attention.

In my worlds, the persistent and relentless harm never seems to count or to be enough. For students at the Sister Jean Hughes Adult High

School, who were formerly incarcerated and are struggling to build lives in a city where they are not recognized as fully human, the violence they experience never seems to matter to all the powerful institutions and structures:

Cheryl finally found a job, the midnight shift, cleaning at the fancy sports fitness center, a three-mile bus ride from her house. While working, accidently, she locked herself out and had to call the gym's private security company. The gym fired her. Desperate for money, she is considering all options. Cherise was doing well in all her classes until her son's health declined and she had to drop out to care for him. As she is not in school, she lost her free housing. She is in a temporary shelter with her kids, a place she feels is unsafe, and she would do anything to get out of there. Charles is working, just above minimum wage, at a military base a two-hour bus ride from his house. They changed his work hours to the lunch/afternoon shift. He wants to finish high school, but he will be an hour late to school every night. He can't switch his shift and needs this job to survive. Nolan, picked up on parole violation for shoplifting soap and personal hygiene items at a drugstore because he wanted to be clean, spent months lingering in Cook County Jail while his public defender, clearly overloaded and frazzled, worked through her caseload. Naomi, locked out of living wage employment because of her record, struggled in her late thirties to see possibilities and life in her future of low-wage service work and, in the end, could not. Wesley, caught in the new classification of "gang probation" that includes strict movement restrictions, is trapped in his mother's house, and the cops are primed to pick him up if he steps onto the street. His two life options: her porch or the penitentiary.

Yes, there is resistance and survival and joy and transformation, but there is also pain and death that never seem to count as enough.

Project

Rooted in daily struggles while working to engage a wider analysis of power, this book brings focal theoretical and practical attention to existing forms of activist thinking/organizing. Chapters examine the circulation of key artifacts, including the child, and the affective economies that suture these artifacts to carceral landscapes. This labor requires an antidisciplinary analysis or the synthesis of seemingly divergent fields. Moving beyond disciplinary boundaries is particularly important to inquiries that relate to youth or the child, as social science research centered on children or adolescents can assume that developmental categories are fixed and natural, rather than flexible, sociopolitical constructs. To build for abolition requires organizers and scholars to investigate and dismantle these containers that function as technologies to advance and authenticate practices and visions of punishment, policing, and prisons.

This book engages four significant overlapping and undertheorized areas in contemporary work in critical carceral studies, educational policy studies, and gender studies with a fierce eye on movement assessment. The first two chapters in part I, "Childhoods" ("Magical Age" and "The Trouble with the Child in the Carceral State"), explore how shifting conceptions of children and childhood have been central to the buildup and maintenance of the prison nation. The child surfaced repeatedly in pro- and antiprison campaigns and struggles while the United States engaged in the world's largest prison construction project. Deployments of the child, never a neutral container or image in these debates, perform a kind of temporal magic by collapsing our organizing horizons and demanding commitment to the child-futurity. The child also masks key social and political transactions. Notably, the artifact of the child also houses, redefines, and racializes the category of innocence and simultaneously protects this concept from scrutiny. As Kathryn Stockton writes in *The Queer Child*, "Innocence is queerer than we ever thought it could be" (2009, 5). New sites of resistance and mobilization are created by unpacking who counts as a child in this political moment and how heterogendered and racialized forms of innocence are reproduced through the use of the child in campaigns.

Part II, "School and Prison," interrupts prevalent analysis and organizing around the school to prison pipeline. Chapter 3, "Beyond Reform: The Architecture of Prison and School Closure," and chapter 4, "Restorative Justice Is Not Enough," reframe the problem of the criminalization of young people as wider than a failure of school-based disciplinary policies. Community-based organizations, in concert with a number of scholarly initiatives (including my own), have popularized the image and the metaphor of the school to prison pipeline and a wide range of corresponding, and overwhelmingly school-based, intervention strategies. Yet the criminalization of nonwhite and/or poor young people in schools cannot be separated from a wider carceral landscape that targets select youth and communities and their surrounding geographies for disposability or participation in low-wage economies. Engaging with and reframing a body of scholarship and organizing that focuses on the STPP, these chapters both explore the punishing artifacts that prison or carceral reforms produce and argue that a turn toward an *abolition politic* provides a needed reframing for those working against the criminalization of youth, particularly in schools.

Furthermore, this book explores political facets of the affective dimensions of public safety and how the artifact of the child shapes adults. The work to challenge policing or incarceration as a public safety strategy is made difficult by how commonsense the ideas of incarceration and child protection appear to be, as well as how frightening the prospect of dismantling the current criminal justice system can seem. While economics fuels recent engagements with decarceration and sentencing reform, dismantling investments in punishment requires more than structural policy work or making the right economic argument. Our prison nation requires grappling directly with questions and feelings of safety and, in particular, with how heterogendered and racialized fears of (child) sexual assault are publicly deployed to augment the prison system. To effectively understand public attachments to incarceration and not simply transfer old fears (of the drug dealer, serial killer, or home invader) to new bodies (terrorist, sex offender, undocumented migrant) requires more than structural policy work. Synthesizing recent scholarship in affect theory with grounded examples of strategies to build alternatives to prisons and policing, parts III and IV—encompassing chapter 5, "Life and Death: Reentry after Incarceration"; chapter 6, "Registering Sex, Rethinking Safety"; and chapter 7, "Not This: Building Futures Now"—explore feelings of safety and protection and raise grounded challenges in the work to transform the concept and the practice of public safety.

Working across disciplinary boundaries and building from an activist and organizer platform, this book dismantles these *child-facets* of our carceral state and engages fresh questions in the struggle to build sustainable and flourishing worlds. As states depopulate prisons under policies fueled by economic rather than justice-based arguments, as the "crimmigration" wave—or the growing industry of immigration prisons and punishment—expands, as neoconservative political figures push for reforms to shrink big government, and as select jails and prisons become cognizant of nonheterosexual and non-gender-conforming lives, an abolitionist vision is needed now more than ever. This book argues that challenging our prison nation and building more-just communities requires interrupting commonsense investments in childhood, exploring emergent practices of public safety, and interrogating the institutions and ideas—such as juvenile justice or innocence—upon which prison expansion was built and that contain the racial and gendered investments at the core of the carceral state. An examination of these self-perpetuating ideas and how these containers advance and authenticate policing, punishment, and incarceration reveals pathways to the world we need now.

I

Childhoods

1

Magical Age

In 2013, Ethan Couch, a sixteen-year-old from Texas, drove while drunk and high and killed four people and critically injured two others. Buttressed by a crack legal team and a defense of "affluenza"—that Ethan had not been properly parented but instead had been afforded too much luxury and freedom by his wealthy parents—Ethan's culpability was diminished. Instead of prison time, Judge Jean Boyd sentenced Ethan to ten years' probation and time in a private treatment facility, with the annual price tag of $250,000 paid for by Ethan's parents. The psychologist Gary Miller persuasively testified for the defense that while affluenza is not a recognizable illness within the American Psychological Association, the death of four people was not murder because Ethan did not understand the consequences of his actions (Rosenberg 2013).

In 2012, Cristian Fernandez was charged as an adult with first-degree murder in the beating death of his brother. Cristian was twelve years old when he slammed his two-year-old brother David into a bookshelf. Media reports highlighted that Cristian grew up in a poor and violent family: when Cristian was eleven, his stepfather shot himself in the head when he learned he was to be arrested for beating Cristian. In 2013, Cristian agreed to a deal and pled guilty to manslaughter; he will remain in a juvenile prison until his nineteenth birthday (Schoettler 2013; Associated Press 2012). Media coverage of Cristian routinely reported pending charges of another "heinous crime"—what was described in the news as Cristian's "sexual battery" against another brother. Yet Ethan's own defense team offered the example of his prior police contact—Ethan was found in a pickup truck at age fifteen with a nude fourteen-year-old girl—as evidence of his diminished capacity. There are no reports of Ethan being charged for sexual assault or sexual battery or of Ethan being identified as a sex offender.

These two young people grievously harmed others but received two different pathways through the criminal justice system. One white and wealthy boy is afforded protection, consideration as a juvenile, and an almost a priori association with diminished capacity, and subsequently the family is offered the right to purchase access to a rehabilitative facility. The other, Latino and poor, is quickly constructed as predatory and an adult. Even with a seemingly widespread acknowledgment that Cristian is someone the system—child welfare agencies, schools, health care organizations—has abjectly failed, at twelve Cristian is now a lost case. Childhood has never been available to all. Historically, childhood was a category inaccessible to nonwhite communities. In the United States, the criminal justice system is at the forefront of defining the boundaries surrounding adulthood and childhood and masking the institutionalization of racial inequities. Legal and social protections are extended to some individuals categorized as children but denied to many others, including Cristian. These benefits are not based on race but on access to childhood.

While Cristian and Ethan learn the malleability of the boundaries between childhood and adulthood, others acquire another lesson. While some, such as Ethan, benefit from childhood's diminished culpability, nonadults are also subject to additional forms of surveillance and punishment. *Preteens* are increasingly charged and convicted of sexually based crimes (Finkelhor, Ormrod, and Chaffin 2009, 1–2). According to a 2009 research brief from the U.S. Department of Justice, "Juveniles account for more than one third (35.6 percent) of those known to police to have committed sex offenses." Consider this example from Human Rights Watch's 2013 report examining the increased number of juvenile sex offenders, *Raised on the Registry*: "In 2006, a 13-year-old girl from Ogden, Utah was arrested for rape for having consensual sex with her 12-year-old boyfriend. The young girl, impregnated by her younger boyfriend at the age of 13, was found guilty of violating a state law that prohibits sex with someone under age 14. Her 12-year-old boyfriend was found guilty of violating the same law for engaging in sexual activity with her, as she was also a child under the age of 14 at the time" (Human Rights Watch 2013, 35). While twelve and thirteen might very well be unwise or even harmful ages to engage in sexual activity or to become a parent, this assessment of vulnerability is significantly different than criminal conviction and state punishment. The turn to criminalization to negotiate vulnerability not only negates the possibility of agency and links "age" to "consent," producing fixed ideas about psychological or developmental norms; it also harms people. Unable to legally consent, at thirteen and twelve, these two people are criminals: convicted sex offenders.

While the increase of juveniles on the registry can be partially attributed to the expansion of laws that require registration as a sex offender, the growth of juveniles on the registry is also a result of the *legal strangeness* of children, a term used by the literary theorist Kathryn Stockton (2009, 29). Across jurisdictions, a matrix of laws and administrative regulations limits juveniles. Behavior and mobility are constrained by laws that police a juvenile's ability to drink alcohol, to smoke cigarettes, to assemble (loitering and curfew), to engage in sexual activities, to work, to travel, to sign a legal contract, to wear particular clothing, to vote, and more. Sexuality, in particular, continues to be a prime focus of surveillance and regulation for all youth, particularly cisgendered girls (Schaffner 2006; Coalition for Juvenile Justice 2014). While Ethan and Cristian offer examples of the flexibility of the borders between child and adult, the status of nonadult is not necessarily a privileged position. Not being an adult renders a person not fully free, not a full citizen, and subject to a host of regulations and additional forms of surveillance and policing.[1]

Ruth Gilmore (2007) defines racism as "the state-sanctioned or extralegal production and exploitation of group-differentiated vulnerability to premature death" (Gilmore 2007, 28). *The child* continues to produce, and simultaneously attempts to mask, traces of a racialized and heterogendered production: group-differentiated vulnerability. Age holds magical powers. As Ethan and Cristian illustrate, some are simply excluded from inhabiting the categories of childhood or youth, including twelve-year-olds charged as adults or nine-year-olds held as juveniles in detention centers. Yet, as the young people classified as sex offenders demonstrate, being a child or a juvenile also confers diminished capacity. Who counts as a child? What are the political and economic possibilities available, or denied, to children? What evidence is marshaled to define the child?

Flexible Bodies

Childhood, as a formal life stage, is a relatively recent creation. Seventeenth-century shifts in the modes of production and in religion altered family and kinship structures across Europe (Ariès 1962). As infant mortality declined, literacy rates increased, and discourses about human development emerged, children began to be understood not as smaller versions of adults but as *future* adults. Age began to possess a significant legal and social meaning. The historian Holly Brewer outlines how this invention of a childhood—specifically, a white male childhood—is today manifested in the United States:

> We would not now elect a thirteen year old to the House of Representatives (and certainly not have him give a keynote speech on an important bill at fourteen). We would not accept a will signed by a four year old. We could not permit a fourteen year old, regardless of wealth, to judge (as a juror) someone's guilt or innocence. We would not hang an eight year old for arson. We would not permit an eight year old to legally marry. We would not allow a five year old to bind himself to labor—and force him to abide by his agreement until he reaches twenty-four. Yet the laws and legal guides made these practices acceptable in sixteenth- and seventeenth-century England and Virginia. (2005, 9)

Brewer's scholarship demonstrates how central racialized childhood was to the social contract and to enlightenment theories that shaped conceptions of representational democracy in the United States. In particular, she details how between the sixteenth and nineteenth centuries, access to rights and full participation in civic life became defined through childhood and (non)consent. Democracy required both consent and adulthood and, therefore, also nonconsent and nonadulthood. Racialized from inception, childhood concurrently shaped forms of association and life beyond the figure of the adult and the child.

Nineteenth-century constructions of childhood were exclusively white. As understandings about humanity shifted from Calvinistic beliefs of the child born in sin, or infant damnation, to the framework of John Locke's "tabula rasa," the status of childhood, for some, changed. The belief that individuals are influenced by an environment and capable of self-governance reconfigured childhood. These political and religious shifts create childhood for some, but not all. The historians Robin Bernstein and Karen Sánchez-Eppler suggest that the category of "pickaninny" was invented precisely as white American childhood appeared. The nonwhite child emerged as an "imagined, subhuman black juvenile"

(R. Bernstein 2011, 34). Bernstein argues that while the "pickaninny" circulated across a range of mediums and domains, fulfilling varied purposes, a defining characteristic is the lack of sentience: "animalistic or adorable, ragged or neat, frightened or happy, American or British, but the figure is always juvenile, always of color, and always resistant if not immune to pain" (R. Bernstein 2011, 35). White children were innocent and sentient, and therefore fully human, while black children were excluded from innocence and access to sentience, not fully human, and therefore not a part of childhood (R. Bernstein 2011). Cognizant of the possible benefits associated with childhood, those who owned enslaved people organized to ensure that black children could not be understood as children. "As early as 1670, the Virginia Legislature effectively disqualified African children from claiming the role of child as defined by English custom" (Duane 2010, 131). Laws, popular culture, and tradition regulated and racialized access to childhood.

While the history of the deeply racialized construction of the child is documented, the continuation of this legacy is less visible and not popularly understood. *Child* continues to be a kind of "legal strangeness" (Stockton 2009, 16). *Juvenile, adolescent, teenager, kid, youth, minor, young adult*—are all classifications that hover between childhood and adulthood. This categorization further stalls entry into key capital-producing institutions: the workforce, politics, marriage, and the military. A child, according to Kathryn Stockton, "is a body said to need protections more than freedoms. And it is a creature who cannot consent to its sexual pleasure, or divorce its parents, or design its education—at least not by law" (2009, 16). Juvenile or youth is the transition between the child and adulthood, yet, like the "strangeness" of the child, there is no clarity or consensus about this transition.

Inconsistencies about the boundaries of the child are starkly apparent even with the most cursory review of any body of laws surrounding age(s) of consent. Most nations (and sometimes the jurisdictions within nations) establish laws that demarcate at what age youth can give informed consent to participate in civic life and to engage in a range of practices that might be considered harmful. Globally, differing age of consent laws (including absence of such laws) regulate employment, participation in sexual acts, voting, alcohol and tobacco consumption, and driving. Within jurisdictions, the establishment *and enforcement* of such laws vary across gender, race, sexuality, ability, class, and geography. For example, compulsory school attendance laws for all young people were not enforced for Mexican American youth in the 1920s throughout the Southwest because white farmers and landowners expected these youth to work in the agricultural industries. White officials and white communities subsequently created narratives that Mexican American families did not care about schooling (San Miguel 1997, 138).

While laws and regulations create a fixed age of consent for many acts, including sex, these ages are not, and have never been, neutral or bright lines. In the sixteenth century, according to Holly Brewer (2005), "all contracts by those children over age seven were valid" (332), including marriage contracts, yet by the twentieth century white women under the age of sixteen could not contract any valid marriage (333). Throughout the twentieth century, many age of consent laws relating to marriage or sex applied only to white women. When white men were subsequently included, regions and governments frequently established different ages of consent for men and women (233–37). Age of consent laws often did not apply to nonwhite populations. Enslaved people were denied the right to participate in marriage for a host of reasons, including, by the nineteenth century, "by comparing them to children in their right to contract" (330). When homosexuality began to be decriminalized in 1967 in the United Kingdom, the age of consent was twenty-one for what was defined as homosexual sexual acts (sodomy) and sixteen for what the state identified as heterosexual acts ("Commons Approves Bill to Lower Gay Age of Consent," 2000). The age a person can consent to sexual activity (or marriage) is not fixed but is intimately hinged to other sociopolitical norms.

Contemporary age of consent laws, particularly those related to sex, remain uneven. While those who are fifteen in the United States can be culpable and tried for crimes as adults, the state protects that same age cohort through the enactment of laws that stipulate that a fifteen- or sixteen-year-old is not able to consent to sex, except in some states where a girl of said age may marry a man with parental consent (Fine and McClelland 2006; Schaffner 2002). Most states require and sanction an abstinence-based sex education curriculum based on the belief that schoolchildren are too young to be sexually active. However, the courts do not blink when sentencing a fifteen-year-old in an adult court or requiring a twelve-year-old to register as a sex offender.

Even for those who are considered nonadults, and therefore legally incapable of consent, state-enforced protection is complex. Children or juveniles might be able to access rehabilitation within the criminal justice system or serve a shorter sentence in a prison that has access to education and other resources, and after release from prison their records might be sealed. Yet, while diminished capacity legitimates access to these considerations and resources, this classification also ensures that children and juveniles are denied the right to vote, to consent to sexual practices, to control their living arrangements, to consent to education, to be independent from their parents or guardians, and more. For the child, experience itself becomes a double bind. Remaining innocent (the defining category of childhood) requires the negation of experience. Knowledge becomes tricky. For example, it is nearly impossible to name youths' sexual agency and pleasure, particularly within a culture of persistent sexual violence that targets young people.[2]

While these laws that regulate and produce juveniles are now facially neutral, or do not specifically discriminate against nonwhite people or other targeted populations, the enforcement of age of consent laws is uneven. While the "pickaninny" has disappeared from our landscape, the affiliated meanings have not. Innocence is still attached to childhood but routinely denied to those nonwhite, poor, queer, and/or disabled. While our culture purports to be focused on child protection and interrupting harm to children, the pain and sentience of select white children is visible, prioritized. Unlike Ethan, Cristian is classified as a sex offender, predatory, and not fully human.

Varying ages of consent demonstrate the flexibility of the boundaries between child and adult. Yet, as indicated, this suppleness of *childhood* and subsequently *adult* is neither new nor arbitrary. Eligibility for participation in any of the categories of child, youth, or adult and their accompanying legal, political, and social conditions is never produced in isolation from race, sexuality, gender, ability, geography, socioeconomics, and more. Yet, classification as a child, or a body that merits state-regulated protection, is also not necessarily beneficial.

Juvenile Injustice

The criminal justice system continues to define the boundaries between child and adult. The first juvenile justice court was established in 1899 in Chicago to obtain different treatment for people under the age of seventeen within the criminal system: another court, alternative institutions, confidentiality, and fewer rights (including initially no right to due process or legal representation) (Krisberg 2005; Feld 1999; Willrich 2003; Wolcott 2005). Widely understood as a Progressive Era child-saving reform with a focus on preparation for adulthood and therefore full citizenship, the *juvenile* necessitated the creation and mobilization of a bureaucratic and professional army: social welfare policies, juvenile detention centers, social workers, truancy officers, child development experts, and more. Diminished capacity, a hallmark of juveniles and children, requires expert management. Once established, these child- and family-saving bureaucracies both required and reproduced the very categories they were set up to monitor and police. These "child-saving" reforms were unevenly available.

Geoff Ward's *The Black Child-Savers* (2012) documents that early white reformers who created juvenile justice systems did not see black children as juveniles or as future citizens. Juvenile justice was a "racial project" from inception (33). Across the United States, early reformatories and systems designed for juveniles, including houses of refuge, were either categorically unavailable to youth of color or segregated by race (and gender). In the nineteenth century, as compared with their white counterparts, black youth in the northern states spent more time confined in houses of refuge and had more-limited apprenticeship options and fewer opportunities after release (57). Across the northern states, the early part of the twentieth century translated into "less violent but more benign forms of neglect" as black leaders and communities continued to be denied access to juvenile justice institutions (110). At "best and worst," nineteenth- and twentieth-century juvenile justice systems "variously organized to perpetuate black second class citizenship and white advantage in what remained a white democracy" (75). Ward argues that black women's associations, not white juvenile justice reformers, enabled black youth to have moderate access to the juvenile justice system, and yet this did not ensure equitable treatment or beneficial outcomes. In many southern states, black children were excluded from any access to juvenile justice systems until 1940 (60).

Geoff Ward also persuasively argues that Progressive Era reforms sought to construct a parental state that aimed to "underdevelop black citizens deemed delinquent and black civil society generally and, thus, to maintain the boundaries of white democracy" (G. Ward 2012, 47). The historian Khalil Gibran Muhammad suggests that Progressive Era reforms aimed at improving the welfare of people overwhelmingly benefited white communities while concurrently solidifying the category "white." Muhammad specifically outlines how the outcome of the discriminatory application of state programs designed to secure communities' well-being was used to reinforce white supremacy: "Thoughtful, well funded crime prevention and politically accountable crime fighting secured immigrants' whiteness, in contrast to the experiences of blacks, who were often brutalized or left unprotected and were repeatedly told to conquer their own crime before others would help them. . . . Progressives used crime statistics to demonstrate the suffering of poor and working-class immigrants and native whites" (K. Muhammad 2010, 273). Many of these reforms, such as state-supported social work (and teaching) provided white women entry into the public sphere yet simultaneously circulated narrow and racialized frameworks for family and childhood that rendered many, specifically those who were nonwhite and/or poor, unfit or deficient. In 1923, the U.S. Children's Bureau reported that black youth were twice as likely to be sentenced to "a prison, a reformatory, a jail or a workhouse" as white youth (K. Mohammad 2010, 231).

As youth and families of color began to access juvenile justice systems and child and family welfare programs, the focus of these programs shifted from any pretense toward assimilation, welfare, or rehabilitation toward punitive and carceral functions. The 1954 *Brown v. Board of Education* decisions that struck down forms of de jure segregation did not eradicate profoundly unequal prisons and systems for juveniles in the North, and Ward suggests that instead black youth became "more alienated in legally integrated court communities" (2012, 217). Desegregation was not an affirmative stance, and it did not ensure that youth of color would receive equal treatment within criminal justice systems, nor did it disappear profound practices and histories of the criminalization of blackness.

The category of juvenile delinquent also proved a versatile weapon to push back on politically active youth leaders. Beyond differential treatment for specific kinds of crimes—murder, theft, rape—the juvenile justice system has historically *produced* categories of crime and illegality—truant, delinquent, runaway—or "status violations" that are applied only to juveniles. Status violations can emerge in tandem with prevailing public anxieties. In the 1960s, Brenda Travis, a black teenager and a leader active in the civil rights movement, was "labeled delinquent and committed to a reformatory to deter her and other youths from becoming involved in Mississippi's civil rights movement" (G. Ward 2012, 205). While Travis was eventually freed after her second arrest and received an indeterminate sentence, Ward identifies "hundreds of similar cases" where white-controlled courts and law enforcement were able to criminalize free speech and assembly. Young people, often forefronted in the civil rights movement through manifestations such as the Children's Crusade because of their "moral and emotional influence," faced specific hurdles when adjudicated as juveniles (G. Ward 2012, 206, 207).

Access to the juvenile justice system and the associated hard-fought "rights and liberties" gained during the civil rights movement were not "leveraged to advance more progressive racial politics within juvenile justice" (G. Ward 2012, 231). Geoff Ward's research identified an increase, starting in the 1980s, in the number of court-involved youth of color, or young people who experience "disproportionate minority contact." In our current political moment, children under the age of eighteen do not have equal access to the facets of the criminal justice system nominally framed as rehabilitative. Contemporary child- or family-saving programs—the "multiracial parent state" (G. Ward 2012, 234), including the juvenile justice and child welfare systems—are much more likely to investigate, seize, and remove black children from their families (Roberts 1997, 2003). Although the United States still locks up more people under the age of eighteen than any other nation—approximately 105,000 per day in 2010—and although in 2013 the rates of juveniles in the system were the lowest in thirty-five years, people under eighteen are still held in adult facilities. According to the National Prisoner Statistics program and the Annual Survey of Jails, "on an average day in 2010, some 7,560 youth under age 18 were held in adult jails, and another 2,295 were in adult prisons" ("Reducing Youth Incarceration in the United States," 2013, 1–2). Some states have lowered the age at which a child can be held accountable and tried in a juvenile court and raised the number of children moved into the court system. These shifts expand the definition of who is culpable and therefore punishable. Approximately 250,000 youth are tried as adults every year, across every state ("Youth in the Adult System," 2015), and research suggests that youth who are tried as adults are more likely to reoffend (32 percent) than youth adjudicated through the juvenile systems for the same crime (Lanza-Kaduce et al. 2002).[3]

Youth of color, particularly African American, Latino, and First Nations, are disproportionately transferred into adult court. The National

Center on Crime and Delinquency documents the staggeringly dispro-portionate incarceration rates for youth of color at every level of the sys-tem and highlights that youth of color are significantly more likely than white youth to be removed from the home, transferred to adult court, and sent to adult prison (Krisberg 2007; "Reducing Youth Incarceration in the United States" 2013). While the total number of juveniles locked up has continued to decline over the past thirty-five years, African American youth are still five times more likely than white youth to be behind bars ("Reducing Youth Incarceration in the United States," 2). Sixteen- and fifteen-year-old black and brown youth, particularly boys, count as adults.

Notably, young people continue to get in trouble with the law even if no harm happens. In the past decade, laws and bills that target "baggy pants," criminalize homelessness or loitering, and establish age curfews, in conjunction with zero tolerance school policies, seek to control bodies, movement, and assembly, particularly for low-income urban youth of color. Identified by some jurisdictions as "ungovernable" or "incorrigible," juveniles are picked up for these violations, perhaps under the frame-work of protection, but the result is the criminalization of increasing numbers of youth. Again, particularly impacted by status violations are young women of color. As indicated in the report *National Standards for the Care of Youth Charged with Status Offenses* by the Coalition for Juvenile Justice (2013), "girls make up 61 percent of all runaway cases, and spend twice as long in detention facilities for status offenses as boys" (39). Ward reports that since the 1970s, available research on youth in the criminal justice system illustrates a racial pattern in the classification of juveniles as normal or serious delinquents: "White youth tend to be categorized as normal delinquents. . . . Black and other nonwhite youths are assigned to the undeserving status of serious offenders" (G. Ward 2012, 234).

With this analysis of how the juvenile justice system continues to shape young people for participation in a racialized democracy and to reproduce flexible categories of child and juvenile, I do not mean to mini-mize other significant factors that shape the production and circulation of these categories, for example, capitalism. The concept of the teenager emerged in the 1940s through the efforts of the market/capitalism to produce a postwar category of consumers with a leisure-seeking, "fun" identity. As Dick Hebdige, an early theorizer of the concept of the teen-ager, wrote: "The invention of teenage is intimately bound up with the creation of the youth market. Eventually a new range of commodities and commercial leisure facilities are provided to absorb the surplus cash which for the first time working-class youth is calculated to have at its disposal to spend on itself and to provide a space within which youth can construct its own immaculate identities untouched by the soiled and compromised imaginaries of the parent culture" (Hebdige 1988, 29–30). What was viewed as the teenager's way of life (one never uniformly accessible to all young people) also produced concordant moral panics, creating tension between "youth-as-fun and youth-as-trouble" (19). The demographic "tweener" is also a current product of an insatiable and flexible economy that is perpetually seeking to identify and shape new consumers. These categories—youth, teenager, juvenile—are not simply flat constructions by adults, the market, or legal systems. These structural forces play significant roles and yet are resisted, inhabited, and torqued by many, including those who count as youth.

Bad Girls

Early juvenile justice courts functioned to control racialized forms of sexuality for girls. A 1912 study of the first decade of Chicago's juvenile court found that 80 percent of the 2,440 girls who went before the juvenile court during this time did so because "their virtue is in peril, if it has not already been lost" (as cited in Schaffner 2006, 39). Defying racialized heterogendered constructions placed one in trouble with the law. Progressive Era juvenile reformers were often also participants in related temperance, antivice, or other moral movements. While not directly focused on juveniles, these organizations and movements sought to regulate gender and sexuality. The American Social Hygiene Association (ASHA), a national organization formed in 1913, used emerging science to control vice and diseases believed to be sexually transmitted. Between 1914 and 1916, ASHA's Legislative Committee "visited 80 cities in 25 states" to successfully convince state legislatures to adopt their proposed law to reclassify prostitution from a crime of public order to a sexual crime (Luker 1998, 614–15). This change effectively criminalized the contexts and acts associated with sex work, including the places where prostitution happened and all involved in these transactions.

On the heels of the development of the juvenile courts, these new prostitution laws created "women's courts," built new reformatories and prisons for women, increased the amount of time women faced in prison when convicted of a sex crime, and permitted the profiling and preventive detention of "sexually suspect" young women (Luker 1998, 616). The criminalization of sex work not only brought innumerable white women, particularly young women, under state control and surveillance but also expanded the regimes of punishment through the construction and staffing of new prisons, courts, reformatories, and asylums. While some female reformers advocated for the criminalization of prostitution because they believed that this would create more equality between white men and white women by helping to eradicate the sexual "double standard," these laws and associated surveillance structures overwhelmingly regulated women's lives, particularly their sexuality (Luker 1998, 625).

Nonwhite women and girls, particularly black girls, were outside of this gendered "double standard." As Progressive Era reforms such as women's courts and the juvenile justice system emerged to ensure that the state acted as a patriarch, delinquent nonwhite girls had the least access to any of these institutional resources. A study of the jail population in Chicago conducted in 1913 by Hull House found that "black girls and women made up nearly one-third of all females in jail," while black people constituted less than 3 percent of the city's population (G. Ward 2012, 85). Not only were black women disproportionately picked up and held in jail for longer terms; rehabilitative services were not made available: "Barred from private institutions, and accepted only in small numbers at the state-run institution, they remained in detention longest. Thus dependent black girls had virtually no access to rehabilitative services through Chicago's early juvenile court" (G. Ward 2012, 85). In 1913, the president of the board of Hull House, Louise deKoven Bowen, who was also the president of the Juvenile Protective Association of Chicago, wrote in a report that this racial disproportionality was "startling." This report also stated that black girls received differential treatment from white girls, and specifically that black girls were sent from the jails to associated employment agencies that found them "work as maids in houses of prostitution." It noted that "such referrals would never be made for white girls," given what it called their "moral fragility" (G. Ward 2012, 111).

Race, class, and ability have long shaped who counted as fully human and merited protection or even recognition as a sentient being. Ida B. Wells-Barnett evocatively charts how lynching, primarily in the southern states but across the United States, was often perpetrated based on false accusations of criminal activity (or for no reason at all) and often for accusations that black men had raped white women. Wells-Barnett out-lines not only how many of these charges were groundless but also the racial bankruptcy of the state's and the community's stance of "protect-ing women and children." In 1892, while white citizens in Nashville, Tennessee, tortured and murdered Ephesians Grizzard after he was falsely charged with raping a white woman, "a white man was in the same jail for raping eight-year-old Maggie Reese, an Afro-American girl. He was not harmed" (Wells-Barnett 2002, 37). And months earlier, accord-ing to Wells-Barnett, a white man, Pat Hanifan, was given six months for "outraging" a little black girl who, "from the physical injuries she received . . . has been ruined for life. He was jailed for six months, dis-charged, and is now a detective in the city" (Wells-Barnett 2002, 37). Wells-Barnett's research acutely chronicles precisely whose pain matters, who is worthy of protection, and whose invented or real harms will galvanize (white) mobs. While race, ability, and class demarcated who counted as a girl or woman and whose bodies counted as subjects worthy of protection or prosecution within the law, age also shaped which white female bodies were the most innocent and most worthy of protection (Pliley 2014).

Research suggests that during the postemancipation Progressive Era there was no explosion in prostitution or crisis of sexual trafficking or slavery, but rather mounting public anxieties surrounding immigration and industrialization (Luker 1998; Pliley 2014). Immigration exploded and women moved into cities and into labor markets, and these changing contexts created a fertile context for the manufactured fears—the immi-nent dangers of sexual slavery facing white girls (and women)—which in turn fueled criminal justice shifts (Bernstein 2007, 2010; Pliley 2014). The sociologist Kristin Luker identifies social movements—"temperance to suffrage to birth control to eugenics to anti-vice commissions to anti-obscenity groups" (1998, 606)—that, under the guise of morality, sought to regulate race, gender, and sexuality in this emerging new world order. The 1910 Mann-Elkins White Slavery Act, or the White Slave Traffic Act (popularly known as the Mann Act), sought to prohibit white female slavery and criminalized the transport of white women across state lines for immoral purposes. Supported by erroneous media representations of an epidemic of young white girls snatched off the streets and forced to be prostitutes, the Mann Act was, as many historians outline, shaped by post-Reconstructionist anxieties about race, gender, and sexuality (Pliley

2014). Reconstructionist laws and regulations that specifically targeted and criminalized nonwhite people—often known as the Black Codes—already policed women of color. The Mann Act did relatively little to prevent the exploitation of women or to catch sexual predators; instead, the act policed consensual sex acts.[4]

Biopolitical Borders

The evidence used to rationalize boundaries among child, juvenile, and adult provides a key window into how the intertwined—and often lethal— histories and associations between heterogendered white supremacy and innocence are disappeared within developmental categories. Increasingly, scientific research plays a key role in attempts to fix boundaries between child and adult, and therefore between innocence and culpability.

Over the past decade, mainstream media coverage of scientific research related to cognitive and neurological development has exploded. Examples include a *Harvard Magazine* article, "The Teen Brain" (Ruder 2008); a National Public Radio broadcast, "The Teen Brain: It's Just Not Grown Up Yet" (Knox 2010); and a *Discover Magazine* article, "The Brain: The Trouble with Teens" (Zimmer 2011). A 2011 *National Geographic* cover article, "The New Science of the Teenage Brain," summarizes the contemporary core research developments: "A National Institute of Health (NIH) project that studied over a hundred young people as they grew up during the 1990s showed that our brains undergo a massive reorganization between our 12th and 25th years. The brain doesn't actually grow very much during this period. It has already reached 90 percent of its full size by the time a person is six, and a thickening skull accounts for most head growth afterward. But as we move through adolescence, the brain undergoes extensive remodeling, resembling a network and writing upgrade" (Dobbs 2011, 43).

This upgrade, as the *National Geographic* summary suggests, produces the characteristics of adolescence: "excitement, novelty, risk, the company of peers" (55). Much of this research contradicts earlier findings that posited that a child's brain finished developing at age ten. Instead, this new body of scientific research suggests that the adolescent brain has not fully developed. The impact of this research suggests that adolescents do not necessarily fully understand the consequences of their actions and that they are more open to learning and also more susceptible to addiction and other compulsive behaviors (Ruder 2008).

This "explosion in scientific research on adolescent brain development" (Bronner 2012, para. 2) has had a significant impact on the status of those under eighteen years of age within the criminal justice system. This brain research has translated into less legal culpability and more access to state protection or services marked as rehabilitative. Neurological research informed the U.S. Supreme Court's 2005 decision to outlaw the death penalty for crimes committed by people under the age of eighteen (Lane 2005). Statements from organizations such as the American Bar Association translated this research for wider audiences: "Along with everything else in the body, the brain changes significantly during adolescence. In the last five years, scientists, using new technologies, have discovered that adolescent brains are far less developed than previously believed" (American Bar Association Juvenile Justice Center 2004, 1). Research on the neurological development of juveniles also influenced the 2010 Supreme Court decision (by a 6–3 vote) to abolish life without parole (LWOP) for juveniles convicted of nonmurder crimes. Justice John Paul Stephens wrote: "Knowledge accumulates. We learn, sometimes, from our mistakes" (as cited in Liptak 2010). In 2012, in a 5–4 decision, the Supreme Court prohibited states from imposing a life sentence on juveniles convicted of murder. Justice Elena Kagan's majority opinion drew not only from the problematic paradigm of "common sense" but on a possibly equally elusive foundation, science: "Our decisions rested not only on common sense—on what 'any parent knows'—but on science and social science as well" (as cited in Barnes 2012). Emerging neurological research is a strong foundation for these decisions. Commenting on these Supreme Court decisions and wider shifts in how the criminal justice system treats juveniles, the *New York Times* cites retired Florida judge Irene Sullivan: "These cases are a recognition of the fact that we are at a level of objective scientific certainty with the brain science that calls for policy changes" (as cited in Bronner 2012, para. 9). Psychology and, most importantly, neurology provide evidence that juveniles are different than adults, need protection, and merit the opportunity to change.

My focus here is not to critique this brain research, which is infinitely beyond my scope. Instead, the circulation of this research within a deeply unequal heterogendered and racialized landscape has profound consequences. Dorothy Roberts raises pointed questions, in *Fatal Invention:*

How Science, Politics, and Big Business Re-create Race in the Twenty-First Century (2011), about this shift to biologize inequalities that are rooted in sociopolitical environments: "When scientists report genetic explanations for negative behaviors like gangbanging, absentee fatherhood, and teenage sex, which the public stereotypically associates with blacks and Latinos, it seems more plausible that genes cause social problems. The race-gene claims simultaneously confirm the myths that races exist in genes and that genes can tell us everything about ourselves. Together, they support a biological explanation for the widening racial chasm in health, incarceration, and social welfare" (299). While Roberts's work focuses mainly on genetic research, her analysis helps unpack the burgeoning body of research, advanced by child advocates, that seeks to focus not on the relationships between race and poverty and the criminalization of youth but on brain development.

Roberts (2011) also suggests that liberals or progressives have strongly advanced this current wave of "race-neutral" biopolitics and "cast the horrors of racial science as aberrant errors of the past" (295). An intense focus on science as value-free and neutral, as Roberts argues, erases demands for structural changes to systems that produce deeply inequitable life pathways. While Roberts identifies this moment as a contested "dawning era of biocitizenship" with the potential "for people dedicated to social justice to intervene collectively in bio-politics" (225), "technologies of the self" as defined by Michel Foucault (1988) have a long lineage. A mechanism of governance, these technologies of the self demand self-regulation and individuation and shift attention away from structural forces—such as poverty—to the body of the individual.

The lawyer and juvenile justice advocate Patricia Soung (2011) terms the shift toward basing juvenile justice reforms on biopolitics, specifically neurological research, *neurolaw*. Soung offers key questions, linked to Roberts's analysis, surrounding the use of science by advocates in recent juvenile justice reform initiatives: "Interpretations of the science [are] too often laden with deficits-language, even describing youth as a form of mental deficiency. Moreover, the application of neuroscience to a juvenile and criminal justice system disproportionately populated by people of color perpetuates and naturalizes associations between race, criminality and intellect. In the end, biologizing youth and race in the same moment distracts from a fuller social understanding of how youth, race and context interact, and what measures should be taken to address youth crime and racial inequity" (439–40). For Soung, the use of neurolaw obscures the root causes and contexts that produce youth, particularly low-income youth of color, as criminals. The shift to "biologizing" youth of color, Soung argues, also simultaneously ensures that youth are not understood as shaped through ideological contexts and histories.

Deracialized neurolaws also reproduce a discourse of youth as unique or different. This strategy of exceptionalism assumes that adults, or those over the magical age of culpability, have fully developed brains, are capable of reason, and therefore can and should be culpable and fully punished. Psychology and neurology provide evidence that juveniles are in need of state protection. Yet the inverse of this research posits that adults—or those over the age of consent—are culpable. Rehabilitation, transformation, and protection are available because of the delayed, temporal status of the child-juvenile.

New developmental categories also illustrate the flexibility between adult and juvenile. The psychologist Jeffrey Arnett proposed the category "emerging adulthood," defined as between eighteen and twenty-five years old, as a temporal stage: "It is a period characterized by change and exploration for most people, as they examine the life possibilities open to them and gradually arrive at more enduring choices in love, work, and worldviews" (Arnett 2000, 479). Emerging adulthood is a new developmental phase for college-educated young people for whom the secure markers of their class (and often racial and gendered status), including marriage, employment, and home ownership, have yet to be achieved (P. Cohen 2010). Some psychologists use this new life stage to refer to those who return home after college to live (Henig 2010). Almost concurrently, Becky Petit, Bruce Western, and other scholars have identified another development life stage (Petit and Western 2004). For other segments of the population, different factors emerge as "life stage" events. For young black men, going to prison has become akin to entering a new life stage, similar to joining the military or getting married. While black men (and black women) from low-income families are moved directly from childhood to adulthood and effectively denied adolescence (Petit and Western 2004), more-affluent young people who are not able to secure a foothold in a restructured economy (the growth of a just-in-time, low-wage service economy) are granted a new status and attendant benefits, such as extended access to their parents' health insurance (Arnett 2000).

Science, particularly neurological research, is not infallible. Poor people, women, queers, and/or communities of color have painful, and ongoing, histories of disqualification and dehumanization through scientific research. In particular, anatomy has historically provided scrupulous evidence of innate inferiority: brain weight, hair texture, nose length and width, cranial shape, genital size, and on and on (Stern 2005; K. Muhammad 2010; Roberts 2011). In the late 1800s, researchers and scientists used bodily measurements and skin color to determine where people from various cultures were placed on a hierarchical human ladder (Winfield 2007). Eugenics provided a "science" for white supremacists to "prove" that nonwhite people were inferior. From 1920 through 1940, across the United States, eugenicists striving for a racially and genetically pure society disseminated propaganda in the form of films, literature, and state fair displays (Snyder and Mitchell 2006). Propaganda moved into educational conferences and classrooms as scientifically based information to advance the health and well-being of able-bodied children. This literature routinely justified segregation in schools and other institutions under the frameworks of health and safety to keep "social degenerates" from preying on unsuspecting children. Testing and assessment proved essential to eugenics movements: "Eugenics provided scientific legitimacy to racism by affiliating with and influencing the developing field of mental measurement" (Ferri and Connor 2004, 67). These tests were used to measure intelligence, to prove racial superiority, and to identify people considered defective in some way. In 1931, C. Croft Williams, a public welfare official, speaking at the annual meeting of the American Prison Association, rationalized that the large number of "Negro offenders" was related to their "low mental power" and as biology shaped behavior, he opined that "perhaps studies in glands, nerves, brain, and blood may some day give us new conceptions of the Negro" (as cited in K. Mohammad 2010, 245).

Even after eugenics was formally discredited (by some), nonwhite people continued to be *objectively* identified as deficient, amoral, asexual, hypersexual, and/or sexually aggressive (M. Wallace 1979; Roberts 1997; Harris-Perry 2011). In the 1980s, "crack mothers" and "crack babies" emerged as a public policy panic. Based on scientific evidence that babies born to addicted mothers were creating a "generation damaged for life" in the 1980s and 1990s, this research opened the door to treating women who admitted to or were suspected of using crack cocaine as unfit to be mothers and in need of state management when pregnant or parenting (Winerip 2013). Decades later the body of scientific evidence that formed the foundation for this panic was dismissed as flawed. Children born to mothers addicted to crack were not damaged for life. In the 1990s, Charles Murray and John Dilulio produced social science research, now widely discredited, on the teenage superpredator that convinced many that black and brown youth possessed deficient intelligence and, as Dilulio predicted, an army of remorseless adult criminals would emerge if these teenage superpredators were not halted (Dilulio 1995).

Entangled with these eugenicist histories and frameworks, contemporary neurolaw strategies can possibly purchase slivers of protection for some juveniles—for instance, those who might otherwise have faced the death penalty or LWOP—but with collateral consequences. The response to the hyper-incarceration and criminalization of low-income communities of color is individuated. White supremacy, misogyny, colonialism, poverty, compulsory heterosexuality, and other forces that produce inequitable access to life pathways are erased. This turn to science by progressives in this political moment, as Roberts argues, is particularly distressing: "The liberal faith in scientific objectivity has generated an approach to the genetic definition of race that sounds remarkably similar to the conservative one. Like conservatives, liberals separate racial science from racial politics to retain a supposedly scientific concept of race as a genetic category. Liberal scientists erect a wall between their objective study of racial difference in the lab and racial politics at play in the outside world" (Roberts 2011, 293).

Even with the best of intentions, this strategy of advancing color-blind science to address complex injustices rooted in racial inequalities is flawed. Science, in particular neurology, is divorced from histories of eugenics and produces a biopolitical regime defining that youth, particularly youth of color, have diminished capacity. Adults are fashioned as the culpable, unchanging body for whom *difference from* must be established.

Childhood's Affects

While policing, punishment, prisons, and associated carceral systems continue to unevenly define the boundaries of adulthood, the category of the child also shapes artifacts central to everyday life. Innocence and consent are key characteristics associated with childhood. When the boundaries surrounding childhood move, innocence and consent also reconfigure. While previously associated with sin and the possibility of eternal damnation, eighteenth-century discourses of childhood created children as holy, angelic, and, persistently, innocent. In her rich analysis of the racialization of childhood in the United States, *Racial Innocence: Performing American Childhood from Slavery to Civil Rights* (2011), Robin Bernstein charts the seamless pairing of childhood and innocence: "By the nineteenth century, sentimental culture had woven childhood and innocence together wholly. Childhood was then understood not as innocent but as innocence itself; not as a symbol of innocence but as its embodiment. The doctrine of original sin receded, replaced by a doctrine of original innocence" (R. Bernstein 2011, 4). Yet childhood, and therefore innocence, was always a racialized, heterogendered project. Just as the "pickaninny" was constructed to categorize and desensitize the black child, the innocence embedded in and produced through childhood was blindingly, and seemingly invisibly, white.

Childhood not only shaped a racialized form of innocence but provided a "perfect alibi" for this ideological work. Bernstein contends that while nineteenth-century abolitionists had some success arguing that enslaved African Americans were capable of feeling pain (and were thus human), the "libel of insensateness" and its attendant meaning did not fade with the abolition of slavery but instead "stealthily" moved into "children's culture," where innocence "provides a cover under which otherwise discredited racial ideology survives and continues, covertly, to influence culture" (R. Bernstein 2011, 51). The abolition of slavery did not eradicate white supremacy. Bernstein and other historians suggest that categories such as children, still widely understood as race-neutral developmental markers, function as the perfect containers to house and reproduce deeply racialized (and heterogendered) conceptions of innocence.

The child continues to produce gendered and racialized forms of innocence. *Ethan is a child, but Cristian and Trayvon Martin and Michael Brown are not children.* Racial disproportionality at every level of the justice system—surveillance, arrest, removal from home, conviction, sentencing—clearly shows that youth of color do not have the same access to innocence and are not understood as sensate in the same way that white youth are. While innocence is "a lot like the air in your tires: there is not a lot you can do with it but lose it" (Kincaid 1998, 53), within our contemporary political landscape the a priori association with innocence is a potent asset. Through categories such as the "pickaninny," eighteenth-century writers excluded nonwhites from childhood and restricted access to characteristics such as innocence. How are similar disqualifications enacted today?

In addition to innocence, childhood is also defined by a lack of reason and therefore an inability to consent. Meaningful consent is the social contract underwriting democratic states, according to the seventeenth-century philosopher John Locke. Power and political status were not inherited or the product of birthright but based on "reason, merit and virtue" (Brewer 2005, 344). During the eighteenth and nineteenth centuries, meanings surrounding childhood and adulthood shifted as did the "nature of the boundaries between different stages of life" (351). The construction of children with their "almost complete inability to exercise judgment" functioned to "elevate reason beyond other human attributes" (351). The literary scholar Anna Mae Duane, building from Brewer's analysis, suggests: "The child effectively came to represent all that should exclude a subject from citizenship" (Duane 2010, 6). Incapable of reason, children were unfree, yet with the potential to adjust their status at adulthood.[5]

Concurrently, the child and her lack of reason and inability to consent also created structures that enabled the control and management of other populations. Historian Holly Brewer (2005) outlines how the construction of a child not yet capable of reason functioned to disqualify other groups: "Children became subjects incapable of consent, because they did not have reason. But the emphasis on their informed consent provided an excuse to deny equality and consent to others on the same grounds. Comparing women, blacks, and other groups to children in their reasoning abilities would become common in the wake of the Revolution for those who sought to legitimate elements of the older order" (341). While the status of a child could potentially be useful, many groups—including women, African Americans, people with disabilities, and indigenous communities—have been, and still are, assessed as childlike. This classification, far from providing benefits, ensures that these communities do not have the rights attached to full citizenship. Once children were established as without reason and incapable of full citizenship, infantilization functioned to disqualify others.

To justify slavery, advocates invoked images of enslaved people as children, a tactic exemplified by George Fitzhugh in *Sociology of the South* (1854): "Would the abolitionists approve of a system of society that set white children free, and remitted them at the age of fourteen, males and females, to all the rights, both as to person and property, which belong to adults? Would it be criminal or praiseworthy to do so? Criminal of course" (as cited in Brewer 2005, 359). Enslaved people were childlike and required the management of white adults. Diminished capacity easily translated into disenfranchisement, enforced sterilization and other restrictions on parenting, confinement, and premature death. To be "childlike" severed access to due process and rendered one potentially subject to a host of state-sanctioned violations.

The residential boarding school movement throughout Canada, the United States, and Australia provides just one example of a state's classification of an entire group of people as childlike, not fully human, and therefore not full citizens. Residential schools across the United States and Canada aimed to colonize First Nations children between 1890 until as late as 1990. Often removed from their communities by force, First Nations children were placed in schools where they were starved, beaten for speaking languages other than English, forced to conform to Anglo-Christian norms and values, often sexually assaulted, and trained for low-wage work. These schools had widespread support from settler-colonial communities, including religious, political, and philanthropic groups. Scientific evidence was marshaled to illustrate how the students' savagery and primitive ways demanded (white) civilization and intervention: child-stealing and land grabs (Adams 1988; Haig-Brown 1988; A. Smith 2005). Across Australia, Canada, and the United States, indigenous peoples were not seen as fully human, as adults, or as capable of reason. In Australia, Aboriginal people were classified as flora and fauna until 1967 (Marks 2013). Entire communities were denied autonomy and self-determination, and lands and resources were stolen, fracturing kinship networks and nations. Often these practices were legitimated through the veneer of protection. Sylvia Wynter outlines that forms of self-perception continue to animate this life-defining taxonomy: "to realize ourselves as normally human in the Western bourgeoisie's always already biocentrically chartered, therefore sociogenically encoded and semantically activated, *symbolic life's* opiate- rewarded (placebo) terms" (Wynter, in McKittrick 2015, 59). The disability studies scholar Lennard Davis argues that rather than being "childlike," people of color and indigenous communities are instead viewed as disabled. Davis writes that nineteenth-century eugenics classified as undesirable people who "were clearly delineated under the rubric of feeble-mindedness and degeneration as women, people of color, homosexuals, the working classes and so on. All of these were considered to be categories of disability, although we do not think of them as connected in this way today" (L. Davis 2010, 266).

Child-rearing manuals from the eighteenth and nineteenth centuries, as the literary theorist Ann Laura Stoler writes, often compared white children to racialized others to discipline them: "Children are invariably othered in ways that compare them to lower order-beings, they are animal-like, lack civility, discipline, and sexual restraint; their instincts are base, they are too close to nature, they are, like racialized others, not fully human beings" (Stoler 1995, 151). To become an adult translated into acquiring reason, modeling civility, and distinguishing oneself from "lower orders." Middle-class white children's bodies and sexualities, Stoler argues, were schooled through discourses of racialized class difference (1995, 151). Stoler suggests that the racial other is the fixed referent, while middle-class white children's identities were more flexible (163).

Reproductive rights for all women and for people with disabilities are still contested. Many indigenous nations across Australia, Canada, and North America struggle for self-determination including the right to parent and to control access to education and health care. In the United States, many nonwhite kinship systems are still chastised as deficient, not normal, and potentially dangerous for children. Nonadults are not permitted the right to object to mandatory schooling. People who were formerly incarcerated are also often seen as infantile and in need of constant monitoring. Many communities are still formally and informally characterized as childlike and therefore constrained by the logic of diminished capacity.

Age is an integral and yet subsequently undertheorized category within our legal (and democratic) structures. The naturalization of children as incapable of agency and in need of protection cloaks the reproduction of profound inequities that impact those who are considered children, but also all of us, particularly members of other marginalized communities. Holly Brewer argues that it is critical to unpack the naturalized associations between age and consent, not necessarily to alter our understanding of children, but to rethink our understanding of consent:

By naturalizing the position of children, we not only distort the past but make it impossible to understand the debates over authority during this period and the transformations in social order and ideology for all of society. Unless we pay attention to those who are unequal in this theory of equality, to those who cannot consent in this theory of consent, we cannot see what the theory really meant, in the abstract and as it shaped the logic of the laws. We cannot understand how people could manipulate this theory to create a new structure of privilege, one that could be twisted to justify—even slavery. The construction of consent, grounded in an ideology of reason, deeply affected norms in a supposedly unchanging legal system. With its abstract principles it projected an ahistorical system of values that cover and obscure historical struggles over power. If we cannot see these connections, we lose the ability to justify or understand many modern norms. (Brewer 2005, 12)

Reason scaffolded the development of a new regime of governance—a democratic republic—produced against the backdrop of slavery. Childhood is emblematic of a lack of reason. Unpacking the magical age of childhood illustrates not only how the category of child shaped the life pathways of people who counted as children but also how ideas about children and childhood supported wider political and economic regimes. Consent and innocence, frameworks intimately linked to children, shape institutions beyond those directly attached to childhood.

As a legal category conferring particular privileges, neither "childhood" nor "juvenile" is available to all. Not only are the boundaries of childhood dynamic, but *who counts as a child* and what evidence is used to make these claims informs our political moment. Ethan's affluenza renders him innocent, a privilege available because of his ability to be understood as a child and incapable of reason—diminished capacity. Cristian, however, is not seen as a child by the state and does not benefit from an association with innocence. Informing and naturalizing conceptions of innocence and guilt, consent and freedom, *the child* shapes key foundations of the criminal justice system and democracy.

2

The Trouble with the Child in the Carceral State

In the late summer of 2008 I attended a meeting on the west side of Chicago. The focus was to debate a proposed zoning bylaw change to permit a community-based organization, St. Leonard's Ministries (SLM), to convert a building in the vicinity into housing for women and their children and to open a coffee shop. The apartments and the café would house and employ formerly incarcerated women. A visible organization with over fifty years in the neighborhood, over the last three years a number of condominium buildings had popped up, and the demographics of the community changed.

Most of the people at the meeting were new local condo owners who contrasted with the few residents and staff members of SLM at the meeting, who were predominantly black and Latino.

The members of the local condominium association were opposed to any SLM expansion, including additional housing space for formerly incarcerated women in the neighborhood. The meeting turned into a speak-out against any proposed zoning changes that might make it possible to offer more temporary housing for people exiting prisons and jail, as well as providing other forms of low-income housing. Many expressed concerns about safety. At the tail end of the meeting a woman stood up and stated that she did not want any more "ex-cons" living in the neighborhood because it was not safe. *More dangerous men in the neighborhood and I cannot let my children play in the street.* The few in the room trying to advocate for housing for women coming out of prison—our motley crew—had no public rejoinder. Housing for mothers and children was (temporarily) halted by other mothers and their children.

Demands for child safety that turn on restricting access to rights and resources for others are not unusual. Children represent an almost unassailable future-oriented goodness. Yet, when invoked, demands for childhood safety do not just create images of a child. Claims surrounding the needs of children (real and imagined) also often define and police all that childhood is not: adulthood. The poet and scholar Fred Moten observes:

> What is it about adults that's so distasteful? You see a kid on the street or in your house, you know you're supposed to feed them, right? And then that same kid hits eighteen and all of a sudden you say, "I'm not feeding you." What's so vulgar and gross and smelly and distasteful about the average adult that you wouldn't just assume that he should get something to eat? I mean, you've gotta be sick to come up with something like that. I mean, who's the worst person in the world? Even he should have something to eat. (Moten, in Harney and Moten 2013, 157)

Yet what if Moten's question were inverted and expanded? What makes (some) children exempt from disgust? What enables children to be afforded certain rights and privileges, and not adults? What are the costs, to children, and to others, of these privileges? How can child safety shut down a community meeting on expanding housing access for people coming out of prisons and jails?

The sentimental figure of the child, as Lee Edelman (2004) chronicles dismally in *No Future*, "remains the perpetual horizon of every acknowledged politics, the fantasmatic beneficiary of every political intervention" (2–3). Yet, while Edelman describes the heterosexualized white child who dominates futurity, an analysis supported by this chapter, not all children represent the future, and not all access childhood. José Esteban Muñoz (2009) reminds us that the symbolic child has little to do with the material lives of those who are black, brown, queer, or poor: "The future is only the stuff of some kids. Racialized kids, queer kids, are not the sovereign princes of futurity" (95). The category of childhood, as the previous chapter outlines, continues to be unavailable to nonwhite communities and to produce racialized and heterogendered affects. Particular forms of harm experienced by specific black, brown, and/or other marginalized children can mobilize the carceral regime (often to act against their own parents and communities), yet the futures of white youth matter more. While tropes such as "family values" are critically deconstructed by organizers and scholars, the use of children, or of empty signifiers such as "child protection," receives less scrutiny. Deconstructing the circulations of the child in contemporary campaigns offers windows into thinking about the most central questions in justice work today. Our criminal system counts on these bright lines between innocence and guilt.

This chapter explores the circulation of real and imagined children in movements that surround the carceral state: the harmed black or brown male child/youth fights the school to prison pipeline; the sexually innocent (white) female child demands protection from sex offenders and sexual traffickers; the white (male) gay student requires laws to fend off bullies; and the undocumented (Latina/o) youth merits immigration reform to secure adulthood. In these four contexts, material children are invoked, but, as importantly, ideas about youth and childhood circulate through these campaigns. Not finite or discrete, representations of the child within these movements and campaigns perform a wide range of political and affective labor. The child reinforces the legitimacy and the perceived ahistoric neutrality and stability of concepts—such as innocence and consent—that undergird the criminal justice system and, as Moten suggests, also feed our disgust and distaste for unfamiliar adults.

While young people's lives can be extraordinarily precarious, movements that make visible their vulnerability to demand protection, often through criminalization or through visibility in a carceral regime can augment the very precarity of young people. These strategies also often animate a "penology of racial innocence," as legal theorists Naomi Murakawa and Katherine Beckett outline: "the study of punishment obscures the operation of racial power in penal practices and institutions" (Murakawa and Beckett 2010, 696). Exhaustive research on the status of the juvenile in our justice systems, often chronicling deep racial disproportionality, has not been able to arrest the treatment of young people of color in our nation's streets and schools. Neither the category of the child nor the criminal justice system are race neutral, therefore reforms predicated on the status of the juvenile or on tinkering with the procedures and process in the institutions and systems that regulate young people, will ensure justice. A reading of the use of the child in each of these campaigns illustrates how the invocation of children/childhood, even with the best of intentions, functions to strengthen regimes of racialized and heterogendered criminalization that make everyone, even the *child*, less secure.

Harmed Black or Brown (Male) Youth

A December 2012 congressional hearing on ending the school to prison pipeline featured twenty-year-old Edward Ward, a volunteer member of Blocks Together, a community organization that works to support the efforts of residents of the near west side of Chicago to change their community. Ward, now an undergraduate at a Chicago university, spoke about his experience at Orr High School. For the black and brown students at the school, Ward testified, Orr was "like we stepped into prison": "From the moment we stepped through the doors in the morning, we were faced with metal detectors, x-ray machines, and uniformed security." Orr security officers "spoke to us as if we were animals" and "being in detention was like being in solitary confinement." Like many nonrestrictive-enrollment schools in the Chicago public school system, Orr had "a police processing center so police could book students then and there. The officers don't get any special training to be in the school so they don't treat us like we are misbehaving; they treat us like we are committing crimes" (E. Ward 2012). Ward's testimony highlighted how youth are treated within a prison-like institution: disrespected, harassed, threatened, profiled, and preemptively detained.

In research and organizing work surrounding the school to prison pipeline, the focus frequently centers on harmed male youth of color such as Edward Ward (Herbert 2010; Petit and Western 2004; Lochner and Moretti 2004; Justice Policy Institute 2002). Young men of color do experience high rates of suspension and explusion and school-based racial profiling. They are frequently not viewed as child-like and the harm they experience does not seem to count. The criminalized black male youth is the statistic and the body most frequently circulated, even when young women of color constitute the fastest-growing population of those locked behind bars and research consistently illustrates that black girls also face high rates of punitive school discipline (Crenshaw 2015; Wun 2016; Lawston and Lucas 2011; Sudbury 2004). Sexual and gender violence pushes girls out of school, and researchers have linked interpersonal sexual violence as a "powerful indicator" of young girls' future incarceration (Simkins et al. 2004; Winn 2010). Research also highlights that "consensual same–sex acts more often trigger punishments [from schools and courts] than equivalent opposite sex behaviors" (Himmelstein and Bruckner 2011, 50). These queer and gendered narratives are often minimized or erased in public examples describing the school to prison pipeline, erasing a more nuanced and complex analysis of identity and subjugation.

The choice by those working against the school to prison pipeline to represent the figure of the harmed and criminalized black and brown male youth is not surprising. Just as the state identifies that specific white female bodies require protection from particular forms of sexual violence, historically, the punished black male body has represented of freedom denied. Angela Davis, in her introduction to the 2010 reissue of Frederick Douglass's biography, highlights the gendered complexities of abolitionist narratives. Slavery was often narrated as the loss of the natural rights attached to patriarchy and masculinity. Davis (2010) writes that "lurking within the definition of Black freedom as the reclamation of Black manhood is the obligatory suppression of Black womanhood" (24). Robin Kelley also argues that "manhood rights" were understood as strategies of black liberation across the nineteenth and early twentieth centuries, as "servility of any kind was regarded as less than manly" (2002, 26).

In contemporary depictions of black (and brown) youth trapped in the pipeline, the danger and cost of imprisonment are often framed as a loss of manhood. Freedom is the regeneration of black manhood, de facto heterosexualized and gendered. These framings are reflected across the political spectrum in contemporary interventions to the school-to-prison pipeline (STPP). As the STPP is framed as a crisis for black boys and men, responses often reinforce conceptions of gender (and race) as static: manhood or family curriculum that do not address patriarchy, single-sex schools and boys' after-school programs that require or assume compulsory heteronormativity, and ongoing attempts to coerce marriage to solve the problem of poor single mothers, who are often framed as responsible for the rise in imprisonment rates for black youth, particularly males (Goldberg 2014). The 2014 "My Brother's Keeper" White House initiative that focused on young black men and boys and sought to "help break down barriers, clear pathways to opportunity, and reverse troubling trends" was roundly critiqued for its reliance on personal responsibility and also by its erasure of gender and sexuality and the lives of black women and girls (Jarrett and Johnson 2014: McClain 2014).

Yet making the case that the nonwhite male body is being harmed, and counts as a child, is not a shallow move. In struggles for liberation worldwide, many subjugated people fight to be understood as sensate.

Historically, pushing the association between children and those enslaved was a tactic deployed primarily by early white abolitionists. To be seen as a child was (and often still is) to inherit a thicket of affective possibilities, particularly a status that one's harm, vulnerability, and pain will ensure full and unfettered access to the positionality of "victim." To be harmed, a body must be sensate, be capable of experiencing pain, and count as fully human. Establishing this point through a linkage with childhood was an early white abolitionist strategy that met with mixed results. White audiences might pity individual enslaved and harmed children but be unable to critically engage the political systems, or their own relationships to these structures, that created this harm (E. Bernstein 2010; Duane 2010; McBride 2001). These associations between children and enslaved peoples also produced a range of affective possibilities, including sentimentalism and paternalism, in addition to the potential revolutionary resonances attached to childhood.

The overwhelming majority of current "schools, not jails" organizing centers the harmed black and brown child, generally male, often for (white) policy makers, politicians, educators, and other public school workers. These campaigns work to ensure that the bodies harmed by the STPP count as children, and they often feature personal examples of experiences of policing, detention, repression, and arrest in schools. The circulation of the black and brown *male child* in strategies to resist the STPP not only functions to reproduce heterosexualized and gendered constructions of freedom; these campaigns also invoke ideas of children and innocence as neutral and a priori categories. Risking the evocation of sentimentality that does not produce structural shifts through the use of the child and childhood, the racialization of innocence is both masked and reproduced throughout anti-STPP campaigns. Claiming nonwhite youth as children or juveniles does not allow for a critical exploration of the conception of innocence: who benefits, who does not, and why. Nor does widening the category of who might have access to childhood (and therefore possibly innocence) unpack the underlying nexus of other associations tied to childhood.

Criminal justice reformers have used innocence and an array of proxy terms and concepts for decades in attempts to wrest some sort of reform from our nation's addiction to punishment and incarceration. Some of the most visible prison reform campaigns over the past twenty years have focused on the treatment of mentally ill inmates or have worked to free those falsely accused. A core legal strategy is to assert that juveniles and youth are "categorically less culpable" (Soung 2011, 439). Yet, just as childhood needs adulthood, innocence requires guilt. While the work to dismantle the STPP does not aim to reify innocence, and the youth centered in these campaigns are often refused access to the category of children by the state, the demand to claim childhood for those harmed by the pipeline erases how the category of childhood itself shields the racialized reproduction of innocence.

Innocent (Girl) Child

Child sexual safety is a central spoke justifying carceral expansion: the "worst of the worst"—those who commit acts of sexual violence against the most innocent/children—necessitate a punishing state apparatus. Hyperbolic media coverage of "stranger danger" augments the penalties and restrictions associated with conviction as a sex offender, leading to an increase in, and the naturalization of, the surveillance and policing of public spaces, including parks, school grounds, and the Internet. For example, there is no evidence that sex offender registries and notification systems reduce persistent sexual violence against anyone; as the criminologist Wayne Logan (2009) writes, their expansion has been "based on a mere verisimilitude of empirical justification" (99).[1]

In the past twenty years, high-profile media coverage of sexual violence against children has almost uniformly focused on white children (Levine 2002; Lancaster 2011). The names of laws passed throughout the 1990s and the first years of the twenty-first century with the aim of protecting children from sexual violence reflect this focus, including Megan's Law, Jessica's Law, and the Amber Alert, all of which represent white female children (Lancaster 2011).[2] While children of color also experience sexual violence, their bodies command less white empathy, and the child's innocence (or the mother's) is not assumed and must be proven. The abduction and sexual assault of children of color by strangers does not garner national attention, nor do they fuel national laws to "protect" children. The political traction received by the figure of the innocent white child is in direct proportion to the devaluation and stigmatization of the black child (and black mothers). Historically, the status of *child* (and later youth or juvenile) and its associated protections in the labor market and the legal realm were simply unavailable to nonwhite bodies.

Similarly, the privileges and protections that accompany motherhood were also unavailable to nonwhite mothers (Roberts 2003).

The definition of motherhood, and of who can wield this status to influence public policy, is still intimately interconnected to race and national reproduction.[3] Registries were built with the support of this maternalist model, constructed on narrow definitions of vulnerable children (and mothers). Bodies that do not fit—undocumented, black, disabled, queer, and/or non-gender-conforming—do not command the same empathy or political capital. Black mothers and families continue to be viewed as deficient, and "child safety" too often translates into removal of the child from the home. Interpersonal sexual violence experienced by children of color does not propel public policies but rather contributes to the demonization of mothers of color and legitimizes child seizure (Roberts 2003). The decades of work by feminist legal scholars and grassroots organizers that changed rape laws were not evident in these public, often maternal, strategies to create and to augment sex offender legislation. The feminist legal scholar Rose Corrigan, in her detailed research, points out that "the most threatening aspects of feminist rape law reform—its criticisms of violence, sexuality, family, and repressive institutions—are those that supporters of Megan's Law erase in rhetoric and practice" (2006, 276).

Feelings about children, public spaces, race, and sexuality continue to be harnessed to expand the carceral state. The image of the vulnerable female child/potential victim juxtaposed with the figure of the sex offender stirs feelings of fear and anger. In some spheres, sex offenders have become synonymous with and representative of all people behind bars, thus making decarceration challenging. Carceral expansion required intricate parallel affective economies to scaffold the "worst of the worst." The desire to protect *the children* still halts decarceration initiatives, requiring and remaking the child, and suturing innocence to the white girl-child body.

In the past several years other representations of child sexual violence have emerged to augment punishment and policing practices within and outside U.S. borders. Antitrafficking legislation aims to protect children (and women) who are forced into "modern-day slavery." Antitrafficking organizations cite a range of numbers to signify the amount of people currently enslaved. The website of the organization End Slavery Now cites an "estimated 20.9 million people trapped in some form of slavery today" and "4.5 million victims of sex trafficking" (http://www.endslaverynow .org/learn/slavery-today). The website for the Not for Sale organization states, "Slavery is not dead: Human trafficking enslaves more than 30 million women, children and men every year" (https://notforsalecampaign .org/). The Polaris Project, while not offering any definitive numbers, states, "There are more people enslaved today than at the height of the transatlantic slave trade" (Ocasio 2013).[4] The website for New Yorks' New Abolitionists, cites "5.5 Million: Number of children worldwide who are victims of human trafficking each year" (http://www.newyorksnewabolitionists.com/). Children are, as all sources identify, the most likely to be trafficked, and while organizations often mention that people are trafficked for labor, sexual trafficking is highlighted.

The U.S. Victims of Trafficking and Violence Protection Act (VTVPA), passed in 2000, while designed to stop human trafficking, focuses especially on "the sex trade, slavery, and involuntary servitude." The VTVPA created new enforcement agencies and new systems of criminalization and made trafficking a federal crime. The U.S. government also initially required all organizations receiving federal funds for the purpose of combating domestic or international trafficking to include a statement that they opposed both sex trafficking and prostitution. In 2013 the Supreme Court ruled that the federal government cannot require groups to endorse a viewpoint, and this policy of requiring all organizations that work against sex trafficking to publicly adopt an antiprostitution stance was revoked (Barnes 2013). The feminist scholar Elizabeth Bernstein, who has written extensively on the global antitrafficking movement and its alliances with U.S. Christian forces, writes that organizations that sign on to end sex trafficking are required to take "a carceral loyalty oath" or to legitimate that the criminal justice system is the primary and effective response to harm (E. Bernstein 2010).

Despite the passage of a federal law and corresponding state laws, there have been few arrests or convictions. In 2009, the *New York Times*, in an article titled "Despite Law, Few Trafficking Arrests," Joseph Berger noted that the state of New York, after the passage of an antitrafficking law in 2007 and law enforcement's prioritization of trafficking, had made only eighteen arrests, resulting in one conviction (Berger 2009). In 2013, despite this low record of arrests or convictions, New York established eleven special courts across the state to provide services to victims of trafficking and to address prostitution cases (Rashbaum 2013). Such responses are not unique to the United States; in 2009 the United Kingdom started a law enforcement crackdown on sexual trafficking, Operation Pentameter. Yet, despite raids on sex workers, the UK police failed to produce any trafficked people or traffickers (Davies 2009).

Researchers and activists suggest that, far from "catching" international traffickers or "rescuing victims," this focus has created a "misguided moral crusade" (Thrupkaew 2012). Infamously, in 2014 journalists publicized that Somaly Mam, an internationally known activist working against sexual trafficking, invented her biography of being sold as a child sex slave and that her teenage daughter was also captured and trafficked. Her fabricated life story was used to garner resources to support million-dollar international missions to countries such as Cambodia, where (often forcibly) "rescued" sex workers reported harm and violence from the rescuers (Gira-Grant 2014). Protecting girls and women from the threat of sexual trafficking often legitimates and masks the increased policing and criminalization of consensual domestic sex work and regulates sexuality and gender beyond U.S. borders (Kempadoo 2005; Soderlund 2005; Agustín 2007; Chapkis 2003; Vance 2011).

In efforts to secure child sexual safety, state responses naturalize a carceral apparatus and bury underlying tensions tethering sex (including sex work) and age to consent. Sex work is understood by some as always harmful and coercive—a form of modern slavery.

(Dead) Queer Child

Harm experienced by LGBTQ youth is also used to expand punishment and to extend policing practices further into schools. In 2008, a fifteen-year-old boy named Lawrence "Larry" King was shot in the head and killed in his middle school computer lab by a classmate, Brandon McInerney, aged fourteen (Cathcart 2008). Brandon was horrified that Larry flirted with him in public. King's murder was followed, in 2010, by a concentrated and well-publicized wave of suicides by gay youth, including Tyler Clementi, Seth Walsh, Asher Brown, and Billy Lucas. These suicides, like Larry's murder, were preceded by intense sexuality- and gender-policing by peers and teachers and triggered a series of antibullying initiatives.

The high-profile media attention that centered select (often white and male) examples of antigay bullying spurred state legislatures to act. States that already had school antibullying programs, including character education or legislation, broadened these policies. For example, in 2011, New Jersey implemented what has been described as "the strongest anti-bullying legislation in the country" after Rutgers freshman Tyler Clementi's suicide (Education Law Center 2013). Called the Anti-Bullying Bill of Rights, the New Jersey law requires teachers to report bullying to administrators, requires school superintendents to report bullying to the state board of education, and allows the suspension or expulsion of students accused of bullying (Friedman 2010). In 2012, a law criminalizing cyberbullying passed in North Carolina. In an effort to protect school employees, this law makes it a crime for any student to post real images or make any statement online—even if it is true—that provokes harassment. Other prohibited acts by students are signing teachers up to receive junk mail, posting pictures of teachers online, and making fake websites. In North Carolina, those who are sixteen are treated as adults under state law; therefore, if convicted, a student could face thirty days in jail or a $1,000 fine (Miller 2013). As of 2015, all states have antibullying laws (Child Trends 2015).

Meanwhile, despite the increased media focus on particular kinds of youth violence and focused support for antibullying legislation, nongender-conforming and nonheterosexual young people continue to harm and be harmed in classrooms, on playgrounds, and online. Stories splash across media outlets every day. A New York fourteen-year-old, Jamey Rodemeyer, contributed a video statement to the online It Gets Better archive in May 2011 and, after experiencing physical, verbal, and online harassment about his perceived sexuality, hanged himself in September 2011 (Praetorius 2011). On June 5, 2012, Kardin Ulysse, a New York City middle school student, was blinded in one eye after being assaulted by a group of boys shouting antigay taunts in the cafeteria of Roy Mann Junior High School (Cannold 2012). Also in 2012, in New Jersey, Pine Lake Elementary School student "C.O." routinely returned from school "bruised, crying, and depressed" from being verbally and physically harassed about his perceived sexual orientation. His parents asked the school to intervene in a culture of pervasive homophobia that included classmates yelling homophobic slurs at C.O. from his own front lawn, and being called "gay," "fag," and "girl" every day at school. C.O.'s parents were told that he "should attempt to 'make new friends.'" When C.O. was as-saulted on a school bus with a metal seat belt and the school and the district still refused to intervene, the family moved and C.O. transferred to a differ-ent school (Armstrong 2012). While most of the attacks that become high profile or receive media or other attention target cisgender boys, others, in-cluding trans youth in particular, are certainly not exempt from violence.

These acts of interpersonal and structural heteronormativity or trans-phobia, of course, are neither new nor surprising. Heteronormativity—the structures and systems that "legitimize and privilege heterosexuality and heterosexual relationships as fundamental and 'natural' within soci-ety" (C. Cohen 2005, 24)—is pervasive in most institutions, including schools. Fear of the queer, or all the meanings and associations attached to non-heteronormativity, leads schools to suppress teachers and creates cultures that facilitate harm toward non-gender-conforming and non-heteronormative youth. Instead of excavating heteronormativity in schools, legislative responses to bullying define the "problem" narrowly and posit punishment and criminalization as the response. These laws are predi-cated on the concept that if we removed or changed the few bad kids, schools would be safer for queers. While this practice could purchase a temporary reprieve, a few bad kids in schools are not the root problem. These initiatives are not capable of excavating heteronormativity. Beyond individuating what is in fact a structural and institutional problem, anti-bullying laws and their accompanying punitive sanctions operate in al-ready highly attenuated spaces for surveillance and punishment that are neither race- nor gender-neutral. School suspension rates for African Americans, in particular for African American males, are significantly higher than for their white counterparts (Office for Civil Rights 2012; Losen and Skiba 2010; Skiba et al. 2002). Excessively punitive disciplinary measures that disproportionately target the most marginalized students in school contexts (including queer youth) made national headlines in 2011, highlighting the educational cost to young people when they are pushed out of school (Losen and Skiba 2010; Phillips 2011; Schwarz 2011; Himmel-stein and Bruckner 2011). Given this preexisting landscape, when "disruptive behavior" and "other" are the dominant reasons for suspensions, it is not a stretch to predict that antibullying laws will be unevenly implemented and that particular students will be disproportionately targeted and punished.

While the majority of the laws passed nationally are also intended to act preventively, the sanction and punishment measures are generally most powerful. In 2011, California made bullying illegal with the passage of "Seth's Law," yet all language requiring counseling or restorative justice practices was pulled from the final version of the bill. Rather than being proactive, the bill is retroactively punitive, involving spot checks of schools to see if they are in compliance (Gould 2011). In 2011, New Jersey enacted its Anti-Bullying Bill of Rights tightening the relationship between schools and local law enforcement. The law forces schools and officials to report incidents more quickly and to hire school-based antibullying specialists, and increases penalties for bullying; it also provides for a Crimestoppers telephone line, which makes "reporting easier, but . . . also ups the ante by involving law enforcement rather than resolving issues in the principal's office" (Hu 2011). In 2014, Carson, California, proposed charging anyone who cyberbullies or physically bullies anyone of school age, up to age twenty-five, with a misdemeanor and/or fining them (C. Muhammad 2014). These laws deepen already existing relationships to law enforcement and also falsely assume that law enforcement is free of violence or bullying. Police and other security forces are often key perpetrators of sexual and other forms of violence (Richie 2012).

The suicides of white male queer youth engender the most public response, perhaps because of the images of the grief of white heterosexual parents. For example, in the deaths of Seth Walsh and Jamey Rodemeyer (and, earlier, the death of Matthew Shepard), the maternal and paternal losses are mobilized to support antibullying or hate crimes legislation. After his 2009 murder by peers in Chicago, sixteen-year-old Derrion Albert was repeatedly identified in the national media as physically slight, an excellent student, and a "Grandmomma's boy" (C. Cohen 2012, 126). Meanwhile, Albert's family was rarely visible in mainstream coverage; instead the media focused on violent, unruly black male youths. For dead white gay youths, the families' loss is often highly visible.

LGBTQ young people face persistent violence in schools, and numerous reports highlight the interpersonal violence that non-gender-conforming and non-heteronormative students experience at the hands of peers, teachers, and other staff members (Kosciw et al. 2010; Pascoe 2007; McCready 2010). Yet interpersonal violence is precipitated and shaped by state violence. A 2009 national study of LGBT students of color, *Shared Differences: The Experiences of Lesbian, Gay, Bisexual, and Transgender Students of Color in Our Nation's Schools,* identified the curricular and systemic erasure and marginalization of LGBTQ youth of color:

> Few LGBT students of color had access to LGBT-inclusive curricular resources in school. Less than a fifth of students had been taught about LGBT-related people, history, or events in their classes, or had such information available in their textbooks (14% each). Furthermore, only 38% reported that they could access LGBT-related resources in their school library. Less than a fifth of all LGBT students of color (18%) reported that their school had a comprehensive policy to address in-school harassment and assault, which provided specific protections based on sexual orientation and gender identity/expression. (Diaz and Kosciw 2009, 13)

Violence is a problem, and yet the question gets framed very narrowly: If not antibullying laws, then what? This chapter's analysis outlines that the state's responses to violence mask the problem. These laws transfer structural factors that perpetuate and reward heteronormativity into individual pathologies and also suggest that the route to ending homophobia is to punish perpetrators. The symbolic figure of the dead queer white male child and, as importantly, the kinship networks that the child is attached to are used to pass these laws. Queer youth, who are often criminalized for their sexual practices, restricted by ordinances and statutes that deny transgender and non-gender-conforming youth gender-affirming bathroom access, and can be placed on the sex offender registry for consensual sexual acts, appear to incite less concern from the state while alive or when unharmed.

Harm and violence experienced by the child, in conjunction with desires of communities for systemic change, advance agendas that do little to make communities actually safer, particularly for those who are non-heterosexual and/or non-gender-conforming. An increase in criminalization means that those most vulnerable—including queers and those involved in survival economies such as the sex and drug trades—will be caught up in the criminal justice system. More people in the system means more people subjected to racist, gendered, and heteronormative judicial proceedings. Conviction means detention and confinement in institutions predicated on gender normativity, compulsory heteronormativity, and racial oppression.

Undocumented DREAM-ing Student

In 2009 the student and/or child emerged as a powerful figure within public debates surrounding immigration, recalibrating the political landscape for immigration reform. Young people across the nation began to speak publicly about their immigration status and to demand immigration reform. The 2011 campaign of the Chicago-based Immigrant Youth Justice League was titled Undocumented and Unafraid, and many members of this group (and others across the United States) publicly outed themselves as undocumented at rallies and in interviews with mainstream media sources. Some participated (and were arrested) in high-profile public mobilizations in Georgia, Washington, D.C., Arizona, and Illinois. These actions were the result of careful training and collaborative consultation processes within the wider immigrant justice movement. Increasing numbers of young people publicly coming out as undocumented and organizing deeply altered the landscape for immigration movements across the United States (Marcum 2010; O'Neill 2012; Olivo 2010).

If "coming out" sounds familiar, it should. In 2012, in front-page articles for the *New York Times* and *Time* magazine, the journalist Jose Antonio Vargas (then thirty-one years old) came out as undocumented (and as gay). Vargas explicitly makes the connections between gay liberationists coming out and the outing tactics of the contemporary (youth) undocumented movement:

> While closely associated with the modern gay-rights movement, in recent years the term coming out and the act itself have been embraced by the country's young undocumented population. At least 2,000 undocumented immigrants—most of them under 30—have contacted me and outed themselves in the past year. Others are coming out over social media or in person to their friends, their fellow students, their colleagues. It's true, these individuals—many brought to the US by family when they were too young to understand what it means to be "illegal"—are a fraction of the millions living hidden lives. But each becomes another walking conversation. (Vargas 2012)

The wave of young people publicly naming themselves as undocumented students, and as hard-working young people brought to this country by their parents as children or babies, educated audiences about the impact of punishing immigration policies. Concurrently, these practices of coming out also engendered some limited public sympathy for young undocumented people, generally at the cost of framing their parents and others as the real criminals.

While estimates vary, approximately twelve million to seventeen million people undocumented people live and work in the United States. With a staggering increase in the number of noncitizens detained daily, from 7,475 to 33,330 between 1995 and 2011 (Meissner et al. 2013, 11), Immigration and Customs Enforcement (ICE) shapes communities across the United States:

> There are now 16.6 million US residents in families with at least one unauthorized immigrant. Nine million are part of "mixed-status" families that contain at least one unauthorized citizen parent, and one child born the United States. Of the 10.2 million unauthorized adult immigrants living the United States, 63 per cent had been in the country for a decade or longer. In 2010 52 per cent of Latinos in the United States reported that they worry that they, a family member, or close friend could be deported. One-quarter of all Latinos polled reported that they knew someone who had been deported or detained by federal authorities in 2011. (Meissner et al. 2013, 134–35)

While the United States has a history of racialized and heterogendered immigration policies (Ngai 2004; Canaday 2009), since the 1960s federal legislation has provided some people working and living in the United States without legal papers options for legalization and/or relief from the threat of deportation. While limited, these reforms, which included amnesty initiatives, made it possible for millions of people in the United States to access pathways for legalization. The most recent legislation that included an amnesty component, the Immigration Reform and Control Act (IRCA) of 1986, offered approximately three million people who are undocumented a pathway for legalization. Since IRCA's passage the only significant legislation related to immigration reform that has received any traction—yet as of 2016 had not passed—is linked to providing pathways only for young people to adjust their status.

The Development Relief and Education for Alien Minors (DREAM) Act, first introduced in 2001 by Senator Orrin Hatch of Utah, attempted to provide a legal path to citizenship for undocumented students. Tereza Lee, now an internationally recognized pianist, is widely credited as the youth who inspired the DREAM Act in 2001. Her trajectory started by coming out as undocumented to a teacher, spurring local education and elected officials to assist undocumented students (Lee later achieved U.S. citizenship through heterosexual marriage) (M. Brown 2012). The last iteration of the DREAM Act, in 2012, offered undocumented students who arrived in the United States before the age of sixteen, have lived in this country for at least five years, and are of "good moral character" temporary residency for six years, during which time they must obtain at least an associate's degree or complete two years of military service. After satisfying these requirements, a young person could be eligible to apply for permanent residency. Those who do not meet the requirements could be subject to deportation. As Latinos have low rates of college entry and college completion (Kelly, Schneider, and Carey 2010), many termed the DREAM Act a de facto racial and economic draft. Yet after ten years of repeated attempts, the DREAM Act still failed to pass.

Organizing that centers the harmed migrant youth has achieved outcomes that many characterize as a success. Visible youth-led coming-out organizing pushed President Barack Obama, on June 15, 2012, to make an announcement offering a reprieve from deportations for some undocumented youth residing in the United States through the Deferred Action for Childhood Arrivals (DACA) program. Janet Napolitano, secretary of homeland security, indicated the following: "I am setting forth how, in the exercise of our prosecutorial discretion, the Department of Homeland Security (DHS) should enforce the Nation's immigration laws against certain young people who were brought to this country as children and know only this country as home. As a general matter, these individuals lacked the intent to violate the law and our ongoing review of pending removal cases is already offering administrative closure to many of them" (Napolitano 2012). This program provides a form of administrative relief and, literally, some potential protection from deportation for select youth, specifically those who arrived in the United States before age sixteen, have lived in the United States for at least five years, are in school or in the armed forces, and have not committed a crime.

While the program has indeed provided temporary relief from deportation for some eligible young people, DACA, similar to the failed DREAM legislation, recirculates tropes of innocence and merit associated with the status of a child or youth. This strategy separates a population that typically accrues more sympathy—youth—and acknowledges that this group merits access to differential pathways. Other groups who are unable to engender sympathy do not benefit from these options, and the wider context that frames people as illegal, and borders as legitimate, remains unchallenged, invisible. Against the backdrop of young, undocumented people claiming innocence and merit, others—including day laborers, domestic workers, or those over thirty—are the undeserving or guilty immigrants. The mobilizations surrounding DACA and the DREAM Act created sympathy for young, undocumented college students who therefore might merit legalization, but this narrative required an opposite.

Marginalized migrant communities, in attempts to secure their own rights or power, have historically struggled to separate themselves from other stigmatized populations, specifically during economic downturns or war (Ngai 2004). According to research by Yen Le Espiritu (1992), prior to the 1960s, rather than joining to combat racist forces, Asians in the United States sometimes distanced themselves from one another so as not to be mistaken or blamed for the presumed transgressions of one particular ethnic group: Chinese Americans displayed buttons proclaiming "I'm Chinese" during World War II to clearly avoid being viewed as, or assumed to be, Japanese and therefore potentially be subject to incarceration (23). Sectors of the current immigration justice movement seek, strategically, to differentiate themselves from the figure of the criminal. Being hard-working, not lazy or a criminal, is a prerequisite to being recognized as fully human. In the fall of 2012, Israel Lopez Bautista, picked up by ICE in Chicago's working-class Albany Park neighborhood, captured this sentiment precisely: "'I'm not a criminal, I'm a worker, pronounced Israel Lopez Bautista, 43, a father of 3" (Rezin 2013). Antiblack racism is reproduced when communities distance themselves from markers representative of criminalization. Khalil Gibran Muhammad, in *The Condemnation of Blackness: Race, Crime, and the Making of Modern Urban America* (2010), analyzes how the "ideological currency of Black criminality" (3) builds the United States. Muhammad argues that between 1890 and 1940, the relationship between "crime" and blackness solidified through the production and circulation of crime statistics: "Although specially described race-conscious laws, discriminatory punishments, and new forms of everyday racial surveillance had been institutionalized by the 1890s as a way to suppress black freedom, white social scientists presented the new crime data as objective, color-blind and incontrovertible. . . . From this moment forward, notions of blacks as criminals materialized in national debates about the fundamental racial and cultural differences between African Americans and native-born whites and European immigrants" (4). Presented as objective and color-blind, these "crime facts" ignored the significant contextual legal and ideological forces that shaped why black people were overrepresented in prisons and arrest records.

Centuries of institutionalized white supremacy in the United States produced blackness to be "absolute dereliction" (Wilderson 2003, 18). Specifically, the artist and scholar Frank Wilderson writes that blackness and the black body have come to represent the very antithesis of civil society (2003, 25). Wilderson's analysis is not unique, and a robust body of scholarship and activism supports how antiblackness is central to contemporary criminal justice systems. Dorothy Roberts's *Killing the Black Body: Race, Reproduction, and the Meaning of Liberty* (1997) chronicles how state agencies, notably child and family services agencies, pathologize black families and demonize black mothers. Child welfare agencies disproportionately restrict black women's access to the right to parent. Roberts's work consistently demonstrates how black mothers are, in policy and practice, constructed as unfit. Beth Richie's *Arrested Justice: Black Women, Male Violence, and the Build-Up of a Prison Nation* (2012) outlines how the concept of a merit-worthy victim of domestic violence developed to exclude women of color, poor women, and/or queer folks.

The institutional arrangements and linked practices of dehumanization that shaped the intimate relationship between blackness and criminality make our current carceral regime possible and, by association, also harm and dehumanize nonblack people locked behind borders or in cages. Simultaneously, these structures of dehumanization also create the promise that disassociation with blackness might provide access to civil society for marginalized communities. Just as some in immigration justice movements claim to be workers, not lazy, or students, not gangbangers—claims that attempt to distance oneself from black-ness—other nonwhite groups negotiate pathways for survival within this regime. Wilderson argues that the struggles of "civil society's junior partners (i.e. workers, white women, and immigrants)" require and re-produce antiblackness: "Put another way: How is the production and ac-cumulation of junior partner social capital dependent on an anti-Black rhetorical structure and a decomposed Black body?" (2003, 20).[5] While some individuals and organizations have shifted to reject this "I am not a criminal" logic, many others have not. Undocumented youth reproduce, reflect, and resist the tropes surrounding youth and innocence, including antiblack racism, represented in mainstream media.

While some young people have achieved legalization through DACA, the costs of privileging youth within this regime mount. A focus on young people within immigration justice struggles has, predictably, collateral consequences. DREAM organizing hindered the ability of pop-ulations regarded less sympathetically by society, such as workers or adults, to achieve any form of immigration relief. The relentless focus on youth and students deepens a wider logic suggesting that other im-migrants—those not children or students—are unworthy and criminals. Not only do undocumented adults merit unjust and inhumane treatment, but criminals deserve to be treated as less than fully human. A de facto racialized discourse, in the United States crime and blackness are co-constructed through the strategy of privileging children as worthy innocents.

After Childhood?

Children—imagined and real, harmed and not—continue to surface re-peatedly in campaigns for a wide range of affective and political ends. In Chicago, after some struggle, eventually SLM's second-stage housing for women and their children, with the coffee shop on the first floor, was ap-proved over the local condominium association's objections. The possi-bility of the child harmed by ex-cons did not outweigh the needs and the organizing capacity of the longtime residents of that community—those formerly incarcerated—and their children. Yet, as this chapter outlines, children—imagined and real, harmed and not—continue to surface re-peatedly in campaigns across our carceral terrain for a wide range of affective and political ends.

In this chapter's examples, the harmed child (or its close proxies, youth or student) reinforces criminalization and a wider carceral regime. Child safety is demanded, yet these very forms of child protection—including increased punishment, surveillance, and/or policing—invariably function to harm many, often the very populations these strategies purport to protect. In these demands for recognition, for black or brown young people to be seen as children, for (white) girls to be protected from interpersonal (male) sexual violence, not only do these state responses—criminalization or recognition, for example—not produce safety for the bodies at stake, but they augment precarity for too many others. These child-saving strategies reproduce deracialized and gender-free associations between childhood and innocence. The core characteristics of childhood—including its dangerous malleability—remain invisible.

At this political moment, as some are rethinking facets of "mass incarceration," the work is not only to rethink policing or to shut down prisons but to restructure and open the doors of the supposedly democratic institutions that have locked out too many. The foundational building blocks of how civil society is understood—including the idea of the child—require and extend the racialized carceral apparatus. While the façade of authenticity places children outside of history, as something timeless, natural, and universal, supposedly neutral or private categories such as the child redefine and refine the category of innocence and simultaneously shield this concept from critical engagement. While innocence is a racialized, gendered, sexualized, and flexible construct, the child is able to mask these genealogies and distract audiences from seeing the histories of power and other political and economic forces. Instead of identifying the forces that shape our reading practices and condition a body to be an adult or a child, innocent or guilty, the gaze is narrowed, and reading practices collapse.

This analysis moves beyond these campaigns and invites a radical rethinking of how the category of the child, naturalized across multiple domains, forecloses liberation for many. If select children can access rehabilitation, does that require adults to be constructed as static and therefore targeted and eligible only for incapacitation? If we cannot separate out the construction of the child from histories and practices of child saving that create bureaucratic and intimate surveillance systems, what are the local, narrow moves that are possible for those who work in schools, detention centers, and courts? While the terrain of criminal justice reform often appears to be fixed—for example, to championing an individual's or community's innocence or guilt, or fixed on forms of interpersonal violence rather than state violence—this chapter urges a closer analysis of campaigns and movements that center ideas and representations of young people and their proxies, to build a politics and movement where no one is disposable.

II

School and Prison

3

Beyond Reform

The Architecture of Prison and School Closure

On May 22, 2013, after a contentious meeting, Chicago's school board voted to close fifty public schools—forty-nine elementary schools and one high school—affecting approximately forty thousand students in primarily black and brown communities on the south and west sides. Many of us had picketed, participated in too many school closure hearings, and attended packed meetings of the mayoral appointed, not elected, school board. We knew that the educational opportunities youth received at these schools were not exceptional or often even adequate. Yet, while operating within and often reproducing a punitive and racialized regime, these schools in nonwhite communities were sites of possibility, spaces that merited defending. What the closure foreshadowed for Chicago's youth of color was unacceptable: privatized public schools run by (generally white) philanthropic agencies that are not accountable to the community, using experimental educational programs and employing fresh-faced and energetic but also underpaid and predominantly white teachers. Since 2011, 150 public schools in low-income black and brown communities across Chicago had been closed, restructured, or turned around—harming neighborhoods and not increasing the academic success of local youth (Lipman, Vaughan, and Gutierrez 2014). School closures displaced the "problem" of "low academic achievement" back onto communities and young people instead of shining a light on wider structural inequities that guaranteed wide gaps in access to educational opportunity, including uneven state funding formulas and a punitive test prep culture that continually flagged youth of color as deficient.

Schools were not the only public facilities Illinois struggled to close. In 2012, in an odd moment of jubilation for antiprison activists, the governor, recognizing that the state was broke, proposed the closure of a number of prisons (Long and Garcia 2012). Dwight Correctional Center, a maximum-security prison eighty miles from Chicago for people the state classifies as women (Sudbury 2011), was on this list (Lowe and Erickson 2013). Many argued that Dwight, originally opened in 1930 as Oakdale Reformatory for Women, merited closure for a number of reasons, including the recent decline in the number of women in Illinois prisons, a growing commitment in the state to support alternatives to incarceration for women, and, for some, the dismal conditions at Dwight, including lack of potable water. Dwight was operating under capacity, with approximately 900 people caged in a prison with 1,212 beds, and, most centrally, the estimated first-year savings from Dwight's closure would be $36,900,000 (Porter 2012, 2). Shutting down Dwight was not uncontested. All state prison closures were met with fierce opposition from labor unions that represented prison workers as well as from members of the surrounding community and most sectors of the law enforcement community (Lowe and Erickson 2013; Garcia 2012). Arguing that incarcerated women had special needs only this prison could address, a key prison reform group charged with improving the lives of people in prison and shrinking the number of people locked up also resisted Dwight's closure.

Beyond prisons and schools, other public facilities across the state of Illinois central to the regulation of the lives of poor and often nonwhite communities shut their doors. As part of a larger policy aim by Governor Pat Quinn's administration to balance the budget, the state shut a number of facilities confining people with disabilities (a process often called deinstitutionalization) (WistTV10 2012).[1] By 2014 the "rebalancing initiative" in Illinois aimed to close fourteen major state institutions (including prisons).[2] The city of Chicago, through the administration of Mayor Rahm Emanuel, shut down six of the city's twelve public mental health clinics in 2012 (Ballout 2013). Cuts to Chicago's public housing that began in the mid-1990s ramped up. Cabrini Green Housing Project, which once housed up to thirteen thousand people, vanished by 2012 (Chachkevitch 2012), while the Ida B. Wells Homes—once also home to up to thirteen thousand people—began to be dismantled in 2002 (Olkon 2008) and were totally demolished by 2011.

The restructuring of public institutions that regulate the lives of those most marginal is an uneven but strong nationwide trend. Between 2001 and 2011, 1,069 public schools across the nation closed, primarily in urban communities of color such as Washington, D.C., and Los Angeles (E. Brown 2013; Isensee 2014). Public housing vaporized; a quarter million units were lost over the past decade according to the political scientist Edward Goetz, author of *New Deal Ruins: Race, Economic Justice, and Public Housing Policy* (2013). States are also shuttering their psychiatric hospitals and developmental centers for people with disabilities. By 2011, eleven states had closed all state-operated institutions for people with intellectual/developmental disabilities (Braddock et al. 2011). Of course, when public facilities close, the budget lines and the associated public resources tied to these institutions are not released and made available to the populations these facilities once enclosed.

Often framed as progressive initiatives to improve the lives of those most vulnerable, prison reform and educational reform illuminate the complex reconfigurations of the state and capital. Through one narrow lens, it could be argued that fighting for prison closures requires that public schools stay open, and fighting to keep public schools operating requires shuttering and defunding prisons. This analysis is clearly represented in campaigns against the school to prison pipeline that feature slogans such as "Fund schools, not jails" or "Educate, not incarcerate." However, these are not the only linkages between these public sites, as is particularly visible during these moments of restructuring, reform, or rebalancing. Yet more of the same public schools will not solve the prison problem in the United States. Prison closures alone will not improve the educational pathways of youth of color. This moment of reform necessitates careful attention to emergent forms of capture beyond physical structures. This requires a wider understanding of punishment and control within a dynamic carceral regime.

Paying careful attention to the logics used to rationalize school and prison reforms is crucial during these moments of transition. Who would be against safety for children or against prisons built specifically for the needs of women? Who is against stronger schools for communities of color? The very grammar produced by liberation movements is often absorbed and used to extend punishing apparatuses. The framework of the *carceral state* refers not only to those held in prison but also to the population under formal supervision; the number of those on parole or probation or subject to other forms of state surveillance is almost triple the number of people who are locked behind bars. This concept also points to how the logic of punishment shapes other governmental and institutional practices, even those not perceived to be linked to prisons and policing, such as health care or education. Across the United States, those who seek food stamps are subject to mandatory and/or random drug testing; postsecondary educational applicants who seek federal or state financial aid are required to disclose histories of arrests or convictions; and migrants must face ICE, the largest enforcement agency in the United States.

Building from this political moment of reinvestment, restructuring, or rebalancing, this chapter maps the logics surrounding Illinois's prison and school closures (and resistance to such closures) to illustrate the value of critically analyzing reform practices, particularly those that mask carceral expansion. This chapter analyzes how safety, discipline, and difference continue to advance the logic of white supremacy and the enclosure of minorities within public schools, and how gender continues to be used to expand the prison system. As people move between different forms and scales of cages and as patterns of surveillance and punishment morph, new forms of capture *and resistance* are possible. Moments of transition, such as prison or school closures, offer opportunities to anticipate new forms of capture but also to continue the ongoing work of building the communities we need.

Schools

Chicago's recent wave of public school closures were not unexpected. In the fall of 2012, the Chicago Teachers Union went on a two-week strike to push back on a city government that sought to extend the working day of teachers without compensation, assess teacher competency through student achievement on standardized tests, and weaken the growing power of the union. While the strike was widely considered a political win, as the union built strong relationships with parent and community groups, school closures were not a contractual issue. In early 2013, rumors began circulating about the existence of a list of proposed schools that would be closed at the end of the school year. The alleged number of closures fluctuated widely, and at one point the media reported on a list of 200 schools under consideration for closure in a district with 681 schools. The short list of 54 proposed school closures was announced on March 21, 2013, while Mayor Rahm Emanuel was on a family skiing vacation in Utah. Many of the schools targeted, serving 100 percent students of color, not only employed veteran teachers of color but were also named for dead African American political and cultural icons, including Marcus Garvey, Mahalia Jackson, Benjamin Banneker, and Garrett Morgan.

This announcement did not go uncontested. With an international media spotlight and under pressure from outraged communities, the city was forced to put in place a process to solicit feedback from community members on these proposed closures. This process was artfully cumbersome and designed to dissipate resistance, with hundreds of meeting dates set in neighborhoods and schools across the city. These lengthy and multiple meetings were widely considered to be what Democratic county commissioner Toni Preckwinkle called "a charade" (Mihalopoulos 2013). By the start of the 2013–2014 school year, despite sit-ins, marches, and protests, the city shuttered fifty schools. Although a few of the closed public schools were leased to charters (Schlikerman and Spielman 2013), most remain locked and unused in black and brown neighborhoods that already lack services, employment, and resources. Young people who formerly attended these schools were moved elsewhere, generally to schools with academic success rates similar to those that were closed (Lipman, Vaughan, and Gutierrez 2014).

The official rationales for these reforms fluctuated. Previous closures or school "turnarounds" (involving a change in all personnel and a retooling of the entire school) had advanced the argument that the targeted schools were underperforming. However, researchers, reporters, and parents investigated and found that schools not targeted for closure had lower attendance rates or test scores. The schools targeted for closure also often had successful programs. As this critique emerged, the stated rationale for closure shifted. The city claimed that the schools targeted were underutilized. Yet researchers and reporters also quickly unpacked this claim. Some of the city's assessments about capacity were calculated using older building plans that did not account for how space was actually being used (for example, assessing a classroom as empty when in fact it was in use as a library); others failed to take into consideration that some schools had never been at full capacity; and, perhaps most importantly, some evaluations negated the reality that "under capacity" might mean, for many in the school, an optimal learning environment—a smaller school and possibly smaller class sizes (Lutton 2013; Lewis 2013; Lipman, Vaughan, and Gutierrez 2014).

In Chicago, as in many urban centers, the actual rationale for school closures is much more complex than the official explanations, and any engagement with public school closures is impossible without a meaningful understanding of the linkages between public schooling and race, labor, housing markets, and geography. While the gentrification reshaping Chicago's previously Latino and/or poor white neighborhoods had stalled by 2008 with the mortgage and housing crisis, repopulating and whitening schools continued to be key to restructuring neighborhoods. Real estate, public education, and white supremacy have lengthy and intertwined histories. If prospective white homeowners perceive a public school to be affluent and white enough for their children, the value of the houses in that neighborhood increases. Whiter urban schools with more affluent parents demand and receive more resources. When one of the largest vertical housing projects in the country—the Robert Taylor Homes—was dismantled, the young black and brown students who used to live there were not able to move from their decrepit existing school, which had no functioning bathrooms or playground, to the fancy new incredibly well-equipped school that was built to accommodate the new (white) homeowners (Schultz 2008). School closure and school restructuring are about real estate and race.

Closing public schools also widened the door for charter and other privatized schools. The overwhelming majority of teachers at charter schools locally and nationally are not unionized and instead are "at will" workers who can be fired at any time. A nonunion workforce is flexible— without the contractual right to due process and tenure, they are expendable—and cheaper. The number of charter schools in Chicago doubled between 2005 and 2012. By 2012, 14 percent of Chicago schools were charter or contract schools, and there were plans to open more, all privately run, while closing public schools. Over the past decade in Chicago, as schools were closed and "turned around," newer and whiter nonunionized teachers, often with little experience and no connection to the school and the surrounding community, were hired as predominantly older and African American unionized teachers were laid off (Ford 2012). School closure is also about dismantling a strong labor union (Ustinova 2012; Vevea 2012).

Yes, many of the schools that were closed were not "successful"—if the measures of success are scores on standardized exams and attendance.

Yet, the reasons their students struggle will not be found in the schools alone. Communities are hungry. The closed schools were in neighborhoods with double-digit unemployment rates, food deserts, and histories of laws and practices that produced racial isolation. State and district school funding formulas guarantee that whiter and wealthier schools receive more resources. Standardized testing shrank the curriculum and ensured that it has even less relevance to poor communities of color.

These conditions are not unique to Chicago. Across the nation, public school closures accelerate, and the communities most affected are also those that generate the most bodies for the prison nation. These are heavily policed neighborhoods with the highest rates of street violence. Mainstream media reported that school closures would further destabilize vulnerable communities and also put students at risk, but their coverage did not address the hyper police presence in most of these neighborhoods. Nor did reports address the fact that the Chicago police, as the journalist Ta-Nehisi Coates (2013) writes, are also another violent gang that must be negotiated, particularly by young people.

Narratives of *discipline* and *safety* underscored these school closures. Privatized public schools such as charters and those operated by non-profit agencies that hire employees with yearly contracts are represented as necessary because the lazy (and overwhelming female) teachers hired by traditional schools, needlessly protected by tenure and unions, are unable to control and regulate students. Military-themed public schools run by the Department of Defense (DOD) are essential because urban youth of color are undisciplined, unruly, and even dangerous, and need to be controlled (Quinn and Meiners 2009; Lipman 2003). Youth, nearly all low income, and often Latino and African American, are targeted for enrollment in charters and DOD schools because they need more control, perhaps even military-style discipline, and strong male role models.

Even if discipline is a valid goal and not just a code for racialized control, the school-based routes to discipline offered to the children of the most privileged in society involve the acquisition of expertise. Art education (dance, music instruction, theater and performance, visual arts), sports and physical education, after-school activities, and clubs ranging from chess and debate to radio journalism (and many more) all cultivate discipline but are not available equally to all youth. These programs build focus and expertise and teach responsibility, community, and discipline. In Chicago 20 percent of principals report that their public schools offer no arts programming at all, with children in low-income communities of color less likely to have school art instruction than students in wealthier, whiter neighborhoods (Arts Alliance Illinois 2005, 15). In 2010, 164 public schools in Chicago had no libraries (Ahmed-Ullah 2010).

Discipline and safety have a specific and complex resonance in all policy discussions tied to schools, particularly in recent Chicago history. On September 24, 2009, the death of Derrion Albert, a student at Christian Fenger Academy High School on Chicago's south side, ricocheted across the globe. Albert was beaten to death with boards by other young people, an event that was filmed by peers on a camera phone and posted online. For many, Albert's death became emblematic of the "brutality common in Chicago's toughest neighborhoods," as reported in the *New York Times* (Saulny 2009, para. 5). In conjunction with an increased focus on youth gun violence, dramatic headlines proliferated: "Chicago Homicides Outnumber US Troop Killings in Afghanistan," "More Young People Are Killed in Chicago Than Any Other American City," "Chicago under Fire," "Another Deadly Weekend in Chicago," "Deadly Distinction." Failing schools with lax security often figured prominently in media representations of this epidemic of youth violence. Disinvestment in urban communities of color, the history of race and public schooling in Chicago, and any discussion of the dearth of school finance reform were invisible in mainstream media coverage about youth violence. School closure destabilizes neighborhoods, engineers conflict, and exacerbates violence. For example, in the 2009 death of Derrion Albert the policy of school closures was partially culpable. Students from the neighborhood of Altgelt Gardens were moved to Fenger High School after their school, Carver High School, was transformed into a restrictive-enrollment public military academy. While the Chicago Public Schools do not acknowledge that school closures were a factor in Albert's death (Karp 2009; "Derrion Albert's Death May Be Rooted in School Closures," 2009), many attribute the violence at Fenger to the instability of public schools in this region: "Chicago police have acknowledged that Albert's slaying was related to the mixing of students from different neighborhoods, but they didn't respond to questions from The Associated Press about whether the violent deaths were related to school closings" ("Derrion Albert's Death," 2009, para. 15).

Hinged to the need for more control over youth of color (and their communities) is the implicit ongoing failure of (unionized female) teachers. If students are not learning, it is because teachers are not teaching. Common sense tells us that education is all about the teacher, hence the media's love affair with the standout teacher, and the unchallenged presumption that there are too many incompetent teachers, protected by unions and prepared by mediocre teacher-certification programs. Are some teachers ineffective? Yes, just as there are ineffective people in any profession. But this focus on the individual masks the bigger picture, especially the more structural aspects of public education that can help to explain why disparities persist. Media coverage of evil unions that protect veteran teachers' rights while stamping out the light of better (and often whiter), newer (and cheaper) teachers catapulted teachers' unions to public educational enemy number one (Kumashiro 2008).

To take a visible and ongoing example: Rather than increasing racial justice in schools or supporting the self-determination of young people of color, educational developments within "special education" pathologize inequities and continue to ensure that too many students are tracked toward undereducation or noneducation. Students of color are grotesquely overrepresented in a number of disability categories (Losen and Orfield 2002; McNally 2003; R. Smith and Erevelles 2004; Harry and Klingner 2005). Before school even begins, many white teachers believe that they will refer an African American student for special education services (Garda 2005, 1092). Through one lens these classifications may appear to involve access to additional resources and differential treatment within the school system, but students labeled with these disabilities receive less access to high-quality education, are not tracked toward college, experience higher rates of suspension and expulsion, and are disproportionately represented in juvenile justice prisons (Losen and Orfield 2002; McNally 2003; Harry and Klingner 2005). Classification as special education masks segregation, and pathologizing "students of color as disabled allows their continued segregation under a seemingly natural and justifiable label" (Reid and Knight 2006, 19).[3] Special education, a reform established in the waning era of de jure segregation in the United States, provided a race-neutral cover for the reproduction of racialized and heterogendered ideologies of achievement and intelligence within schools to enclose black, brown, and First Nations youth.

Prisons

The proposed closure of Dwight Correctional Center arrived after a bumpy recent history of prison reform in Illinois. In late 2009, information surfaced that the governor of Illinois, Pat Quinn, and the head of the Illinois Department of Corrections, Michael Randle, had implemented a program to permit people to accrue "good time" and potentially be released from prison early—days or weeks before they had served their full sentences. Decarceration seemed fiscally responsible when Illinois topped the list of the most financially strapped states and because the prisons were bulging at the seams. The state prison population increased from approximately "18,000 in 1986 to more than 46,000 in 2009 (a 150% increase compared to statewide population growth of just over 4%)" (Eisenman 2010). When information about this "good time" program trickled out, many of us who worked on antiprison campaigns rejoiced. Some of our language was being used by the Illinois Department of Corrections: *Locking people up was expensive and not helpful to the community!* While our motivations did not necessarily overlap with the state's rationale, overcrowding and lack of resources forced a Democratic governor to rethink the number of people behind bars, and the end product, we rationalized, was the same: people were being let out of prison.

Once information about this program hit the mainstream media, the conversation exploded. The headline "Illinois Prisons Shave Terms, Secretly Release Inmates" characterized the tone of most of the immediate mainstream media coverage that criticized Governor Quinn and the head of the Illinois Department of Corrections, whom the governor had "hand picked" (J. O'Connor 2009). On March 18, 2010, the *Huffington Post* published a completely misleading piece titled "Murderers Released: Illinois Prisoners Freed in Budget Shortfall." The *Chicago Tribune* ran relentless coverage scrutinizing this program (Garcia 2009), and, in a violent echo of the 1988 Willie Horton debacle, a Democratic challenger for the gubernatorial nomination in Illinois circulated advertisements against Governor Quinn that featured mug shots of some of the men released during this "good time" program ("Murderers Released" 2010).[4]

Quinn halted the program in December 2009 after only four months. In total, the program had allowed 1,745 incarcerated people to accelerate their "good time credit" and be released, on average, thirty-six days early. When the program was canceled, of those released under it, fifty-six people were back in custody (less than 2 percent) and forty-eight of the fifty-six were picked up for status violations, or violating the terms of their parole or probation, not for acts of violence (Garcia 2009). Yet the damage was done. Under pressure, Michael Randle resigned with the tacit encouragement of Governor Quinn (Dai 2010), and a hastily assembled partisan investigation launched after the program was disbanded released a report stating that the program was an "ill-conceived path that traded protecting public safety for saving $3.4 million" (Garcia and Heinzmann 2010). Quinn worked to distance himself from the program: "Clearly, mistakes were made," he said. "I take accountability for the mistakes, the director who made the mistakes takes responsibility for them" (Garcia and Heinzmann 2010).

In Illinois, those of us invested in this early release program, sprinkled across Chicago in community organizations, churches, prisons, and families, watched as the governor's attempts to let people out of prison were halted by local economic arguments and the triggering of a range of racialized and gendered fears related to crime and criminals. Disconnected and overwhelmed, we tried to engage from within our small community groups as individuals. We contacted our state representatives and demonstrated our support for this program. We wrote opinion pieces and letters to the editor (sometimes published after edits, generally not) that highlighted the crisis of incarceration in Illinois and its false promise of safety and—point by point—dismantled the mythologies that circulated around this early release program. Largely shut out of mainstream press coverage, our letters to the editor were left unprinted, and the debates quickly moved and left us behind. Advocates of the early release program were widely shut out of mainstream media outlets—talk radio shows, TV news coverage, newspapers—or reduced to sound bites and then disappeared.

This moment left us so deflated. *Who were we, anyway? The motley fringe of the leftie crew? How dare we imagine that we could have an impact or even win in this terrain?* Even though we were shut out of mainstream media, our vision and analysis felt incredibly logical, in sync with what could actually work and with what people (and not just those locked up) needed but simultaneously desperately out of touch with what the media represented as everyday people's desires.

With this experience still fresh, in February 2013, the John Howard Association (JHA), a globally recognized prison reform organization active in Illinois, came out with a statement against the proposed closure of Dwight. It advocated for the prison to remain open despite the fact that in 2010 a monitoring report from JHA identified a number of significant problems with Dwight, including an overuse of psychotropic medication, a high number of women on suicide watch, and crumbling facilities that required "extensive rehabilitation": "Roofs are visibly deteriorated. The ceiling of a freshly painted corridor in one cottage is already disfigured by water damage. Cells are covered with peeling paint. Mold is visible in some areas. Windows are drafty and plaster is crumbling" (John Howard Association 2010, 5). In 2012, JHA had supported the proposed closures of the supermax that housed people the state considers men and of a number of youth prisons and publicly affirmed a commitment to a smaller system in Illinois. However, JHA opposed the closure of Dwight. Titled "Without a Plan to Safely Reduce Illinois' Prison Population, Closing Dwight Will Make a Bad Problem Worse," JHA's report outlined several key reasons. First, despite the declining number of women in state custody, the overall system in Illinois is overcrowded. The proposal to move women from Dwight to Logan Correctional Center, 180 miles from Chicago, would place an undue burden on the many families who already struggled to maintain connections to their children, mothers, aunts, or sisters.

Without naming it as such, JHA also used a "gender-responsive" frame, or an analysis seemingly grounded in feminist scholarship that has highlighted the gendered pathways women often follow that led to prison, to argue why Dwight should remain open: "Over the years, Dwight has trained its staff, hired larger numbers of female correction officers, and created a culture to address the unique needs of female inmates, most of whom come from backgrounds of serious trauma and physical, sexual, and emotional abuse. If Dwight closes, Illinois risks losing the significant investment we have made in creating this rehabilitative environment that protects public safety" (Maki 2013, para. 3). When JHA's statement was released, many of us in the vibrantly ragtag prison abolitionist community and/or those working toward decarceration in Illinois scratched our heads. This memo was relatively unexpected—a pointed intervention in the Democratic governor's attempts to shrink the system; it originated from an organization that had not opposed the closure of prisons for people the state identifies as men and raised a number of points that we found troubling.

A number of activists across the city started to identify why JHA's response was flawed and crafted a response that other antiprison organizations could endorse to support the closure of Dwight and oppose JHA's statement. Our initial draft highlighted a number of facts: in the past two years the number of women in Illinois prisons had declined significantly, and thus the prison was not needed; the conditions at Dwight were abysmal; and we objected to the zero-sum game of gendered frames, or that doing something for women will harm men and therefore cannot be done. Also, many of us were deeply disturbed by the memo's use of what some of us perceived as paternalistic language, including the statement that this prison had an adequate "culture" to address survivors of deep forms of sexual violence and the implicit and related assumption that prison was even potentially an adequate rehabilitative site to deliver these services.

In Illinois between 1983 and 2002, the number of women in prison for drug-related crimes skyrocketed from 32 to 1,325, a 4,041 percent leap (Institute for Metropolitan Affairs et al. 2006, sec. 1:4). Nationally, close to 70 percent of incarcerated women are nonwhite (Díaz-Cotto 2006; Johnson 2003). Between the ages of thirty-five and thirty-nine, 1 in 100 black women, 1 in 297 Latinas, and 1 in 355 white women are imprisoned (Pew Center on the States 2009). Research clearly documents that incarcerated women are undereducated, under- or unemployed, frequently homeless prior to entering prison or jail, and have a significantly higher rate of experiences with sexual or physical violence (Richie 1996, 2012; Faith 2005). Poverty is a "common denominator," as, "if a woman is not poor when she enters prison, she will be when she leaves" (Faith 2005, 5).

The idea that women require specific forms of punishment, control, and rehabilitation is not new. Historically, women—specifically white women—were criminalized and incarcerated because of frameworks rooted in limiting notions of race, class, ability, and gender (Freedman 1981).

Reformist good intentions that translate into carceral expansion continue in contemporary efforts to introduce "gender-responsive justice," which seeks to develop programs and protocols specific to women (Bloom, Owen, and Covington 2004). JHA's argument for keeping Dwight open, while not named as such, animates a gender-responsive logic. While this approach may seem simply to acknowledge the unique or different pathways to imprisonment for women and their experiences during and after incarceration—for instance, women are more often the primary caregivers of children—there are larger implications and expansionist outcomes that result from such an approach. The obvious and problematic corollary to this approach is that it reinforces stereotypes of men as violent, dangerous, and, in the specific context of incarceration, in need of harsh conditions and lengthy sentences, as well as undeserving of and uninterested in contact with children and family. This framing reproduces dualistic, obsolete, and constraining conceptions of gender and sex, excludes those who do not conform to normative notions of male and female, and supports the work of the state in promoting compulsory heteronormativity and gender conformity. Yet, beyond the ways in which it polices and requires gender conformity, this approach increasingly has material consequences for the expansion of the system. The purported need for women-specific responses can be used to justify more programs and more "community-based" prisons or "alternatives to incarceration."[5]

The recent attention some prisons and jails have focused on transgender people both provides another example of the limitations of a gender-responsive frame and exemplifies how gender is used to expand the prison system. In 2012, the Los Angeles Police Department (LAPD) opened a twenty-four-bed module specifically for transgender people. Segregation is not a new tactic. The historian Regina Kunzel (2008) notes that jails and prisons have a conflicted and storied history of isolating people identified by the state as gay, lesbian, or non-gender-conforming; by the 1970s, placing these individuals in protective custody (isolation) was a routine practice.[6] In 2012, at least one transgender group advocated for a separate facility for transgender people in prison: "'This is a new LAPD,' said Karina Samala, a transgender woman and chair of the Transgender Working Group, which was formed in 2007 to collaborate with the department on changes in its policies. 'The chief of police is now listening and really paying attention to our issues'" (Quinones 2012, para. 9). While transgender people (particularly folks of color) are disproportionately locked up and experience much higher rates of harm while in cages, the construction of new punitive facilities, or even the creation of new spaces specifically for transgender people within existing jails, expands the prison nation.[7]

Our ragged group struggled through a response to JHA's argument that Dwight should be kept open, and, somewhat predictably, could not agree. We worked to circulate a draft memo among local and national organizations that we knew supported the closure of Dwight, and we met roadblocks even from allied organizations that shared a similar political vision of decarceration. Justice Now!, a California-based abolitionist organization working with people in prisons for women, refused to sign on because they perceived our draft response as potentially suggesting that a different prison could be a "better" place for women. One group in Chicago that has historically had strong ties with people at Dwight, Chicago Legal Advocacy for Incarcerated Mothers (CLAIM), was in a period of transition and would not take a public stand either against or for the closure. The Transformative Justice Law Project, a Chicago-based abolitionist organization that works with criminalized transgender folks, also stepped back from signing on because their members who are locked up at Dwight (or in Cook County Jail [CCJ] pending transfer to Dwight) wanted to be geographically closer to Chicago. To reach outside of the anti-prison community—to radical mental health or education advocates—seemed impossible.

In the end, we did not circulate our statement publicly and instead waited and hoped that the governor would move forward with the closure despite the criticism from the largest and most legitimate prison reform organization in the state and protest from law enforcement and the employees at Dwight. While JHA's memo opposing the closure of Dwight made a few small waves, it did not receive a lot of traction or mainstream media visibility.

Although Dwight was closed in 2013, how this facility will be used in the future remains unclear. Media coverage suggests that parts of the prison may be only temporarily depopulated and may reopen to house people in the federal prison system, people from other counties, or immigrants awaiting deportation. Across the United States, the track record on prison closures is too nascent to point to any significant trend in the use of these closed prisons. While jails in urban settings have been retrofitted as bars or boutique hotels, including in Boston, where a former jail is now a bar called Alibi with a "$12 blueberry mojito called the Jailbait" (Kaplan 2012), prisons in rural settings are apparently less marketable. In New York, the prisons closed under Governors David Paterson and Andrew Cuomo have proved hard to sell (Kaplan 2012). In other states, closed prisons remain empty, with reports suggesting the possibilities of using the space for retail or wildlife or, as was done with Eastern State Penitentiary in Pennsylvania, opening a museum (Porter 2012). Empty facilities are potential sites of enclosure for other captured populations.

Shutting down a prison does not mean that the people caged inside will be free. While the push to close Dwight was motivated by a decline in the number of women being locked up and a lukewarm commitment by some state Democratic politicians to move women into treatment facilities or alternatives to incarceration (a shift based in part on the recognition of their gendered "difference"), not all people are eligible for these programs, and while many of these alternatives to incarceration are new and can appear as distinct from the prison system, many are not. Even as prisons such as Dwight might depopulate across the United States, a massive apparatus continues to lock people out of full participation in dominant political, economic, and social milieus. People are regulated through the shifting terrain of capture and punishment: community-based prisons, GPS monitoring, parole and probation and their attendant status violations, the policing function of child and family services departments, employment and housing discrimination against those with criminal records, and more.

Yet after Dwight officially closed, when we learned that staff had been laid off or transferred and people who had been locked up had been moved to another prison or released, I did feel a kind of temporary satisfaction, a kind of "we won." Just weeks later, deflating reports emerged that buildings in Dwight were potentially going to be reopened as a prison space for people locked up in the federal system (Erikson 2013). What is the point of organizing to shut a facility down if a prison will simply reopen, repackaged, with new bodies? How effective or important are these site-specific battles? And if some of the tools and language and analysis produced by liberation movements will simply be absorbed by the carceral state, what are the moves available to those struggling to build worlds without cages?

Intimate Architecture

The struggles around the closure of Dwight and Chicago's public schools illustrate how particular logics are mobilized to advance reforms that might promise temporary relief for some, but often reinforce wider logics that expand and naturalize punishment and confinement. Ideas and affective regimes about difference are instrumental to the construction and expansion of a U.S. carceral state. The unique needs of women and transgender people are circulated to keep prisons open and to expand jails. Discipline, safety, and even learning ability are invoked to shutter, privatize, or racially restructure public schools in communities of color. Often marshaling the very frameworks and analyses produced by communities seeking justice and better lives, these reforms expand systems of punishment and control while masking practices of capture.

Identity has become a particularly salient and mobile tool to shore up carceral regimes. Civil rights and affiliated identity-based movements focused on access to ending oppression, and building state power and the right to self-determination. Yet, decades after these struggles, the goalposts have shifted in communities that "have won formal legal protections but whose constituencies remain criminalized and economically marginalized" (Spade 2011, 28). Or the law is such a limited tool to create the world we need. The political theorist Nancy Fraser (1997) addresses this challenge directly, arguing that often the tactics social movements engage in or the goals sought result in recognition but not redistribution. For Fraser, justice strategies all too often agitate for recognition, thus inviting additive responses that are not capable of transforming systems of power and oppression. Recognition is not an insignificant demand—*it matters*. To be seen, to be valued, and to be recognized are powerful affectively and, potentially, politically. Yet, redistribution demands that power be reorganized.

The anthropologist Elizabeth Povinelli suggests that this political moment, what she refers to as late liberalism, is particularly characterized by demands for recognition of difference that do not transform the status quo. "The subjects of recognition are called to present difference in a form that feels like difference but does not permit any real difference to confront in a normative world" (2011, 31). For Povinelli, those who are marginalized organize to be understood and recognized by institutions and structures that have historically harmed, erased, or ignored these communities. In 2012, CCJ in Chicago established a Pride Group—an LGBTQ support group—for people the jail evaluates as "queer" (Noll 2013). There is no redistribution of power, no commitment to structurally acknowledge how and why, for example, nonheterosexual or transgender folks are disproportionately targeted for punishment. Instead, being LGBTQ is subsequently used to shore up and expand systems of power and oppression.[8] Similarly, while public schools by federal law must support gay–straight alliances (and most urban schools have these student-initiated clubs), the privatization of education through the shift toward charter schools ensures that an increasing number of teachers and other school personnel are "at will" employees. How can teachers support queer learning contexts if they do not have some measure of job security?

Beyond shoring up the status quo, discourses of liberation can also be used to advance forms of willful misrecognition. In 2014, the MacArthur Justice Center at Northwestern University announced yet another new lawsuit against CCJ in Chicago, which confines up to twelve thousand people a day and employs just about the same amount of workers. Similar to many other urban jails, CCJ has a long history of reports of abysmal conditions. In 2008 the Civil Rights Division of the U.S. Department of Justice found systemic Eighth Amendment violations in the jail, including beatings, excessive strip searches, rodents in food, and so on. The 2014 lawsuit documents that violence at CCJ is so pervasive that guards take inmates on "elevator rides"—code for beatings out of view of security cameras. Yet when questioned about the lawsuit and the culture of extreme violence perpetrated by officers against people locked up at CCJ, Sheriff Tom Dart denied these allegations and as reported in mainstream news, he "boasted that the jail is the only one in the country with a transgender unit and that correctional officers receive advanced mental health training for how to deal with many of the detainees" (Meisner and Schmadeke 2014). As noted, CCJ has established an LGBTQ support/treatment group called the Pride Group. Once locked up, people have to apply to be a part of this group, and CCJ officials determine who counts as LGBTQ enough to participate (personal conversation, Ray Noll 2014). In this moment, progressive reform-oriented jail LGBTQ policies signify a form of "pinkwashing" to cover how, as Angela Harris (2011) writes, racialized heteropatriarchy and prisons kill. LGBTQ policies suggest modernity, human rights. The implied response from the sheriff: How could a jail that sets up a treatment unit for LGBTQ folks torture people?

Educational policies that incorporate discourses of liberation but advance willful racial misrecognition are particularly pervasive. In 2007, the Supreme Court struck down school districts' ability to use race as a factor in voluntary programs designed to desegregate highly segregated schools. The majority opinion, authored by Chief Justice John Roberts, aligns in *Parents Involved in Community Schools v. Seattle School District*

No. 1, with the landmark 1954 *Brown v. Board of Education* Supreme Court decision desegregating schools: "The way to stop discrimination on the basis of race is to stop discriminating on the basis of race" (Greenhouse 2007, para. 4). In 2010, Tom Horner, Arizona's superintendent of schools, attempted the elimination of ethnic studies programs in Arizona because he understood these elective programs (which increased graduation rates) as racially unjust: "In the summer of 1963, when I just graduated from high school, I went on the march on Washington, in which Martin Luther King gave his famous speech in which he said we should be judged by the quality of our character, rather than the color of our skin. And that has been among my deepest beliefs my entire life. And so this has made me opposed to dividing students by race" (Precious Knowledge 2011). Throughout these examples and across many others, the very terms and markers of the civil rights movement are used to produce forms of willful (racial and economic) misrecognition. These tactics eradicated the weak state strategies developed to address forms of structural inequities produced through and by de jure and de facto oppression.

This analysis is not a charge to ignore difference but rather to push ourselves to understand how difference is absorbed into the prison-industrial complex and how the very strategies we produce—with our goal of liberation—shape expansion. Simply asking select gays to be recognized as equals through the legalization of same-sex marriage does not redistribute access to all the important resources attached to marriage. Asking juveniles or children to be viewed as different than adults in legal proceedings does not transform the larger contexts that punish particular communities. Building a jail for transgender people is a form of recognition, but this difference strengthens and builds systems that continue to harm communities. As is evident from the analysis surrounding school and prison closure, these reforms hold the potential to deepen communities' vulnerabilities.

Abolition Democracy

Services that provide people with access to housing, food, health care, and education, are desperately needed for many people across the carceral state, particularly those who are locked inside prisons or jails or exiting those punishing institutions. Young people in schools with no art rooms, libraries, or playgrounds need new learning environments *now*. Yet, equally important are struggles for structural and paradigmatic shifts that alter the contexts that produce such high levels of school push-out, uneven schooling experiences, and incarceration. Reforms that promise change but simply expand the life or the scope or even the legitimacy of the prison are not needed. Reforms that further privatize the public sphere and place communities in more vulnerable and less transparent educational contexts increase vulnerability. Reforms that use the identification of specific needs of marginalized communities to create new mechanisms of enclosure do not facilitate freedom.

Reforms that liberate more people, that delegitimize the carceral regime, or that make material differences in the lives of people impacted are nonreformist reforms, as identified by Ruth Wilson Gilmore: "What are the possibilities of non-reformist reforms—of changes that, at the end of the day, unravel rather than widen the net of social control through criminalization?" (2007, 242). The response to overcrowding in prisons is not to build more prisons but to reevaluate and change the policies that move more bodies into detention and confinement. As Gloria Romero, a state senator from California (which has the world's two largest prisons for women), says of overcrowding, "California can't build its way out of this problem" (as cited by Braz 2006, 87). The response to the purported "academic achievement gap" of African American and Latino students is not to close, deunionize, and privatize public schools but to widen what counts as legitimate curriculum and assessment, equalize school funding, remove white control of schools, and name and mobilize around the academic debt or the "opportunity gap" owed to communities of color, not the achievement gap.

Following the money in these moments of restructuring and rebalancing is central. Cook County commissioner Toni Preckwinkle publicly stated in 2012 that the scandal-plagued Cook County Temporary Juvenile Detention Center (CCTJDC), the main juvenile prison in Illinois, should be "blown up" (Kim 2013), and many local organizers cheered. Yet what will happen to the multimillion-dollar annual budget of the CCTJDC? The closure of CCTJDC doesn't guarantee young people's liberation. What is the status of the public schools in the neighborhoods that have historically generated the majority of young people for the CCTJC? How will practices of capture continue to be resisted in neighborhoods decimated by decades of active and racialized disinvestment? If

CCTJDC closes, how will new policing practices, including gang ordinances, shape the continued enclosure of young people? Can the resources used to run CCTJDC be reinvested in communities negatively impacted by public school closures? While many of us are cheering the potential closure of CCTJDC, these are questions that we also ask. Forty percent of the budget of the city of Chicago is spent on policing. Investing in black futures requires defunding policing, a key demand of the national organization The Black Youth Project 100 (Muwakkil 2016).

Even as the debate on shuttering prisons grows or as we struggle to keep public schools open, the need to confine superfluous or disposable bodies remains. These moments of transition provide key opportunities to engage in movement assessment and to consider how the closure of a prison and the struggle to retain neighborhood public schools are intertwined. While physical structures might crumble or close, the ideological frameworks that required and naturalized these facilities do not disappear. Prisons, Angela Davis writes, have "thrived over the last century precisely because of the absence of those resources and the persistence of some of the deep structures of slavery. They cannot be eliminated unless new institutions and resources are made available to those communities that provide, in large part, the human beings that make up the prison population" (2005, 95–96). Challenging our prison-industrial complex means fighting to close prisons, but it also means doing the perhaps more difficult work of opening up and reconfiguring other institutions that have shut their doors to the people who have been abandoned by our punishing democracy. A flourishing and public education system is central to the work to build the world we know we need. An abolition democracy, to use the term favored by Angela Davis and W. E. B. Du Bois, requires reconstructing the traditions and systems that safeguard power and privilege just as much as taking down those institutions that visibly punish and oppress.

4

Restorative Justice Is Not Enough

"Take her! Take her!"

It's 9:00 a.m. on Monday, and the visibly upset kindergarten teacher screams at me from across the hall. She is holding a six-year-old by her wrist. The girl, with a dozen pink and white barrettes framing her tear-stained face, yells, "Get off me, let me go!" The teacher pushes the student toward me.

"When should I bring her back?" I ask.

"Never!" the teacher yells. "I don't want her! Never bring her back!"

Before I make it to the main office at Lockwood Elementary[1]—a K–8 school in a north side Chicago neighborhood—to get the peace room key and sign in, two more students are assigned to me.

At noon I am paged over the intercom: "Ms. C, please come to the assistant principal's office immediately." In Mrs. Edwards's office, I recognize a fourteen-year-old eighth-grader, Trevon, sitting across from her with his head in his hands.

"You are lucky that Ms. C is here," Mrs. Edwards says. "Otherwise, you would be on your way to jail in handcuffs."

Trevon had lashed out in the lunchroom at one of his peers, repeatedly shouting inappropriate and sexual slurs at a female classmate who had touched his neck while he was waiting in line to eat. Two security guards approached him. He continued to shout and was physically removed from the lunchroom and taken across the hall to the administrative office.

As Mrs. Edwards recounted the incident, Trevon interrupted several times. "She started it!" he yelled. "This is unfair, why isn't she sitting up in here?" When Mrs. Edwards suggested that I find a black male mentor to work with him, he laughed derisively. "A what?" he asked. As she tried to explain, he started to laugh uncontrollably and muttered something as he folded his arms across his chest. "Ha ha ha! In *this* neighborhood? At *this* school? *Good luck with that!* Ha ha ha!"

I ask him if he would like to go for a walk with me to see the peace room and talk, and he responds, "Not really."

Mrs. Edwards chimes in from her seat, "Or I can call the police . . ."

At 3:30 p.m., right outside of the middle school building, a fight erupts between two young men. Two students run up to the peace room: "Ms. C, Ms. C, please come to the basketball court. Jesse and Chris are fighting and the police are going to arrest them." By the time I get downstairs, both young men are in handcuffs and being put into the back of a squad car. I ask Officer Hernandez to please not take the young men to the station. I promise to intervene. "I will run a peace circle," I say. "Do you both agree to participate in a circle?" I ask both young men. They nod. Officer Hernandez looks skeptical but agrees to release them. He looks over to the boys and says, "You are lucky Ms. C is here vouching for you, but next time, you are going to the station."

. . .

Risking positioning ourselves as saviors who are outside of a landscape shaped by police and educational policy makers, we offer this grounded snapshot from an average day in the work of Project NIA, a Chicago-based community organization. We sketch our complex and often failed attempts to engage practices to halt the movement of young people from our communities into our prisons and jails. In 2012, at Lockwood over 90 percent of the 540 students were African American and Latino, and nearly 95 percent qualified for free or reduced lunch (a federal designation signifying low income). Almost 20 percent had limited English proficiency. Over the past twenty years, students at Lockwood have consistently tested below national norms. High rates of suspension are the norm.

In Chicago, high rates of suspension in schools with a majority of African American and Latino students are not remarkable. Data from the Department of Education's Office for Civil Rights documents that while African American students represented 45 percent of those enrolled in the Chicago Public Schools (CPS) in the 2009–2010 academic year, 76 percent of students receiving at least one out-of-school suspension that year were black (U.S. Department of Education, Civil Rights Data Collection n.d.). CPS's African American students are five times more likely to be suspended than their white peers. Police officers proliferate. In 2010, there were 5,574 school-based arrests of juveniles under eighteen years of age on CPS property. Unsurprisingly, black youth accounted for 74 percent of these school-based juvenile arrests; Latino youth represented 22.5 percent of arrests (Kaba and Edwards 2012). Police circulate within schools and increase the number of young people with formal relationships with the criminal justice system, even though research does not demonstrate that police presence in schools decreases violence or improves safety (Na and Gottfredson 2011).

With the support of community members and school leadership, starting in September 2009, Project NIA established and ran a peace room[2] at Lockwood, staffed by a team of trained volunteers and interns (supervised by a licensed clinical counselor employed by NIA), to serve as an alternative to suspensions and expulsions. Students identified as "disruptive" by teachers and staff would be taken out of class and sent to the peace room so that the teachers and other students could continue with their work without further interruption. Parents who believed that CPS wanted their children to fail would be given an opportunity to have their concerns addressed, and strategies could be created to ensure better communication and to develop trust among students, staff, and families.

On paper, these goals appeared straightforward and in concert with practices emerging across the city that were explicitly framed as attempts to stem the flow of young people into our juvenile justice system. Room 305—an out-of-use classroom that previously housed countless boxes of old supplies—developed into a space where community members (trained by Project NIA) facilitated peace circles and after-school activities, and young people dropped by the room to be engaged by art projects, discussions, and snacks.

In the two years that Project NIA implemented the peace room at Lockwood Elementary, Project NIA paid staff and volunteers offered peace circles, individual restorative counseling, homework help, referrals to and follow-up with other agencies and organizations that could offer services, home visits, a grandmothers' support group, art projects, field trips, and conflict mediation. Often the work was simply listening, providing students with a chance to talk to an adult. Through one lens, these programs and their attendant cultures were successes because they created possibilities for a wider range of adults to be within the school.

Yet, while the after-school activities were popular, getting teachers to refer students to the peace room during school hours was a challenge. NIA was told that students needed to work on their reading and math skills, not create art projects or that "peace stuff." Many teachers, if not downright hostile, were reluctant to refer students to the room during the school day. "He needs to be punished—not rewarded!" As the principal and the assistant principal were new, their priorities simply did not accommodate helping the space to get established. As NIA pressed for school-wide announcements or a space to introduce the organization in each classroom, the requests fell by the wayside, and the work seemed to flounder.

After two years at Lockwood, Project NIA came to recognize that our model and practices were not only unsustainable but potentially augmenting the carceral apparatus. Keeping a peace room open all day in a school was a full-time job, and neither our small organization nor the school had the needed resources. The district constantly threatened to close schools that did not achieve high scores on state standardized tests, making it difficult to secure clear commitments from administrators at Lockwood to dedicate resources, thought, and time to integrating the work of the peace room into the school. Despite our own alliances with the profession of teaching and experiences in classrooms, we failed to secure key teachers as early allies and did not have a full awareness of the workload and the demands on staff at Lockwood. Despite the system's stated commitment to restorative justice (RJ) alternatives, CPS offered no support, and Project NIA was essentially fully responsible for providing services that we believed should be integral to the school's operations.

Building from our own practice, research, and activism in Chicago, and with more questions than answers, we examine the landscape for restorative justice in our communities and schools. As the opening vignette highlights, not only does this work face deep challenges at the school and district levels, but, in the face of a flexible carceral state, the definition of the "problem" is an ongoing tension. Out of control young people or a racist state? Disengaged and rude youth or an underfunded school and an overpoliced community? After ten years into what was widely acknowledged as a win—getting the language of restorative justice included in the CPS Uniform Discipline Code—Lockwood offers one portrait of this restorative justice political moment.

In the early 2000s in Chicago, radical work was the fight to include language surrounding restorative justice in the district's discipline code and to support schools to build these restorative practices, including peer juries. These struggles knit together disparate groups of parents, community organizations, and students. By 2016, the limits of these reforms are increasingly evident. Written with love, complicity, and recognition of both the value and the limits of critique, this chapter examines the landscape of restorative justice in Chicago's schools.

We foreground the shortfalls of our collaborative and methodological approaches. Our work centers analyses and examples that are geographically constrained, making occasional nods or linkages to work outside of Chicago. We, and others, lack longitudinal data on the use of any of the practices we identify. The very terms and practices we chart here—for example, restorative justice and transformative justice—are understood flexibly across the United States and around the world, making it challenging to generalize from this chapter. Also, we are cognizant that when we write about work in progress—particularly work in which we have deep personal and professional investments—objectivity is neither possible nor desired. Many of the organizations we map are ones that we have supported, developed, worked with or alongside, and more. We struggle to represent this work reflectively and critically, and also with generosity. While potential criticisms are numerous and daunting, we know that analysis of in-process, praxis-related work is vital, and we offer these limitations at the start to contextualize our work. Our questions and challenges do not arrest us, or we hope, our readers. While restorative justice is not enough, we continue.

Chicago: Reframing Justice

Restorative justice is an approach that attempts to empower communities to respond holistically to forms of violence and harm experienced by individuals. As defined by the Chicago organization Community Justice for Youth Institute (CJYI), an RJ model is based on "a theory of justice that emphasizes repairing the harm caused by crime and conflict" (Community Justice for Youth Institute n.d., para. 1). As such, RJ takes into account the needs of all affected by an incident of harm and seeks to rebuild what was lost. Punishment is not the goal. In incidents on school grounds, there is no clear line between "victim" and "offender," and punishment overlooks the underlying causes of the original offense. RJ aims to heal the community from an incident where people were harmed and, ideally, help prevent the same sort of harm from happening again.

RJ practices may include peacemaking circles, restorative conferences, mediation, and other accountability processes.

In most circles, RJ's origin is tied to certain indigenous cultures of the Americas and, to some extent, the world. For example, CJYI mentions that its practices "have come to us by way of Kay Pranis, Gwen Chandler-Rhivers and Sally Wolf, who learned them from the Tlingit Tagish tradition of the Yukon Territories" (Community Justice for Youth Institute n.d., para. 3). Some contemporary restorative justice practitioners also credit South Africa's Truth and Reconciliation Commission as an inspiration. Quaker and Mennonite communities have also long used a circle format as a mode of both prayer and problem solving. Providing an alternative to the model of justice based on retribution or penance (what we refer to as "punitive justice"), these claimed genealogies for RJ suggest other paradigms for justice beyond retribution.

The contemporary RJ movement emerged in response to an era of zero-tolerance policies, anti-gang laws, and stricter drug laws that increased the policing, criminalization, and incarceration of many communities, particularly youth of color. Mainstream media coverage and political scapegoating portrayed youth of color as dangerous criminals and created public support for punishing laws and policies throughout the 1980s and 1990s (Dohrn 2000). In concert with attempts to abolish or reform these laws, communities, including young people, began to call for the development of alternative responses to violence and harm. In Illinois, this restorative justice movement influenced the treatment of youth in schools and parts of the juvenile justice system.

While an in-depth treatment of the history of juvenile justice is outside the scope of this chapter, juvenile justice and criminal reform initiatives have long histories in Chicago. Formed in 1899, the Chicago Juvenile Court was the first juvenile court system created in a major U.S. city and reflected a desire to protect young people from the cycle of incarceration (Willrich 2003; Wolcott 2005). Yet, over one hundred years later, African American youth who are seventeen years old and under in Chicago are transferred into adult courts at rates far higher than white youth, and those seventeen years of age and under, overwhelmingly youth of color, face incarceration in punishing juvenile prisons.

The murky promise of the juvenile justice system as a "kind and just parent," a frame William Ayers (1998) critically engages, continues to motivate communities to resist and to push back on the criminalization of youth. As early as 1997, the newly formed Restorative Justice for Illinois advocated for the broad implementation of RJ within Illinois's juvenile legal system (Ashley and Burke 2009). In 2006, the state formally separated its juvenile incarceration functions from the adult corrections system in an attempt to (again) shift away from a punitive model and toward a model of support and treatment (Illinois Department of Juvenile Justice 2009).

Nationally, activists have popularized the use of RJ in schools as a model that may provide an alternative to engagement with the school to prison pipeline. In Chicago, 20 percent of juvenile arrests occur while young people are on school grounds; police presence in elementary and high schools in poor neighborhoods is the norm rather than the exception (Kaba and Edwards 2012). Over the past decade, RJ practices in schools have taken a number of forms. Peer juries bring together a student who has broken a school rule with trained student jurors. Together, they discuss what happened, who was harmed, and what the student can do to repair the harm. Peer mediation brings two or more students together to resolve a conflict with the assistance of trained youth mediators. Peace circles or restorative circles can be used in a number of settings—to help students get to know one another, celebrate student accomplishments, foster discussion, process a difficult topic, or make collective decisions. Schools often call these practices by different names, but the concepts remain the same (Dardick 2000; Tullis 2013; Zenovia 2014; Alternatives, Inc. n.d.; Transforming Conflict n.d.).

Even with uneven resources and support, RJ practices are growing in schools across the United States. Nationally, RJ has been implemented in public school systems in several states, including California, Minnesota, and Wisconsin. Restorative Justice for Oakland Youth runs programs in schools across Oakland (P. Brown 2013). These processes have also crept into the criminal justice systems outside schools. For example, in 2013, the murder of a young woman by her young lover led her family to seek out a restorative justice process which was chronicled in a sympathetic lead article in the *New York Times Magazine* (Tullis 2013). In Chicago, after a four-year campaign led by local organizations, the school board in 2007 revised the student code of conduct to include RJ as a required response to student misconduct (Ahmed-Ullah 2011b; L. Wallace 2007).

Preliminary implementation of RJ in schools has yielded mixed but promising results. Community-based organizations such as Chicago's

Community Organizing and Family Issues (COFI) have documented positive effects on attendance and behavior as well as reduced suspensions in schools that have implemented community peace rooms staffed by parents and volunteers (POWER-PAC Elementary Justice Committee 2010). In 2006–2008, one Chicago public high school documented decreases in arrests and misconduct reports of up to 82 percent after one year of implementing RJ programming. At Fenger High School in Chicago, which became infamous after the death of student Derrion Albert, the administration has been diligently implementing RJ practices, including victim–offender mediation, conferences, peer juries, and peace circles. At a gathering in March 2012, the principal, Elizabeth Dosier, presented data suggesting that "violent and drug related misconducts decreased by 61 percent from Semester 1 (SY2010) to Semester 1 (SY2012)."[3]

Despite the successful campaign to add RJ to the code of conduct in 2007, CPS has never provided full support to schools desiring to implement RJ; furthermore, the state of Illinois's RJ mandate has never been accompanied by significant, robust, or consistent funding.[4] However, even in the face of school closures, takeovers, and budget cuts, many Chicago schools have nonetheless been implementing RJ projects, including peer juries, peer mediation, and peacemaking circles. Coalitional organizing among students, parents,[5] and community members continues to build RJ in schools.

Young people across Chicago are active leaders in this work. Youth from Blocks Together were involved in the original campaign to add RJ to the CPS student code of conduct in 2007. Also in 2007, Voices of Youth in Chicago Education, a youth-organizing collaborative composed of seven local organizations, was established. In 2011, this group of students released a report that (again) identifies the impact of Chicago's harsh disciplinary policies and calls for RJ interventions. Young people from two Chicago organizing projects (Southwest Youth Collaborative and Fearless Leading by the Youth) struggle to improve conditions in (or to close) the Cook County Juvenile Temporary Detention Center (CCJTDC, also known as the Audy Home). This campaign is led by youth who are directly impacted by juvenile incarceration. In October 2011, county board president Toni Preckwinkle expressed her support for closing the facility and moving young people to community-based programs (Slife and Eldeib 2011).

Community organizations outside schools also play key roles. Parents Organized to Win, Educate and Renew–Policy Action Council (POWER-PAC) was also a leader in the 2003–2007 campaign to add RJ to the CPS student code of conduct. POWER-PAC created the Austin Peace Center at Brunson Elementary School on the west side of Chicago, staffed by parent volunteers who assist with talking circles and mediation. This was followed a couple of years later by the opening of a parent-led peace room at Wells High School. POWER-PAC continues to work to eliminate unnecessarily punitive elementary school policies.

In the fall of 2010, a coalition of seven organizations citywide came together to form the High HOPES Campaign, with the stated goal of reducing suspension and expulsion in Chicago's public schools by 40 percent through the citywide implementation of RJ programs.[6] A 2012 report released by the coalition draws on national and local data to argue that RJ can both dramatically reduce suspension, expulsion, and dropout rates and simultaneously save the school district money (High HOPES Campaign 2012). The group also provides a clear road map for the implementation of RJ throughout CPS via peer juries, peer mediation, peace rooms, and training for all staff. High HOPES proposes that every school should have at least one full-time staff person devoted to RJ programming, a cost that would ultimately be offset by the increase in attendance and the reduction in school security costs, such as cameras, guards, and police. CPS maintains that budget cuts and lack of resources make it difficult to implement wide-scale RJ programs like those recommended by High HOPES. Therefore, despite being hard hit by the state and city financial crises, community groups are generally the key entities that offer training and support for school-based RJ programs.[7]

While these coalitions offer examples of movement building around RJ in Chicago, these connections also build bases of support to respond to other issues in schools and communities. Many of these same groups also fought school closures and privatizations across Chicago.

What No School Can Do

While it may be tempting to see them as such, many problems commonly identified with schools are not in fact school problems and cannot be fixed by educational reforms. De jure segregation and concurrent systemic disinvestment in nonwhite communities engineered racial isolation, concentrated white affluence, and reshaped neighborhood economic bases. Of course, these political decisions impacted neighborhood schools.

Identifying something as an educational problem can distract audiences from understanding other roots to that problem. *New York Times* education reporter James Traub (2000) describes how positing schools as a solution to poverty frames the problem narrowly and, ultimately, ineffectively:

> It is hard to think of a more satisfying solution to poverty than education. School reform involves relatively little money and no large-scale initiatives, asks practically nothing of the nonpoor and is accompanied by the ennobling sensation that comes from expressing faith in the capacity of the poor to overcome disadvantage by themselves. Conversely, the idea that schools by themselves can't cure poverty not only sounds like an un-American vote of no confidence in our capacity for self-transformation but also seems to flirt with the racialist theories expressed by Charles Murray and Richard Herrnstein, who argued in "The Bell Curve" that educational inequality is rooted in biological inequality.
>
> An alternative explanation, of course, is that educational inequality is rooted in economic problems and social pathologies too deep to be overcome by school alone. And if that's true, of course, then there's every reason to think about the limits of school, and to think about the other institutions we might have to mobilize to solve the problem. We might even ask ourselves whether there isn't something disingenuous and self-serving in our professed faith in the omnipotence of school. (paras. 8 and 9)[8]

Traub's observation highlights an ongoing romance between the United States and the idea of public schooling.[9]

Just as schools cannot alone interrupt or undo poverty or alter how capitalism naturalizes extreme disparities in wealth, schools cannot alone stem the nation's material and ideological investments in a racialized carceral regime. Restorative justice purports to provide in-school solutions to what many activists and scholars term the school to prison pipeline, yet this very concept of the pipeline draws attention away from the intricate linkages between schools and prisons and simultaneously constrains our abilities to create sustainable and long-term responses. Fixing school discipline policies is not enough to dismantle any pipeline. Building restorative justice practices in schools is not enough. Dismantling the heterogendered, racialized criminalization of young people in schools requires moving beyond ending the school to prison pipeline and toward linking practices inside schools to sociopolitical shifts in the United States that continue to fuel and naturalize confinement and punishment.

Can the anti–school to prison pipeline work that is rooted in restorative practices somehow exceed the confines that have constrained previous school reform initiatives? We are energized by current multisector and cross-issue organizing that encompasses and also extends beyond work to shut down the pipeline. Beyond the Chicago coalitions previously highlighted that weave together youth, parents, and teachers around school-based RJ practices, coalitions such as Californians United for a Responsible Budget (CURB) form a statewide force pushing for political education, policy shifts, and decarceration initiatives. While not focused on RJ or educational reform, CURB persistently advocates for high-quality public education for all and for curbing the state's investment in prisons and punishment.

Redefining the Problem

Restorative justice often starts from the position that there are valuable relationships to rebuild and restore. Definitions of harm and violence within RJ frequently conform to prevailing logics within the criminal justice system. For example, RJ generally assumes an individuated response to harms that should at the very least be partially understood as structural. Restorative justice practices can produce students, again, as the problem instead of implicating schools and other state actors such as school police. RJ places the responsibility to create peace in schools on students (and teachers). This definition of the problem not only places the burden on young people but also strategically creates a focus on particular forms of violence. Interpersonal violence or harm enacted by young people is made visible, and systemic or structural violence—hyper-racialized school policing—is rendered invisible.

When interviewed by a Swedish filmmaker in 1972 in a California prison about the Black Panthers' use of violence, (a clip used in the 2011 documentary *The Black Power Mixed Tape 1967–1975*) Angela Davis stated:

If you are a black person and live in the black community all your life and walk out on the street every day seeing white policemen surrounding you . . . when I was living in Los Angeles, for instance, long before the situation in LA ever occurred, I was constantly stopped. No, the police didn't know who I was. But I was a black woman and I had a natural, and I suppose they thought that I might be "militant." You live under that situation constantly, and then you ask me whether I approve of violence. I mean, that just doesn't make any sense at all. Whether I approve of guns? I grew up in Birmingham, Alabama. Some very, very good friends of mine were killed by bombs—bombs that were planted by racists. From the time I was very, very small, I remember the sounds of bombs exploding across the street, our house shaking. I remember my father having to have guns at his disposal at all times because of the fact that at any moment, we might expect to be attacked. . . . That's why, when someone asks me about violence, I just find it incredible.[10]

Davis's anecdote illuminates the value of interrupting the definition of the problem. The shift toward seeing communities and young people as responsible for peace when they did not necessarily create their learning conditions is problematic and cruel. While the goal of RJ, for some, is to disentangle young people from relationships with prisons and policing, the location of RJ programs in schools already inherently wedded to the carceral state poses significant challenges.

This architecture is visible in some key RJ tools. The name and the language of "peace room" create the possibility that one space within a school can be isolated and that it is possible to interrupt the school itself as a site of violence. Students are produced as a/the problem needing mediation. And peace without justice is truncated and unjust. In addition, the names of RJ practices can potentially function to mask transactions that fulfill old ends. How different is a peace room from a detention hall? The material outcomes could be different for individual students (for example, in Chicago an in-school suspension is not on your record if you elect to go to a peace room), but equally plausible is that this room occupies that same space in the design of a punishing school or in the mind of a Latino or African American student identified as in need of a peace room for being defiant or disrespectful (the number one reason young people are suspended from public schools in the United States). In Austin, Texas, as part of a restorative justice youth program, organizers developed a program to explicitly train youth of color not to be angry or unruly. Adrian Moore describes this restorative justice program, which was working with ten schools as of 2014, as "aggression management therapy" that teaches students who have been removed from the class for "threatening behavior" or fighting "positive social skills, anger management, empathy, and character education": "'We work with 750 kids a year,' said Moore. 'These kids are angry because they are poor, or have family issues. We help them determine their hot spots and recognize why they get angry'" (Zenovia 2014). When assessed through this lens, these practices of accommodation that often name the structural violence but refuse to engage and remake systems are, unsurprisingly, similar to old, and ongoing, forms of domination, including settler colonialism. Through this lens RJ processes, even with the best of intentions, reproduce the young person as the problem.

Co-optation

Too easily, the tools and resources identified for liberation and resistance become embedded in the carceral apparatus. The most ambitious efforts at social change can and have become arms of the punitive state. The current steps toward integrating RJ system-wide in CPS and in other districts place the movement at risk for co-optation by the school system, whose connections to private corporations, police, and youth incarceration will not end overnight (Shipps 2006). Thus, even slow integration of RJ practices and discourses in a limited number of schools invites pause.

Are young people, individually or collectively, made more vulnerable by, for example, the implementation of peace circles within juvenile justice detention centers? Do these practices become soft extensions of the carceral state and actually extend and even mask the state's ability to punish and harm, presenting a kinder and gentler face of punishment to the public? While schools currently disproportionately suspend and expel black and brown youth, does RJ coerce new, intimate disciplinary regimes? Not enough research is available on the impact of "optional" participation in seemingly softer, often therapeutic carceral models, including peace circles and counseling, or in workshops on self-esteem, parenting, or anger management. These forms of what some scholars term therapeutic governance (Haney 2010) are often predicated on the assumption that the incarcerated body is not eligible for a rights-based discourse but instead requires forms of governance to manage outlaw desires and feelings. Perhaps "outlaw" feelings and actions, as Audre Lorde (1984) writes, are legitimate responses to having one's rights violated and one's family systems attacked.

These tensions are relentlessly local. While at Lockwood, we insisted that student participation in the peace room be voluntary. Students had to affirmatively choose to participate after learning about restorative practices. Our rationale was that mandated participation would mirror the carceral state and become seen as a form of punishment.[11] While school itself is not a choice, and the lives of young people are peppered with agencies regulating behavior, it seemed important to us to hold out a space, however fraught and temporal, that attempted to be less coercive. Similarly, parents and teachers must come willingly to the work. Yet, within the wider educational landscape, *choice* rationalizes wildly uneven access to resources. Students attend the very few restrictive-enrollment and high-resourced public schools because of race, wealth, and cultural capital, not because their parents made the right choice. Can RJ be a choice in a deeply coercive system?

The ability of the carceral state to absorb RJ practices (and their attendant critiques) is aided by the constellation of not-for-profits, local grassroots organizations, and religious groups that conceptualize and deliver RJ work. Working inside and alongside schools, training teachers in RJ practices, and providing services for young people and families, these organizations essentially fulfill functions that were once identified as the purview of the state.[12] When a nonprofit organization is paid to train the majority of RJ practitioners, is consulted on school-based RJ practices, and is respected by local courts as an authority, unelected and unaccountable entities set and negotiate policies and practices that adjudicate people's lives. While school personnel and juvenile justice systems often do not act to support young people's self-determination, the significant role nonprofits play to shape all RJ practices diffuses accountability and reduces transparency.

The expansion of RJ communities is a reminder that the decentralization key to neoliberal policies does not mean that the state withdraws; rather, the state's relationships and abilities to negotiate power shift and potentially expand. This presents potential challenges. At the local level, if RJ practices in a school are being run by largely unpaid or underpaid community workers (often funded by soft money) and these practices are problematic, to whom does the student or parent appeal, in particular when RJ practices are constructed as a choice? Who defines what counts as justice? Are these public systems? Structurally, as public funding for education shrinks or stagnates, how does grassroots-supported RJ remove the responsibility from public schools or public teacher education programs to fund and develop this work? Yet, is institutionalization of RJ a goal, or is the more important ongoing struggle the transformation of public schools and communities?

Sustainability

In our Chicago context, nonprofit organizations with few staffers and small, insecure budgets lead and implement the overwhelming majority of RJ initiatives. This is resource-intensive work, outsourced from schools to community-based organizations and nonpaid workers, sometimes parents (women). Shifting discipline and justice paradigms in schools (as in communities) requires resources to be reallocated and redistributed. For example, in 2011, CPS purchased new surveillance cameras for fourteen high schools, and those $7 million could have been spent to make structural shifts that promote school and community safety (Ahmed-Ullah 2011b). Augmenting the nonprofit sectors' role does not shift the function or the role of schools and legitimizes the devaluation and privatization of this "helping" labor.

Sustainability is also an issue at the individual level. Some of the small community-based organizations identified in this chapter are no longer in operation as this book goes to press. RJ initiatives can be hugely dependent on one individual who works beyond a forty-hour workweek and sustains the organization: delivering programs, writing grants, organizing volunteers, building relationships, troubleshooting, and more. Generally underfunded or unfunded, organizations vanish if one of the two or three charismatic and dedicated leaders has a health, employment, family, or other crisis.

Sustainability is also tied to who is being recruited, trained, and supported to build nonpunitive justice responses in schools. In the example of Lockwood School, Trevon responded to his assistant principal's suggestion that the NIA staff person, Ms. C, find him a black male mentor with surprise and disbelief. In Chicago, while pockets of parents and community leaders of color are actively engaged, the majority of professional or formal RJ practitioners are cisgendered females, often white. As RJ programs are scaled up, not only is gender and racial diversity a tension—do staff and nonpaid workers in community organizations and schools reflect the demographics of the neighborhoods?—but the core racialized and heterogendered logics that define RJ remain. Chicago must involve more people, including cisgendered men, people of color, and/or LGBTQ and non-gender-conforming individuals; we should strive toward initiatives, such as COFI's, that directly engage parents and grandparents in RJ work within their own community. As private foundations push to expand forms of RJ across the city, how will this influx of resources professionalize and potentially whiten the pool of people understood as legitimate RJ practitioners?

School Privatization

RJ practices are also challenged by urban educational policies that support school privatization. Chicago offers an on-the-ground example of the effects of the national trends toward expanding school privatization: the city closed fifty public schools in 2013, but the number of charter schools doubled in the city between 2005 and 2012. The overwhelming majority of teachers at charter schools locally and nationally are not unionized; in Chicago these teachers are prevented by law from joining the Chicago Teachers Union. A nonunion workforce is flexible—without the right to due process that contracts and tenure guarantee—and cheaper. In Chicago, the teachers laid off, predominantly older and African American, were replaced by younger and whiter teachers, often with little connection to the schools and the surrounding community. A nonunion workforce has less ability to push back against regressive policies and to support students.

Public schools in some of the most economically marginalized neighborhoods are closed or reconstituted. The impact of reconstitution is severe: all teachers in the school are dismissed, students are often separated and relocated to other schools, and relationships between schools and local organizations are severed. These disruptions challenge efforts to build new cultures and paradigms of discipline and to establish trust between and among teachers, students, and community members. Earlier, we cited the research from Dyett High School as one of the most promising examples of the impact of RJ in CPS. Dyett was targeted for reconstitution, and the new principal immediately dismantled the promising RJ program. Educational privatization and high-stakes accountability impact the schools with the most vulnerable students first. Notably, while police departments have not been effective in their stated goal of stemming crime, there is little discussion of privatizing or reconstituting these forces.

Neocolonialism

The use of First Nations imagery and histories within RJ practices is neither consistent nor unproblematic. Whereas some RJ trainings, practitioners, and public histories clearly acknowledge linkages to indigenous forms of governance and dispute resolution, others do not. While a failure to acknowledge this trajectory can be a form of cultural appropriation, in a landscape like Chicago, where First Nations people and the histories of settler colonialism are often invisible, this acknowledgment can also feel tokenistic. The use of First Nations histories, and concepts, including the use of terms like *talking stick,* can function to reproduce stale stereotypes of noble indigenous savages. Disconnected from the lives of contemporary First Nations communities, particularly those within urban contexts, the invocation of indigenous people within a landscape where colonialism is often willfully ignored functions to extend colonial domination.

Assessment and Evaluation

Another challenge is that there are few consistent evaluation methods to gauge the success of RJ work. Available research is narrow. Anecdotally, we know that many teachers and some schools collect data and attempt to measure the effectiveness of their interventions.

The growing RJ movement is increasingly pushed to demonstrate its effectiveness by reducing youth violence, decreasing youth contact with police and prisons, or increasing academic success and school attendance. Practitioners, educators, and administrators want tools to gather information about RJ practices. Are young people who participate in peace circles instead of a traditional detention hall less likely to end up getting pushed out of class? But many of us also want to collect information helpful to build other tools to respond to emergent faces of violence and power within our communities. For RJ practices to support some young people, at least temporarily, teachers must be provided with the time and resources, in nonpunitive environments, to unlearn disciplinary frameworks and to support paradigm shifts.

One fear is that the traditional metrics of student success—test scores on state standardized tests and attendance/truancy/graduation rates—will be used against the implementation of any alternative disciplinary systems. In this era of accountability, there is little room to use precious teacher or student time in efforts that do not immediately impact students' scores on standardized state achievement tests. Schools that work with low-income students, immigrants, English language learners, and/or others identified by schools as deficient—generally the most underresourced schools to start with—are often particularly vulnerable.

Pushing the Limits with Transformative Justice

As activists, educators, and researchers who work to combat the widespread effects of the prison–industrial complex within and outside school systems, our limited and cautious use of RJ in schools and in the juvenile justice system sets up several contradictions. Most significantly, while RJ aims to provide a potentially holistic alternative to forms of punishment including detention and suspension, youth who participate in RJ often do so under the threat of formal sanction. For example, in an "alternative sentencing" model, youth may be given the option of either going to court for traditional sentencing or participating in a circle process that could result in a criminal sentence but could also result in actions such as apologizing to the victim(s), returning or repairing stolen or harmed property, or working to rebuild trust with the impacted community. Within schools, particularly heavily policed urban schools, the threat of punitive consequences thus places pressure on youth to participate in a restorative process and limits the possibility for RJ to provide a genuine alternative.

The limitations of RJ have led some to identify more closely with the idea of *transformative justice*. Grassroots community and antiviolence organizations in Philadelphia, Philly Stands Up and Philly's Pissed, worked to implement a restorative justice approach within their communities after members experienced sexual assault from other community members. Yet, as they implemented restorative practices, they also began to shift and question the framework of restorative justice. Esteban Lance Kelly, a member of Philly Stands Up, in an assessment of their work, outlines a salient critique: "Yet, in the process of restoration, *what are we restoring?* Would these efforts lead us to the same troubled, problematic world plagued with patriarchy, homophobia, fat phobia, insecurity, heterosexism, racism, anxiety, depression, ableism, and all of the other conditions that feed into sexualized violence in the first place?" (Kelly 2012, 49; emphasis in original). Kelly's analysis frames a core of transformative justice, the desire to transform the conditions that make harm possible.

Transformative justice is defined in opposition to punitive justice systems in the United States and Canada. According to the group generation-FIVE (2007), TJ is "liberation from violence through a process that would confront state and systemic violence for individual and social justice." Instead of TJ, other groups use the term "community accountability" (Chen, Dulani, and Piepzna-Samarasinha 2011; INCITE! 2003; Kim 2012). The Transformative Justice Law Project of Illinois (n.d.) defines TJ as follows: "Through community-based movements, Transformative Justice seeks to resist state-run responses to violence (such as the police state and systems of punishment, detention, and incarceration) and instead promotes support, compassion, dialogue and community building. In this way, reliance on violent and oppressive State level systems is transformed and replaced with community empowerment." TJ questions whether harm can be healed or justice restored in contexts where structural inequality is the norm. TJ seeks to address violence while fighting injustice. It is an inherently flexible approach, structured less as a single model and more as a political outlook driven by values of prison abolition, harm reduction (the goal of reducing harm caused to an individual or a community by an action regardless of whether the action can be completely stopped or prevented), and holistic healing. In a TJ approach, the prison–industrial complex and schools are generally viewed as sources of, rather than necessary responses to, harm.

Transformative justice practitioners shift language to reframe our ideas about harm. The founder of the Oakland-based organization Creative Interventions, Mimi Kim (2012), writes that a transformative practice requires using new terminology and struggling, in whatever the context, to humanize all participants rather than resorting to the use of concepts from the criminal justice or medical world that carry baggage: "General terms such as 'person doing harm' or 'person who caused harm' are used instead of perpetrator, offender, batterer, rapist or predator. For example, in a specific situation of violence we may say perpetrator of sexual assault. This allows for the possibility of change, without assuming it is inevitable. In concrete situations, we were more likely to use someone's name" (21). Even the shift to minimize the use of the word crime is valuable. Not a neutral or natural category, crime refers to a set of articulated laws and regulations. As the criminologist Nils Christie wrote in *Crime Control as Industry*, first published in 1993: "Acts are not, they *become*. So also with crime. Crime does not exist. Crime is created. First there are acts. Then follows a long process of giving meaning to these acts. Social distance is of particular importance. Distance increases the tendency to give certain acts the meaning of being crimes and the persons the simplified meaning of being criminals" (Christie 2000, 22). A crime might be an act of violence, such as assault, but in jurisdictions across the United States, a crime can also be wearing baggy pants if you are under eighteen, urinating in public, or jaywalking. Historically, crime included wearing clothes the state defined as legal only for the opposite sex, being black or First Nations and in a public place after dusk, engaging in consensual anal sex, and drinking alcohol. When used in popular discourse, crime conjures up images of a grievous harm. To be a criminal is to have harmed another person. Yet all harm is not a crime, and all crime does not necessarily involve harm to another person, to oneself, or to the state. The very terms and concepts at stake—criminal, victim, and offender— often disappear acts of harm and simultaneously naturalize linkages between crime and violence. Deconstructing the sociopolitical category of crime is central to understanding the dynamic nature of the prison–industrial complex.

The scope of projects that identify with TJ is difficult to map, as many groups and practices are small, ad hoc, and based in local communities rather than in formal organizations. Other practices may be located or sheltered under organizations that do not publicly identify with the framework of transformative justice. Still others have been reticent to identify with the term for fear of co-optation by nonprofit or state systems, and others simply avoid the use of a formal title to describe their practices. Much of this work takes place in small corners of communities that might not have a website, appear in a book, or identify themselves with any of the terminology used in this chapter.[13] In particular, for organizations that are primarily focused on direct engagement with state systems such as schools or the criminal legal system, the central framework of TJ is in open contradiction to these systems. We suspect that this is at least part of the reason why some individuals and organizations involved with RJ in schools have rarely publicly identified this work as TJ. To do so might require acknowledging an opposition to some of the basic tenets of the approach to schooling in poor communities of color today, in particular the public schools' connection to and ongoing dependence on incarceration and punishment.

For some organizations and individuals, restorative justice and transformative justice are two distinct frameworks, while others use the two terms interchangeably and aren't concerned with what the work is called, rather are focused on practice. The use of *restorative* or *transformative* can be an indication of different long-term visions and goals, but in practice, RJ and TJ could also end up looking quite similar. Several organizations in Chicago identify at least in part with the framework of TJ, including some of the organizations highlighted above, such as Project NIA, Blocks Together, Gender JUST, and the Transformative Justice Law Project.

Before shutting its doors in 2013, Young Women's Empowerment Project (YWEP), a youth-led organization for young women involved in the sex trade, centered a harm-reduction framework rather than encouraging total abstinence. As an organization with a strong TJ committment, YWEP worked to challenge unjust systems. YWEP conducted a participatory action research project to collect information about young people's "bad encounters" with institutional violence and found that many experienced violence and barriers to access within education systems (YWEP 2012). YWEP developed the Street Youth Bill of Rights in response, demanding the right to an education that respects the dignity and learning styles of all youth. In addition to other demands related to policing, health care, and social services, the Street Youth Bill of Rights calls for more accessibility to schooling, including online school and homeschooling, and child care for parenting teens. (YWEP 2009). TJ challenges us to not think of programs we can add to the existing school systems but, rather, to think about transforming schools to eradicate or reduce violence.

Another group, Gender JUST, an organization of LGBTQ young people and adult allies working for racial and economic justice, has publicly advocated for the implementation of RJ in schools, naming the limits of these initiatives. In 2010, LGBTQ youth organizers with Gender JUST, many of whom experienced violence and harassment due to their gender and sexual identity, successfully campaigned to get CPS to adopt a harassment and violence grievance procedure. Rather than advocating a punitive model, however, the young people insisted that the grievance procedure (1) be based in RJ practices, (2) be student-driven, and (3) be governed by a student oversight committee. Later that year, when bullying of LGBTQ youth became a focus of attention nationwide, Gender JUST (2010) released a statement calling for restorative solutions to violence. This statement pointed out that violence against youth of color is also not new, stating, "As queer and transgender youth of color in public schools, violence is a reality we live daily in our schools, on our streets, in our communities, and in our lives." Instead of creating harsher antibullying laws, which many LGBTQ leaders and concerned adults were calling for, Gender JUST proposed RJ practices as a solution: "Our greatest concern is that there is a resounding demand for increased violence as a reaction, in the form of Hate Crime penalties which bolster the Prison-Industrial-Complex and Anti-bullying measures which open the door to zero-tolerance policies and reinforce the school-to-prison pipeline. At Gender JUST, we call for a transformative and restorative response that seeks solutions to the underlying issues, takes into account the circumstances surrounding violence, and works to change the very culture of our schools and communities" (2010). Gender JUST's work provides a clear example of young people affected by violence engage RJ models while also calling for fundamental systemic change.

Whether a restorative or transformative framework is explicitly named or not, the small groups named in this chapter engage in the challenging work of rethinking what justice, safety, and conflict resolution resemble in communities and schools. These organizations struggle to ensure that the analysis of violence also includes the state and the school and works to ensure that individuals are not pathologized as purveyors of harm in a "neutral" state. A transformative justice framework creates space to not just restore relationships or school conditions to what they were prior to a conflict or incident but to imagine, transform, and build more-just communities and educational systems.

Always Moving

Despite these significant concerns, our work in schools and communities convinces us that RJ and TJ are necessary but not sufficient. The practices associated with RJ and TJ hold the potential to be transformative, to create, even temporarily, different possible life pathways for many. These practices can free individuals and communities from punishing systems, create new language to recognize harm, build community, and reclaim aspects of public safety. Yet these practices also have the potential for harm and to reinscribe within institutions the same old forms of domination and oppression. At Lockwood Elementary the peace room did work for some young people, and many community members and parents, as well as some teachers, were supportive. The challenges were linked to capacity, sustainability, and the persistent challenges faced by social movements. While all tools available are needed in the work to build more-just communities—combined with ongoing and collective critical reflection—the school-to-prison pipeline is a part of a wider commitment to a racialized carceral regime, and restorative justice programs in schools are not enough. Yet RJ and TJ practices have the potential to negotiate some forms of conflict in schools and communities, and to reduce the roles that the police and courts play in the lives of young people. More centrally, and much more difficult, these practices and philosophical commitments hold the potential to create different understandings of community for all stakeholders: janitors, school security staff, parents, teachers, students, and community members. However, as this chapter outlines, these openings also risk engendering and legitimating harm. We move, collectively and cautiously, cognizant of the risk, with others.

III

Adulthoods

5

Life and Death

Reentry after Incarceration

With three overlapping and unfinished reports about "reentry from prison," this chapter illustrates how punishment exceeds prison walls and how meanings and protections associated with the child augment precarity. Moving away from a direct analysis of the child, this chapter explores how this figure influences other facets of the carceral regime. These three mediations on reentry focus on the challenge of living after exiting prison and illustrate the wide and punishing fictions associated with contemporary definitions and practices of public safety. While formerly incarcerated people are often seen as "childlike" or as requiring "close supervision and the systematic monitoring of their behavior through constant participation in prescribed programs" (Thompkins 2010, 597), the figure of the child, barely visible in these narratives, shapes a range of institutions and lives.

The anthropologist Elizabeth Povinelli, in *Economies of Abandonment* (2011), explores how viscerally uneven life pathways necessitate new models of thinking not just about ethics but about corporeality and ontology. In her work in North Australia with and alongside Aboriginal communities, Povinelli (who does not identify as Aboriginal) charts the premature death, rampant staph infections, and chronic life-threatening illnesses while also witnessing resilience and struggle. She marks these everyday forms of harm and resistance as intimately linked to a wider colonial regime that produced Aboriginal bodies as insensate, a part of the flora and fauna, while for white settlers the same regime marked access to power, health, capital, and full humanity. A persistent dialectic: civilization requires savagery; private property produces dispossession; whiteness needs blackness; childhood is defined through adulthood. Not twinned or symbiotic, these dynamics, Povinelli suggests, shape individual bodies to produce a "shared body" (2011, 4), and frame forms of resistance and engagement.[1]

Victim and perpetrator, worker and felon, student and prisoner—subjectivities are intimately and dynamically relational, as the historian Elsa Barkley Brown wrote over two decades ago: "Middle-class white women's lives are not just different from working-class white, Black, and Latina women's lives. It is important to recognize that middle-class women live the lives they do precisely because working-class women live the lives they do. White women and women of color not only live different lives but white women live the lives they do in large part because women of color live the ones they do" (1992, 295). Barkley Brown's point is not simply that black and Latina women's lives are different from white women's lives, but that these differences circulate in close relation. Exploring how conceptions of childhood facilitate policing and incarceration, therefore, requires a close excavation of how meanings attached to childhood and youth shape the lives of adults. This chapter tracks how contemporary "law and order" definitions of public safety augment vulnerability and invites readers to recognize, in unfamiliar settings, the imprint of the child. Premature death, violence, and vulnerability, for example, are reinforced through subtle practices ephemerally tethered to childhood: Who is infantilized? How is harm for many augmented through a commitment to child protection? Who is not recognized as capable of rehabilitation? While mapping the landscape for those trying to exit prisons and jails, this chapter also tracks our shared body, how child protection is tethered to a disposable adulthood.

Awful Acts

In the early spring of 2009, after thirty years locked inside Illinois prisons for convictions for armed robbery and sexual assault, Julius Anderson arrived at St. Leonard's Ministries (SLM), a residence for formerly incarcerated people on Chicago's west side (or "West Haven," a designation realtors recently minted). Affiliated Psychologists, the mental health services agency contracted by the Illinois Department of Corrections (IDOC), had evaluated Julius in 2006 and did not find that he was a habitual offender who required ongoing confinement but instead recommended parole (Main and Hussain 2011). Providing free services for over forty years—food, clothing, housing, and access to services including job training and education—SLM is one of the few residential transitional housing spaces for the tens of thousands of people who exit prisons and jails every year in Illinois and return to six of Chicago's seventy-seven neighborhoods—Austin, Humboldt Park, North Lawndale, Englewood, West Englewood, and East Garfield Park (La Vigne et al. 2003, 2004). In 2012, 30,172 people exited prison and jails in Illinois; across the United States, approximately 643,488 people come out of state prisons each year (Bureau of Justice Statistics 2014).

Like Julius, over 95 percent of people housed in state prisons will return to communities resplendent with underfunded public schools, hyper-policing, high unemployment, food deserts, and shrinking public services. People are released from prison in Illinois after serving their sentences (unless they were given an indeterminate sentence or convicted as a class C prisoner) with only the clothes on their back the day they were admitted, a bus ticket (if needed), and the money in their commissary account. Some prisons might also give a person a few dollars, perhaps fifty, or a cheap sweatsuit.

Approaching sixty years of age, Julius had served his time. According to staff at SLM, soon after his arrival, Julius repeatedly stated to his caseworker, his parole officer, and anyone who would listen that he thought he might harm someone, including himself. SLM, similar to the few other transitional residential programs in the Chicago area in 2009, did not have the capacity or the resources to support GPS monitoring, but the state issued Julius a standard electronic ankle bracelet. Confined to his residence at SLM, Julius was not, despite pleas from his SLM caseworker, granted permission to walk more than fifty feet to access (free) group or individual therapy or support groups.

For the past fifteen years, I have worked alongside many people like Julius who exit prisons and jails in Chicago, coordinating and teaching at a high school for people coming out of prisons and jails. Many of my students live at Grace House, a secular residential program on the west side of Chicago for women exiting prisons and jails. Connected to SLM, Grace House is the largest, longest-running, and most stable residential transition space for women in Chicago and offers free services: housing, employment training, counseling, and education. It is sex-segregated and is often staffed by both religious women and many formerly incarcerated women. Grace House residents (and staff) are required to commit to random and mandatory drug tests, and residents are required to attend a number of therapeutic sessions. Residents can get support to secure more permanent housing, access education, find employment, and rebuild relationships with their children and family. In informal conversations many women report to me that they value the resources and benefits of staying at a place that is fiercely drug- and alcohol-free and where people have a shared history of incarceration. Others chafe at the surveillance, the lack of privacy, the enforced sobriety, and the rules.

The eventual release of people housed in state prisons has supported an exponential growth in reentry agencies. Community-based, nonprofit, and sometimes religious, these organizations survive on a constellation of funding streams, including government grants and foundation and philanthropic giving, as well as through the suppressed-wage labor of the frontline staff, which often includes former residents. While not formally a part of the state's department of corrections or other punitive state bureaucracies, these organizations wield considerable power. The sociologist Douglas Thompkins tracks the development of three of the United States' largest reentry agencies and identifies significant growth in program revenue, an increase in the number of employees, and raises for CEO compensation between 2004 and 2008 (2010, 596–99). The prisoner reentry industry (PRI) is a "super authority" controlling increasing numbers of individuals after their release from prison (Thompkins, Curtis, and Wendel 2010, 428). Generally segregated by the sex a person is assigned at birth, residential facilities provide housing for people exiting prisons and jails and regulate their conditions of parole (or probation), which may include mandatory drug tests, curfews, or participation in employment or counseling programs.

Through one lens, organizations such as SLM participate in the well-rehearsed myth that those who are incarcerated, like Julius, can be reintegrated into society after their release. Yet the logic of reentry produces new exclusionary regimes, other facets to carceral power, and additional tools to regulate people's lives. The language of reentry, of services, offers an individualist therapeutic veneer that masks the reality that for most people released from prison, reentry is not feasible. Perhaps, the social arrangements were always organized such that prior to incarceration, full social and civic participation was neither promised nor possible.

Yet, one of the few spaces in which those exiting prisons and jails have been able to secure employment is in the (growing) field of reentry services to monitor and support others after release from prison. Many of the frontline people working in the PRI, save a very few executives, are "professional former prisoners," as Chicago's formerly incarcerated anti-prison activist Joanne Archibald drily reminded me in the late 1990s, and often do not make a living wage. They often lack professional credentials or a coherent resumé, and incarceration has simultaneously cheapened their labor and produced a semi-marketable form of expertise.

While PRI does regulate growing numbers of people, their experiences are not uniform. Tina Reynolds's stay in Providence House, a transitional home run by nuns, provided her with the resources and the space to reflect and rebuild her life (Reynolds 2010, 453). The founder of Women on the Rise Telling HerStory (WORTH), a New York prison reform advocacy-based organization run by formerly incarcerated women, Reynolds also writes that this facility does not change the wider culture for those whose prison records make acquiring living-wage employment or returning to school a challenge. Nor do these reentry programs work to alter the conditions that create high incarceration rates. Reynolds used the time and strength gained from her stay at Providence House to begin to work as an advocate and then to start her own organization. A New Way of Life (NWOL) in Los Angeles, a residential program that can accommodate up to twenty-five women and children, works with women to navigate barriers after exiting prison. NWOL was founded and is run by a formerly incarcerated woman, Susan Burton, and its staff is also linked to political and social movements that challenge incarceration in Los Angeles and throughout California. NWOL views public political education, leadership development by those most affected, and organizing as central to the "service" work of reentry to build capacity for political and systems change.

After living at SLM for almost two weeks, Julius cut off his ankle monitor and disappeared. SLM immediately reported his departure to IDOC, and the state knew precisely when his monitor was removed. Not an enforcement agency, SLM does not have the staff to search for people if they depart. Staff at SLM worried about Julius and what he might do. A month after he cut off his monitor and left SLM, Julius was arrested for sexually assaulting women in Chicago (Main and Hussain 2011).

SLM's relationship with its neighbors was already fractious. The neighborhood had changed over the past few years, and some of the new homeowners were less comfortable living near formerly incarcerated people. The new local homeowners association, which had previously worked to curb any SLM expansion, found out about the sexual assaults, Julius's arrest, and Julius's connection to SLM. A member of its executive committee, a lawyer, contacted the three women who were sexually assaulted and asked them to join a civil lawsuit against SLM. The women joined the neighborhood association to file suit against SLM and the psychologists whose evaluations led to Julius's parole (Main and Hussain 2011).

Julius's arrest led to a series of articles in the *Chicago Tribune* and the *Chicago Sun Times* as well as a number of city blogs. An article about Julius in the *Chicago Journal* engaged online respondents who identified themselves as neighbors of SLM. The overwhelming majority of comments were deeply critical of SLM, some calling for its closure. Many posts reflected a specific anger against the presence of formerly incarcerated people in the neighborhood, as the following comment shows:

> By Concerned Neighbor from West Town / West Haven
> Posted: 12/16/2009 9:07 AM
>
> I am reading all these comments about Saint Leonard's, and no one recognizes that instead of required GPS and a security guard, the facility has a wonderful GARDEN, instead. I mean, what violent ex-felon would look at that and ultimately resist the urge to attack and rape two more women just days after his release? Hey, at least they raped in different neighborhoods! Who needs security when SLM's focus is to add parking lots for overnight guests? What's next? ex-felon slumber parties @ SLM? (Maidenberg 2009)

Another response suggested that SLM is simply and directly an arm of IDOC and should be publicly identified as such.

> By Karen from West Haven
> Posted: 12/10/2009 2:52 AM
>
> Why house sex offender parolees across from Suder Elementary School? And shouldn't there be signs letting people know this is a Department of Corrections transitional housing site?

A 2011 *Chicago Tribune* article quoted local condominium residents as feeling "unsafe" and "angry" at the way SLM had worked with Julius and suggested that SLM lacked regard for people living in the neighborhood.

One of the sexual assault survivors expressed her ongoing fear, pain, and anger at SLM. The article closed with comments from local residents who did not want SLM to close but opposed its expansion. "Women and children . . . are a little safer now because they stopped taking sex offenders," one local resident said. "We, in the community, believe you cannot really change them" (Main and Hussain 2011). SLM's recidivism rates, less than half the national and state average, were not noted in the article, which focused on identifying the few men who had "reoffended" (recidivism rates for women who return from prison were not addressed). Imagined and potential harm to children defines public safety.

Sexual and gendered violence that targets women, including transwomen, is pervasive. Most advocacy and governmental agencies that collect data have relatively consistent findings about the prevalence of sexual assault in the United States. The Centers for Disease Control and Prevention's 2010 National Intimate Partner and Sexual Violence Survey (NISVS) documents that "1.3 million women were raped during the year preceding the survey [2009]" and that "nearly 1 in 5 women have been raped in their lifetime while 1 in 71 men have been raped in their lifetime" (Black et al. 2011). The National Coalition Against Domestic Violence (2007) identifies that in their lifetime, "one in 6 women and 1 in 33 men have experienced an attempted or completed rape" and "nearly 7.8 million women have been raped by an intimate partner at some point in their lives." The Rape Abuse Incest National Network (RAINN) cites "293,000 victims of sexual assault each year" (RAINN n.d). The Bureau of Justice Statistics estimates that "1.5 million women are physically assaulted by an intimate partner every year" and that "in 2007, women were 70 percent of all victims of the 2,340 murders committed by intimate partners" (Richie 2012, 25, 26). All agencies and organizations that collect data on sexual assault concur that the majority of men who perpetrate violence against women are not strangers to their victims.

Women of color experience disproportionately high rates of interpersonal violence. "Homicide by an intimate partner is the second leading cause of death for Black women between the ages of 15 and 25. Black women are killed by a spouse at a rate twice that of white women" (Richie 2012, 26). The "US Department of Justice estimates that 1 of 3 Native American / Alaskan Indian (NA/AI) women will be raped or sexually assaulted in her lifetime, making the average annual rate of rape and sexual assault among American Indians 3.5 times higher than for all other races" (Greenfeld and Smith 1999). Transwomen and/or those who are non-gender-conforming and/or nonheterosexual are subjected to higher rates of violence, including harm inflicted by those state systems set up for protection that are predicated on gender conformity and heterosexuality (Mogul, Ritchie, and Whitlock 2011; Spade 2011).

While men harm women, a focus on interpersonal violence can impede the recognition of other forms of violence and also ignore how harm is directly produced and shaped by policies, contexts, and institutions. Interpersonal "stranger danger" sexual violence targeting specific white children and women is perhaps the most visible form of violence in the United States. The term *state violence* is used to identify when the harm does not come from an individual but from the state (or from an individual acting on behalf of a state or government) (Richie 2012; Spade 2011; IN-CITE 2006). State violence makes visible other kinds of harm. For example, economic disinvestment is a form of state violence, as are hyperpolicing and racial profiling, underfunding schools, or supporting institutions that reward misogyny and heteronormativity.

The sociologist Beth Richie (2012) developed a model to understand the interplay of interpersonal and state violence. She names other forms of violence, including negative media images, the denial of the significance of victimization, encounters with public agencies that are degrading, victim blaming, and lack of affordable housing. These actions, often scaffolded or enacted by the state, harm individuals and communities and facilitate or enhance interpersonal violence. For example, research illustrating that transwomen, women of color, and/or poor women experience much higher rates of interpersonal violence can all too easily be read as an individual pathology. Poor, queer, and/or black and brown women make "bad choices" in their personal lives and are responsible for the violence they experience—this is too often the stereotype that recirculates in public discourse and is cemented through the circulation of individuated narratives of violence. Yet, if structural or state violence is mapped onto the discussion—that transwomen are often locked out of legal employment, formally and informally denied access to housing and health care, targeted for harassment, and humiliated in some mainstream media outlets—this expanded analysis pushes audiences to understand the roots of the problem beyond individual actions. Experiences of interpersonal violence are inseparable from forms of state or structural violence.

This framework holds the potential to shift dialogues about how to respond to harm and violence. Would more police in the streets address the root causes of why transwomen experience high rates of interpersonal street violence? If harm is facilitated by structural forces, not simply interpersonal actors, transformations must be also at the systems level.

Narrow understandings of violence produce an asymmetrical landscape and an incomplete understanding of where harm originates. Representations of sexual violence perpetrated by strangers targeting particular white women and children historically result in a response of increased criminalization, yet, as the "Critical Resistance and INCITE! Statement on Gender Violence and the Prison Industrial Complex" highlights, this does not eradicate sexual violence against women:

> Law enforcement approaches to violence against women may deter some acts of violence in the short term. However, as an overall strategy for ending violence, criminalization has not worked. . . . The criminalization approach has also brought many women into conflict with the law, particularly women of color, poor women, lesbians, sex workers, immigrant women, women with disabilities, and other marginalized women. For instance, under mandatory arrest laws, there have been numerous incidents where police officers called to domestic incidents have arrested the woman who is being battered. Many undocumented women have reported cases of sexual and domestic violence, only to find themselves deported. A tough law and order agenda also leads to long punitive sentences for women convicted of killing their batterers. Finally, when public funding is channeled into policing and prisons, budget cuts for social programs, including women's shelters, welfare and public housing are the inevitable side effect. These cutbacks leave women less able to escape violent relationships. (INCITE! 2008)

Criminalization fails to end violence against women and can create environments that make the lives of many individuals, including some women, more vulnerable.

While media coverage focused almost exclusively on the acts of violence perpetrated by Julius and the perceived failures of SLM, few salient features about Julius emerged. He was diagnosed in the 1970s with chronic schizophrenia and previously found unfit to stand trial, but unknown is what mental health treatment he received during his thirty years of incarceration or what medical services he had access to after release. Unmet health needs not only make an individual's life much more precarious but also compromise the well-being of the community. Our nation has abandoned those not able-bodied or those with health issues to the private sector, family, or poverty, and this has potentially negative ramifications for both the individual and communities.

Julius's diagnosis of schizophrenia in the 1970s is important to explore. The psychiatrist and feminist scholar Jonathan Metzl's *The Protest Psychosis* (2010) outlines how, in precisely the era in which Julius was diagnosed, schizophrenia shifted from being overwhelmingly a white women's illness to being the stigmatizing and punishing disease for "angry" and "out of control" black men that required confinement and heavy pharmaceutical intervention. Schizophrenia shifted racial and gendered bodies during the Black Liberation struggles of the 1960s. The mental health of black communities had not mattered significantly to the mainstream psychiatric community until then, yet the civil rights movement, as Metzl outlines, "catalyzed research subject recognition" (100). In newly desegregated wards, black patients became visible and the objects of research within a racist landscape: "Studies conflated black schizophrenia with Black Power in order to illustrate evolving understanding of the illness as hostile or violent, or used longstanding stereotypes about manic, crazy black men to demonstrate 'new' forms of schizophrenic illness" (100). The pathologization of dissent has a pronounced and uneasy history. Drapetomania, the mental illness invented in 1851 by the physician Samuel Cartwright, classified as *dyaesthesia aethiopis* the actions of enslaved people seeking freedom who were not submissive and whose behavior Cartwright described as "rascally" (Metzl 2010, 30). Cartwright prescribed whipping and "in extreme cases amputation of the toes" (30).

Although Metzl does not argue that mental health is a political construct, nor does he outline the possibility of how punishing landscapes of white supremacy alter bodies and coerce individuals to exhibit symptoms consistent with or interpreted as hallucinations or paranoia, his work meticulously demonstrates how institutionalized white supremacy, misogyny, and heteropatriarchy worked to shape the medical classification of black men as dangerous, predatory, and aggressive (Metzl 2010). While perhaps not directly relevant, this history merits excavation in the context of Julius's life.

Many scholars have also linked the growth of the prison and jail population in the United States directly to changes in how the state identifies and treats people with disabilities.[2] In 1963, the passage of the Community Mental Health Center Act (CMHCA) signified a national shift in mental care policy, from the institutionalization or warehousing of people with mental illness to a treatment plan centered around the use of community clinics, group homes, and pharmaceuticals. According to critics, the CMHCA was never fully funded, yet the majority of the mental health institutions across the United States were shut down, placing most people with mental health challenges in the streets and in poverty. In the 1990s, more than forty mental institutions were permanently closed, while more than four hundred new prisons were opened (Sentencing Project 2002, 3).[3] Institutions for those labeled as physically or psychiatrically disabled closed in the 1980s, sometimes reopening a few years later as prisons. For example, Alabama transformed three-quarters of its closed institutions into prisons, according to sociologist Liat Ben-Moshe (2013). As state mental health facilities closed, often due to the exposure of these institutions as prison-like and cruel, those housed within often drifted into jails and prisons because of a lack of accessible support services.

Jails and the wider prison system are where many people access needed mental health services. Human Rights Watch identifies the top three institutions in the world that house people with designated mental health issues as the jails in Los Angeles, New York City, and Chicago (Los Angeles County Jail, Rikers Island County Jail, and Cook County Jail, respectively) (Human Rights Watch 2003). In 2013, Cook County Jail housed approximately two thousand to twenty-five hundred people with diagnosed mental health illnesses, with a price tag, excluding medical care, of $190 a day ("Locked In," 2013). In Florida, the number of mentally ill in prisons and jails outnumbers the number of patients in state mental institutions five to one (Sentencing Project 2002, 3). Prisons and jails have never been designed for this purpose, and high-profile media coverage continues to highlight grotesque violations. Also in 2013, the Justice Department's Civil Rights Division found that the conditions in Florida's Escambia County Jail, housing approximately thirteen hundred people, were unconstitutional. The jail practiced racial segregation, did not have adequate mental health services, altered physician-prescribed medication, overmedicated people, and did not provide even the most basic forms of mental health care (Austin 2013).

My political work confirms this landscape. For poor people, particularly people of color, there is no generous and affirming safety net. Affective, cognitive, or behavioral differences—being anxious, queer, depressed, paranoid, angry, or a slow learner—do not garner supportive services or resources. In a context where normal means fit to work, acquiescent to authority, and conformist, those who are different are caught up in punishing institutions and struggle to survive. People self-medicate with street drugs because access to health care systems and/or prescriptions for legal pharmaceuticals are inaccessible. Employers discriminate against people with disabilities, and housing is a challenge for those without a job. For some, jail can appear to be a relatively safe and warm place in a city with few free places to sleep. Unaddressed is how living in communities under surveillance by police, where the only options, as the formerly incarcerated organizer Mark Mitchell reminds me, are the "porch or the penitentiary," induces stress, anxiety, hopelessness, and paranoia. Unelucidated is how our punishing landscape shapes the health of captured people. How does racial profiling shape depression? Anxiety? How does time in jail facilitate affective states?

This discussion could easily be read as an apology for sexual violence: *Where is Julius's accountability in this scenario? Isn't Julius just being left off the hook? Don't these same conditions affect many who do not rape women? With this argument, wouldn't thousands of people feel justified to harm one another and deny any responsibility?* While personal responsibility does matter, so does the context and history. Curiously individual responsibility is often emphasized when politically or economically convenient. Assault rifles cannot be banned in U.S. cities because this would infringe on people's individual right to bear arms, yet banning abortion and constraining an individual woman's right to reproductive choice is rationalized by many because of a collective good.

Missing from the coverage of Julius, SLM, and the women who were sexually assaulted is our massive prison nation, which neither produces public safety nor meets the needs of those experiencing harm. Not present is how the buildup of the prison nation removes people from neighborhoods, specifically black and Latino communities, divest wealth from communities, and destabilizes of city blocks and families. Missing are the thousands of formerly incarcerated people locked out of any meaningful possibility of reentry through punishing laws that restrict employment and housing options and any critical engagement with whether these individuals were ever permitted to be full participants in social and civic life. Missing from the picture is how our carceral landscape has sold communities a false promise of safety and taken over other institutions, such as public schools. The news coverage does not mention this uneven geography of racialized disinvestment, the lack of services for those exiting prisons and jails, or the false promise of public safety.

This context does not excuse Julius. Rather, it invokes collective forms of accountability and widens an analysis of sexual violence, creating and proliferating sites and opportunities for transformation. The lawsuit against SLM identifies the two psychologists who signed off on Julius's release as defendants, but what other actors and institutions are also accountable for creating the conditions that made Julius's sexual assault of these women possible? If free, nonstigmatizing mental health services were available to all, how would life be different? How might, for example, access to free, nonstigmatizing mental health services be a part of an anti–sexual violence road map for the United States?

I wish there were a neat and just end to the lawsuit, a report back on the status of the women who were assaulted, and Julius. It is not that simple.

As an ally who has worked alongside and with SLM for over sixteen years, with friendships or professional relationships with many who have come through its doors, I was enraged and depressed by this lawsuit and deeply saddened by Julius's actions. Narrow media coverage constructed SLM as a grotesquely negligent organization. While the majority of SLM's neighbors had historically been amicable or invisible, a vocal core of new residents had increasingly wielded their power—for example, complaining about the "loiterers" on the corner. The SLM campus (six buildings: for administration, short-term and long-term housing, kitchen and dining facilities, and education/job training) is consistently well kept, landscaped, and always presents as the model of a middle-class community. In response to the media coverage, SLM even reined in the annual neighborhood holiday caroling event in order to have a lower profile.

While my heart hurt at the violence these women experienced, the response to punish SLM was frustrating and would do little to diminish any future possibilities that the harm these women survived would not be repeated. Yet, in our impoverished criminal justice landscape, the range of tools available to seek any kind of redress or accountability is narrow. The survivors of rape pressed charges against Julius and are trying to find out who is responsible and to hold these parties accountable.

Unwilling to let this mainstream media coverage (including a two-page article with color photos in the front section of the popular *Chicago Sun Times*) frame the events and the contexts, I worked with other allies to craft a short rebuttal to submit:

Dear Editors,

For almost ten years we have participated in the educational programs that are linked to SLM. We are honored to be able to learn and to teach alongside men and women who are working to rebuild their lives. We appreciated the *Times'* thoughtful recent coverage of SLM.

With over 2.3 million people incarcerated, the US has 5 percent of the world's population and 25 percent of the world's prison population. Approximately 85 percent of those locked up in state prisons will be released. We believe that organizations such as SLM make our communities stronger and safer, because they ensure, on a less than shoestring budget, that our brothers, sisters, lovers and neighbors who are released from prison after serving their time, have access to the basic necessities: a bed and a roof, food, clothing, and some employment options. And, when all related research on incarceration points to the reality that those in our prisons and jails are often mentally ill, living below poverty, under and unemployed, addicted to drugs or alcohol, survivors of violence and abuse, high school push-outs, we also believe that organizations such as SLM are doing some of the most important justice work in our city.

We know that violence against women that is perpetrated by men is, by any measure, an epidemic. For example, on average, every three minutes in the United States a man rapes a woman somewhere. Our hearts go out to the three women that were sexually assaulted. We are angry that sexual violence against women and children persists. But neither life sentences—inside or outside prison—or denying people who exit from prison any services, make our communities stronger or safer, for women, children and others.

I easily secured over a dozen signatures and e-mailed the director of SLM to let him know that we were going to submit the letter for publication. He responded quickly, stating that while he valued all of our support, the lawyer for the agency advised against any—repeat *any*—public response to the *Chicago Sun Times* article. He respectfully requested that I refrain from sending this letter to the editor. Surprised, I considered sending it anyway. I thought he was wrong, believing from experience that silence is rarely protection.

While I still disagree, my livelihood does not come from working at SLM. I do not live in the neighborhood. I have been a nonpaid worker for many years, and twice-weekly or weekly commitments make me at best an ally and at worst just another nice white lady do-gooder. Without this organization, which is precariously funded, dependent on a range of soft money, and delicately built on reputations, many men and women would not have a place to go after they have been released from prison or jail in Illinois. I was silent.

SLM no longer houses paroled sex offenders. Pending trial, Julius was labeled a sexually dangerous person and committed to a state-run mental health institution in downstate Rushville (Twohey 2009). In September 2013, he pled guilty to three counts of sexual assault and was sentenced to seventy-five years in prison (Hussain 2013). He will spend the rest of his life behind bars. I have no update on the women who were assaulted. After a deliberation of less than an hour, in 2015 a jury found St. Leonard's negligent and awarded the three women $18 million. After the verdict the executive director of SLM, Walter Boyd, disclosed to the media that St. Leonard's Ministries (and their insurance) cannot cover this amount, and as this book goes to press, negotiations between SLM, the insurance agencies and, the plaintiffs are still ongoing (Schmadeke and Lighty 2015).

While Julius is in many respects not a typical person released from prison, reentry challenges surrounding employment, housing, parenting, and access to social services shape the milieu for too many. This discussion of awful acts, particularly sexual violence, against the context of the (civil) death conferred on those exiting prisons and jails outlines significant and intertwined contours of the contemporary carceral landscape. Persistently high rates of sexual assault by men who target women and children, gentrifying neighbors who do not want "ex-cons" on their blocks, a carceral state that does little to make our communities safer, and the forms of death, particularly civil death, offered to those coming out of prisons and jails are all too familiar national stories across the United States. These stories are always about race and power, about what kinds of harm matter and to whose bodies. As wealth disparities grow and the carceral regime locks out more people with an increasing array of technologies, the story of Julius, reentry programs, and our continued failure to meaningfully address the roots of violence, including sexual violence, echoes across the United States.

Working Life

In 2007, the Chicago Transit Authority (CTA) started an apprenticeship initiative to hire formerly incarcerated men and women. Those recommended by a select number of reentry programs in the city would be eligible to be hired on a flexible schedule to work the overnight shift to clean out the El train cars or scrub the graffiti off the trains. Brandell Kemp, a formerly incarcerated apprentice, described the work to a *Chicago Tribune* reporter in 2011: to "rid the cars of candy wrappers, beer cans, lost harmonicas, crumpled newspapers, a mysterious bucket of cement and enough old gum to dull a thousand razor blades" (Schmich 2011). Many were willing to do this work, hoping that it would transition to something more consistent and permanent, ideally a unionized position. The apprenticeship paid $9.25 per hour when the state's minimum wage was only $8.25, and hundreds of people I worked with diligently attended CTA job fairs and tried to secure these positions. *An entry-level city worker position with a wage slightly above minimum! The promise of a unionized position and stable employment! An employer OK with hiring people with records!*

Although the labor market in Chicago, as in many urban centers across the United States, is dynamic, living-wage, full-time, humanizing employment for people with criminal records is scarce. A 2012 data brief from the National Employment Law Project (NELP) highlights that the fastest-growing employment sector is low-wage service work. Nationally, positions that pay less than $13.84 per hour account for 58 percent of new positions created since 2008 (National Employment Law Project 2012).

These are the low-wage positions available for those *without* criminal records, *with* high school diplomas and/or some postsecondary education, and *with* stable housing and employment histories.

Entering even the service economy job market is infinitely more difficult for those with criminal records. NELP estimated that as of December 2013 approximately seventy million formerly incarcerated people in the United States were looking for work, and notes that only ten states have what is termed "ban the box legislation" prohibiting employers from asking criminal status questions on job application forms ("Statewide Ban the Box" 2013). In other states, records related to arrest and conviction can be used to deny employment when relevant. While it is not legal (under Title VII of the 1964 Civil Rights Act) to deny employment when the arrest or conviction is not related to the job opening, these claims under the Equal Employment Opportunity Commission (EEOC) are difficult to pursue. Formal and informal employment discrimination saturates the lives of people with criminal records. According to the report *After Prison: Road-blocks to Reentry,* produced by the national advocacy organization Legal Action Center, in twenty-nine states employers and occupational licensing agencies—from cosmetology to real estate—can deny applicants a job or professional licensure because of their criminal record. In a whopping thirty-seven states, asking a job candidate about arrests that did not lead to conviction is also legal (Legal Action Center 2004). The criminal record background investigation industry continues to grow, and a *New York Times* editorial on the flagrant violations of one company, HireRight, characterizes the industry as having "grown so quickly that no one seems to know how many companies there are" and as producing "flawed and unreliable data." Federal (and state) government has been slow to monitor this industry ("Accuracy in Criminal Background Checks" 2012).

Not only does conviction or arrest function as a barrier to accessing legal employment, but the associations among race, gender, and criminality reshape sectors of the labor market for people without convictions. The background check companies not only control the production and circulation of "criminal" information but also reinforce damaging mythologies about the associations between race and crime. In 2012, Pepsi was investigated by the EEOC, which found that the company's criminal background checks had discriminated against more than three hundred African Americans because those with arrests but without convictions were not hired for a position ("Pepsi to Pay" 2012). A 2008 study of employment barriers for formerly incarcerated women in California, *A Higher Hurdle: Barriers to Employment for Formerly Incarcerated Women*, identified that finding employment is most difficult for black formerly incarcerated women prior to and after incarceration. This study also concluded that race, particularly blackness, serves as a proxy for incarceration for some employers, further hampering black women's ability to secure legal employment (Morris, Sumner, and Borja 2008, 27).[4] Criminal background checks reproduce lopsided associations among race, gender, and criminality, constraining access to employment opportunities.

By 2011, questions about the CTA's apprenticeship program surfaced. Only fifteen of the several hundred apprentices had been hired into full-time positions with the CTA (Heffernan 2013). This program was also in hot water with the CTA's labor union, where salaries start at $25.20 per hour. While CTA union members were laid off, formerly incarcerated people hired through the apprenticeship program were brought on to do work at below union wages. While creating employment opportunities, the apprenticeship program provides cheap labor for the city and potentially threatens living-wage union positions. Yet, the CTA labor union is relatively inaccessible to workers with criminal records who lack education and job experience. Union leaders and members balked at the program. Prominent city members, including the south side priest and activist Father Michael Pfleger, specifically called out Amalgamated Transit Union Local 308 president Robert Kelly for killing job opportunities for formerly incarcerated people (Pfleger 2013). The union, the CTA, and a number of organizations supporting formerly incarcerated people struggled to reach a compromise, and the program was temporarily suspended in 2013 (Schutz 2013).

In response to community mobilization, this program was reinstated in February 2014 (O'Neil 2013), yet, with 265 CTA apprenticeship placements, this program neither provides a living wage nor is capable of employing Illinois's tens of thousands of people released from prisons every year or the hundreds of thousands marked for life by incarceration. The CTA struggle characterizes one facet of the structural challenges faced by attempts to secure employment options for formerly incarcerated people. Many of the employment openings available, even those touted by governments as accessible or even designed to employ this population, are short-term, nonunion positions that involve hard and often dehumanizing labor. Many of the people I work with at Sister Jean Hughes Adult High School, for example, are not eligible for even these positions because they have not completed a GED program or earned a high school diploma, and they do not have any postsecondary education. Also, most of the programs, such as the CTA's, will not hire people with convictions for violent crimes or any sexual offenses.

The term *civil death* refers to the consequences of conviction and incarceration that extend beyond life in prison (Patterson 1982; Rodriquez 2008). Orlando Patterson, in *Slavery and Social Death: A Comparative Study* (1982), describes social death as the state of being enslaved. Patterson's historical overview and analysis of slavery across differing contexts conclude that the state of slavery produced individuals who are "socially dead." Other scholars have built on Patterson's work to argue that criminalized communities experience forms of social death or civil death as their fundamental civil rights are denied through prohibitions on accessing social assistance benefits and as their rights to privacy, parenting, and voting are curtailed (Rodriquez 2008; Gottschalk 2015).

Those with drug-related convictions are routinely denied access to public housing and welfare benefits across the United States (Allard 2002; Mauer and Chesney-Lind 2003). The Personal Responsibility and Work Opportunity Reconciliation Act of 1996 (PRWORA) restructured social assistance programs, building in formal barriers to accessing benefits for people with criminal convictions, specifically drug convictions. The federal government instituted a lifetime ban for people with felony drug convictions on accessing the Supplemental Nutrition Assistance Program (SNAP) and the Temporary Assistance for Needy Families (TANF) program. Over the years, states have gradually moved to modify these bans, but as of 2015, approximately twelve states, including Texas and Georgia, still had full bans on accessing welfare benefits (Beitsch 2015). Patricia Allard's research shows that these structural prohibitions continue to disproportionately harm women, who were overrepresented in drug-related charges and convictions (Allard 2002). In addition, as 80 percent of women who are locked up are parents, these prohibitions ensure that women released from prisons with drug convictions find it virtually impossible to rebuild a life with their children (Valbrun 2011). Another casualty of the Clinton administration was the inclusion in the 1998 Higher Education Act reauthorization of an amendment that delays or prohibits access to federal educational financial aid (including a grant, loan, or work–study position) for those with drug-related convictions (Page 2004).

Barriers to accessing social assistance also include restrictions on public housing. President Bill Clinton also signed the Housing Opportunity Program Extension Act of 1996, popularly known as the "One Strike Law," which required public housing agencies to include in leases a provision that legitimates eviction for essentially any drug-related activity in the vicinity of the tenant's apartment, even if the tenant is not aware of the activity ("any criminal activity that threatens the health, safety, or right to peaceful enjoyment of the premises by other tenants or drug related criminal activity on or off such premises, engaged in by a public housing tenant, any member of the tenant's household, or any guest or other person under the tenant's control") (Moser 2011, 5). In Chicago, the impact of the "One Strike Law" on those in public housing was catastrophic. The Chicago Housing Authority, the agency charged with supporting public housing in Chicago, implemented a more draconian interpretation of this federal law, including using arrests that did not lead to convictions and histories of incarceration as justification to evict people and to deny people access to public housing (Moser 2011).

Beyond the difficulties in ensuring equal access to federal and state programs, including public housing and social assistance benefits, incarceration can also make lose the right to parent. For example, the 1997 federal Adoption and Safe Families Act (ASFA) mandated that states terminate parental rights when a child has been in foster care for fifteen out of the previous twenty-two months, except under specific circumstances (Child Welfare Information Gateway 2010). This federal initiative moved the focus away from family reunification, created subsidies for adoption, and required states to fast-track the termination of parental rights. The impact of this federal law was drastic; as states implemented ASFA provisions, incarcerated mothers could not complete tasks required for reunification in time. Parental rights were terminated for thousands and thousands, and, in many cases, the children removed from their parents were never adopted. ASFA specifically hurt incarcerated women and their children. Despite research suggesting that children who visit their incarcerated mothers regularly adjust better socially, emotionally, and academically, mothers are often locked up in prisons or detention centers hundreds of miles from where their children live, making consistent and meaningful contact with them impossible. In 2005, the Illinois Supreme Court found Detra Welch, one of SLM's former residents, to be unfit and terminated her parental rights based on her history of repeated incarceration (Marlan 2005).

After their release from prisons and jails, many are still disenfranchised (although this is not the case in Illinois). According to a report from the Sentencing Project (2008), "5.3 million Americans, or one in forty-one adults, have currently or permanently lost their voting rights as a result of a felony conviction." The Sentencing Project documents a national landscape of inconsistent disenfranchisement restrictions and cumbersome voting rights restoration processes. The incoherent state and county laws surrounding disenfranchisement and restoration create confusion and misidentify and disqualify voters (Uggen, Shannon, and Manza 2012).

Sanctioned discrimination that restricts access to most social assistance benefits, including public housing and food stamps, plus a lack of access to the right to be protected from employment discrimination, creates the contexts for civil death. Given this landscape, it is no surprise that what the state identifies as recidivism, or the rate at which persons who have exited prison "reoffend" or return to jail or prison, hovers around approximately 67 percent nationally. Recidivism rates are shaped by a number of variables: the number of times a person is locked up, the duration of the sentence, gender, and the nature of the conviction. In a study that followed people released from prison in 2005 in 30 states the Bureau of Justice Statistics reported: "About two-thirds (67.8%) of released prisoners were arrested for a new crime within 3 years, and three-quarters (76.6%) were arrested within 5 years" (Bureau of Justice Statistics 2014). Individuating acts of harm and crime, recidivism rates do not highlight how systems and environments almost guarantee reoffending with formal and informal barriers which ensure that full participation in civic, social, and economic life is impossible. A part of the punitive apparatus, the discourse of recidivism and the associated data collected are used to further justify tighter prohibitions on employment and mobility: *these people are dangerous.*

Recidivism rates also create the perception that people are committing another crime or an act of harm, but often they have violated the terms of their parole: failure to report to parole officers, failure to update an address, failure to comply with mandated programs, breaking curfew, and so on. A student at the Sister Jean Adult High School who worked at a chain sandwich shop was afraid to say no to her boss, who wanted her to work a double shift, and she subsequently missed an appointment with her parole officer. She was picked up for a parole violation and reincarcerated. These stories abound. *Missed buses. Work shifts that ran overtime. Sick children. Weather and car troubles. Life.*

This devastating landscape for people exiting prisons and jails has not gone uncontested. In Illinois, Fighting to Overcome Records and Create Equality (FORCE), begun in 2011, mobilizes formerly incarcerated men and women to fight against employment discrimination. Through its Fair Employment campaign, FORCE has produced public service announcements designed to render visible people with criminal records and has actively organized and supported legislation to remove employment discrimination, particularly to expand the sealing of records for low-level, nonviolent felonies (F.OR.C.E. n.d.). Laws pertaining to sealing records (removing a criminal record from general view) and expungement (having a criminal record erased) vary significantly from state to state and are important after-conviction and release initiatives that make a vital difference in the lives of people.

Across the country, groups organize to "ban the box"—to eliminate (or delay) questions on job application forms that ask about arrest or conviction. First passed in Hawaii in 1998 and subsequently in other states, including Illinois, Nebraska, and Delaware (Stinson 2014), these laws restrict an employer's ability to ask potential workers about their criminal histories, reducing the probability of employment discrimination based on criminal records. The National Employment Law Center reports that as of 2014, twelve states and seventy cities had passed some form of legislation restricting employers' access to job applicants' criminal records. This legislation is uneven and incomplete: most laws cover only state or city government hiring practices, or include exemptions for a "legitimate business reason," as was the case with legislation passed in Washington, D.C. (Debonis 2014); or the requirement simply moves the question to later in the hiring process, prior to a job offer or the second interview. In an era of unequal unemployment, underemployment, and compensation, even if formerly incarcerated people can "ban the box" on job application forms, lack of access to education and forms of cultural capital confines people to minimum wage work that does not provide a living wage.

Student Bodies

Suddenly Regina was just not there. In social studies class the previous week, she had seemed, while upbeat and funny and always trying to get in just another question, a little *off*. We were talking about all the possible reasons behind potential U.S. intervention in Syria, and she just was not following the discussion. I chalked it up to stress. One of a cluster of fabulously fierce and smart black women in the class, Regina was conditioned from years of school failure to hone in on what she was doing wrong: not getting the right answer, not keeping up, not being able to write everything down. When she could breathe and forget about failure, she could learn and teach and be present in the class. It was also mid-November, past the halfway mark in the term, and everyone, including me, was getting restless.

In 2001, I collaboratively started a free high school for formerly incarcerated men and women in Chicago. Started in a church basement on the city's west side with former and current nuns, teachers, and a mishmash of activists, our school offers a community-based learning environment that values prior learning. Most of our students are between twenty-five and sixty years old, and therefore our classes are designed for people who have been out of formal educational contexts for many years. The twenty to thirty students we admit every January and December seek to earn a high school diploma, to learn, and to have some possibility of economic and academic mobility. The majority of our students and teachers are African American.

Always funny and positive, Regina had been one of the students who had consistently reached out to me for help. I assumed we would check in later in the week. But there was no later.

A few days after this class, Regina, at fifty-two, had a seizure and a massive stroke, and while she was being treated the hospital found cancer throughout her lungs and brain. Mercy Hospital, where the ambulance initially took her after the seizure and stroke, would not keep her because the cancer was too advanced and she would not have treatment, and, after being transferred to two different care homes, she died weeks later, on January 5, 2014, surrounded by her sisters.

In my years teaching at this high school, the death toll was unavoidable. Of our very first December 2001 graduating class of twelve people,

all African Americans, only seven were still living by 2015. *Heart attack.*
Gunshot. Cancer. Diabetes. Stroke.
Death occupies a front-row desk. Every term, someone's son or neph-
ew dies. A sister is in treatment for cancer. A sibling's kidneys are failing
and then stop functioning. People in the class are stretched, tired, over-
and undermedicated, wheezing, scarred, gasping. When I first started to
organize and teach at this school, I was surprised by the amount of illness
and death. I am embarrassed to consider these first thoughts. *Students*
are scamming. Must be. Can't be this much death, this amount of illness.
After fifteen years of teaching—funerals, asthma attacks, hospital visits—the classrooms and graduations teem with ghosts.

Not only do punishment and containment continue after people are
released, but, as Ruthie Gilmore (2007) suggests, incarceration facilitates
premature death. A cursory look at the mainstream news media and advocacy reports on conditions inside prison confirms this assessment.
Being locked up shortens people's life spans. With inadequate health
care, substandard food, lack of mental and physical exercise, and vulnerability to physical and sexual assault (from prison staff in particular), incarceration kills people (Gilmore 2007; "SPLC Files Federal Lawsuit over
Inadequate Medical, Mental Health Care in Alabama Prisons" 2014; Bar-
clay 2014; Horwitz 2014). In addition to a plethora of research documenting
that incarceration is bad for your health, research also overwhelmingly
demonstrates that people in prison are much less likely to have formal education (Harlow 2003; Coley and Barton 2006). While many self-educate,
the majority of people in state prisons lack degrees and diplomas. Without
access to the legitimizing function of formal education, including some
of the skills and knowledge acquired from school and university, life
pathways are narrowed. Living-wage jobs often require diplomas or an
institutional acknowledgment of skills and expertise: certificates, recommendations, and credentials. Like Regina, many exit prison without these
legitimate markers and skills, and their economic options narrow. Reentry
into formal educational institutions, while not impossible, is a formidable
challenge.

Adults such as Regina and the other people in the classes I teach at
Stateville Prison are not typically associated with the figure of the student. Even my working-poor university students at the relatively open
enrollment public urban university where I teach, Northeastern Illinois
University, struggle to be recognized as students, as part of a *student*

body. Workers, prisoners, formerly incarcerated people, parents, former addicts—these groups do not map easily onto the collective identity of the student, nor are these groups permitted easy access into educational institutions. Despite movements such as the struggle to end the school to prison pipeline and research that illustrates that access to quality education reduces recidivism and incarceration rates (Steurer and Smith 2003; Erisman and Contardo 2005; Gorgol and Sponsler 2011), people marked by prison fight to access education. Through background checks and employment prohibitions, these folks are often locked out of fields such as teaching, counseling and, social work.

Fred Moten and Stefano Harney suggest that capital and knowledge are institutionally organized so that prison is not in opposition to the university but instead that each institution requires the other: "The slogan on the Left, then, 'universities, not jails,' marks a choice that may not be possible. In other words, perhaps more universities promote more jails. Perhaps it is necessary finally to see that the university produces incarceration as the product of its negligence. Perhaps there is another relation between the University and the Prison—beyond simple opposition or family resemblance" (Harney and Moten 2013, 41). In order to have a restrictive enrollment, curricular-rich university, do we need to have a prison? In order to have an international baccalaureate program, must there also be a Sister Jean Hughes Adult High School? If these institutions and their associated life pathways, for people marked as the "best of the best" and the "worst of the worst," cannot be disentangled, is it possible to redistribute the affiliated resources?

A contemporary public policy shift surrounding education programs in prison illustrates this dynamic, Harney and Moten's potential unelucidated "another relation." The Higher Education Act of 1965 formally brought a federally funded loan-and-work program to postsecondary education, including grant funds for students through the Pell Grant program. Pell Grants enabled people across the United States, including those in prison, to access postsecondary education. The prison uprisings throughout the 1970s—from Pontiac to Attica—pushed for greater access to relevant and quality education for people behind bars. By the 1990s, hundreds of college programs awarding degrees were offered in correctional facilities across the country. Community colleges held contracts with many state prisons to offer associate's degrees and a range of vocational courses. People in prison were students.

In 1994, Clinton signed the Violent Crime Control and Law Enforcement Act (VCCLEA), a large omnibus bill that, among other things, created sixty new offenses eligible for the death penalty, funded ten thousand new police officers, created the Violence Against Women Act, dedicated $9.7 billion for prison building and $6.1 billion for prevention programs, and eliminated access to Pell Grants for people in prison (Page 2004). As a result, roughly 350 college programs in prison closed (Harkins and Meiners 2014). The VCCLEA restricted access for incarcerated people, severely diminishing the ability to offer accredited college programs on the inside that awarded degrees. Politicians supported this ban by suggesting that the general public did not want their tax dollars going to support college programs for people in prison. Senator Kay Bailey Hutchison, a Texas Republican, introduced the ban on Pell Grants for inmates into the VCCLEA. Hutchison stated: "It is not fair to the millions of parents who work and pay taxes and then must scrape and save and often borrow to finance their children's education" (Zook 1994, A32). The conflict that Senator Hutchison constructs between working-poor families' access to Pell Grants and those in prison is not accurate. Only 1.2 percent of the total number of Pell Grants were ever awarded to people in prison, and Pell Grants are essentially allocated on the basis of entitlement—all who are eligible are entitled. Furthermore, the subsequent erasure of Pell Grants for those in prisons did not result in new nonincarcerated undergraduate students receiving any additional financial aid (Page 2004).

Yet, after almost two decades of near-erasure, a few programs are being rebuilt through philanthropic dollars and volunteer labor. In 2013, Governor Andrew Cuomo of New York announced that New York would support (and pay for) degree-granting programs inside New York's state prisons (Kaplan 2014). While all the evidence supports the conclusion that education programs (particularly postsecondary education programs) inside prisons reduce recidivism, Cuomo backed away from this initiative only weeks later due to criticism. Free education for those in prison was "too controversial" because many "law-abiding families are struggling to pay for college," as other New York politicians stated (Kaplan 2014). In response to Cuomo's 2014 proposal, Republican lawmakers in Washington, D.C., even introduced a bill to specifically prohibit any federal money from paying for college classes for people locked in federal or state prisons: the so-called "Kids Before Cons Act" (Kaplan 2014). Despite this significant setback, momentum for college programs in prison continues to grow across the United States (Harkins and Meiners 2014), although the movement for access to quality education for people after they are released from prison is less visible. In 2015 the Obama Administration announced a pilot initiative to reintroduce federal Pell Grants to a small number of people in prison (Schwartzapfel, 2015), and in 2016 Governor Cuomo reintroduced plans to support higher education in New York prisons (McKinley and McKinley 2016).

Regina's death did not go unnoticed by her community at the school. Throughout the term people would reference her humor and questions. Several of the black women she had sat next to in class doubled down on their educational commitment and resolved to finish high school and to do the work to honor Regina's life. Her absence functioned as a political presence. Many people from her graduating class do want to further their education and attend a community college. Many have set short-term goals, including technical certification that might lead to more secure immediate employment: heating and cooling installation, radiology technician, and certified home health care attendant. Even the short walk to these programs, which often do not require punitive entry exams or charge outrageous tuition, is complex. Some days even the local public community college seems to be meant for another planet of people another world away.

6

Registering Sex, Rethinking Safety

"We all know that there is a difference between a healthy and a normal love of children and a love which is sick and freakish." With this oft-cited provocation, the literary theorist James Kincaid opens *Child-Loving* (1992), a book examining representations of the erotic child. While Kincaid's project focuses mainly on the Victorian era, in our moment, crowded with televised child beauty pageants, skyrocketing rates of poverty for those under eighteen years old, and abstinence-only sexual health curricula in schools, heterosexuality is still pervasive and perverse. What is authentic sexual development when heteronormativity, for example, is naturalized? What are children's emergent relationships to sexuality? *What is normal love?* This is not empty rhetoric. The number of juveniles charged and convicted of sexual violence across the United States raises the question of who constitutes a child and whether or how children can possess or engage sexual agency. Public dialogues (and scholarly research) about emergent sexuality and agency are challenging, even in a culture that fetishizes youth and sexuality, while sex offender registries provide a grim and uneven public archive of harm, sexuality, and childhood.[1]

A 2009 research brief from the U.S. Department of Justice identifies that across the United States young people are disproportionately charged with and convicted of sexual offenses: "Juveniles account for more than one third (35.6 percent) of those known to police to have committed sex offenses." Notably, this research brief flags preteens as increasingly charged and convicted of sexually based crimes: "The number of youth coming to the attention of police for sex offenses increases sharply at age 12 and plateaus after age 14" (Finkelhor, Ormrod, and Chaffin 2009, 1–2). According to a 2013 report by Human Rights Watch, *Raised on the Registry*, "in Delaware in 2011, there were approximately 639 children on the sex offender registry, 55 of whom were under the age of 12" (33). In Illinois "fully half" of the juveniles arrested for sexual offenses in 2004, 2006, 2008, and 2010 were fourteen years old or younger (Illinois Juvenile Justice Commission

2014, 15). This increase, not unnoticed by law enforcement entities, has created an industry of sexual recovery for juveniles: "Juvenile sex offender treatment programs saw a 40-fold increase between 1982 and 1992" (Finkelhor, Ormrod, and Chaffin 2009, 2). Mandated treatment and registration are particularly galling, as research suggests that child sexual violence is a cyclical—and potentially a learned—behavior. Children arrested for perpetrating sexual offenses are five times more likely than those who have not been arrested for sexual offenses to experience sexual violence themselves (Illinois Juvenile Justice Commission 2014, 16).[2]

The National Center for Missing and Exploited Children estimates that there are approximately 850,000 registered sex offenders in the various state and local registries across the United States. About 98 percent are men. African Americans are disproportionately represented, accounting for 22 percent of those convicted of sex offenses and only 13 percent of the population (Ackerman, Harris, Levenson, Zgoba 2011). The production of sex offenders and the growing penal architecture of their registration and management are entrenched and powerful facets of our expanding prison nation in the United States (Carpenter and Beverlin 2012; Davey and Goodnough 2007; Lancaster 2011; Levine 2002; Long 2008; Simon 2000). Marie Gottschalk summarizes the statistics: in 2012 between 10 and 20 percent (and in some states as many as 30 percent) of all state prisoners were serving time for sex offenses (2015, 199) and 1 in every 160 males was a registered sex offender, "about double the number from a decade ago" (205).

In many states, civil commitment laws, upheld by the Supreme Court in three separate decisions, aim to detain and segregate certain categories of sex offenders indefinitely after they have served their sentences (Davey and Goodnough 2007; Feuer 2005). Overwhelmed with the work of registering and regulating sex offenders, many jurisdictions struggle to facilitate compliance. In 2014 the Chicago Police Department turned away many who were required to register; subsequently, some of these people have been rearrested. To address this problem, Chicago started construction to expand its criminal registration office (Wildeboer 2014). Restrictions on public space intensify: as of 2014, Illinois's sex offender website outlines a number of public space prohibitions for registered child sex offenders, including living or loitering within "500 feet of a school, playground, or any facility providing programs or services exclusively directed toward people under age 18." In Iowa, convicted sex offenders cannot reside within two thousand feet of schools or places where children congregate, thus effectively prohibiting anyone on the registry from living in an urban center.

Despite this growing infrastructure, registries do not reduce child sexual violence, and "stranger danger" sexual violence against children is the least significant risk (Agan 2011; Wright 2003; Bureau of Justice Statistics 2000). Roger Lancaster, a literary theorist who has studied sex offender restrictions, puts things in perspective this way: "A child's risk of being killed by a sexually predatory stranger is comparable to his or her chance of getting struck by lightning (1 in 1,000,000 versus 1 in 1,200,000)" (2011, 77). Children do experience sexual harm, but the perpetrators are the people in their lives—coaches, not strangers.

Even with this body of evidence demonstrating the inefficacy of registries and community notification laws, my research suggests that few feminist or antiprison movements have developed public campaigns to draw attention to how these registries and laws are public policy failures or to identify how they participate in expanding the prison nation. Visible national feminist antiviolence organizations that work on issues related to violence against women and children have been reticent to publicly challenge the expansion of these measures.[3] Despite the criminalization of those who are nonheterosexual and/or non-gender-conforming, a population historically *defined* as sex offenders, national lesbian, gay, bisexual, and transgendered (LGBT) advocacy organizations have not documented how these laws that require registration and community notification potentially impact those who identify as LGBTQ. Mainstream gay and lesbian organizations have been silent about how these policies and laws do not reduce violence against queers, and they have not initiated any public campaigns or research about how registries and community notification could potentially augment "fear of the queer" by recirculating public discourses of "sex offenders."

A small number of juvenile justice organizations, however, have critiqued registries and community notification laws, not, however, for their inefficacy or for the meanings produced about age, consent, and sexuality. Children (and people convicted as children), as organizations such as Human Rights Watch (2013) or the Illinois Juvenile Justice Commission (2014) argue, do not belong on the registry, as they are less culpable. Scholarship exploring how criminalization produces meanings surrounding children and sexuality is scarce.

These silences testify to a conceptual and material problem that must be addressed by those committed to building stronger and safer communities without augmenting our prison nation. The array of extrapunitive systems created to manage sex offenders, the naturalization of punitive technologies of surveillance, and the very concept of sex offender should be at the forefront of debate and discussion, particularly for queer/antiracist/feminist/antiprison activists and scholars, because the bodies and violence at stake pose compelling material and conceptual challenges.

This chapter argues that critiquing the category of the sex offender and the growth of associated registries and notification laws must be a focal point of work not only for antiprison scholars and activists but for those invested in ending (child) sexual violence. The first section, "Offending Sex," offers a brief and queer history of sex offender registries in the United States and their growth, particularly over the past two decades, and reviews the available data on who harms children and women. The second section, "What's Wrong with Registries," provides an antiracist, feminist, queer critique of registries. The third section, "Registering Children" (deepening the work of chapter 1, "Magical Age"), suggests how the growth in the number of juveniles on sex offender registries produces ideas about age and sexuality that potentially harm many, including children.

Offending Sex

Policing and punishing sexualities and gender identities marked as deviant or harmful has a lengthy history in the United States. In the 1930s and 1940s, across many urban centers police forces kept records of sexual deviants—a malleable category that included "known homosexuals," although such records were not made available to the public. The historians William Eskridge (2008) and Margot Canaday (2009) document that police collected and centralized information on sexual deviants including fairies, inverts, and cross dressers.[5] Sodomy, or simply the intent to perform it in public or private, was a crime in many states and penalties varied (*Lawrence and Garner v. State of Texas* in 2003 ruled antisodomy laws unconstitutional). Men perceived to be engaging in sexual practices with other men were charged with crimes such as "lewd conduct," "lewd vagrancy," and "outraging public decency."[4] Other behaviors were also against the law, including dressing in clothing that was identified as marked for the opposite gender.

In the 1950s many policy makers increasingly sought to use policing practices to track known sexual offenders, including homosexuals. In 1950, the Federal Bureau of Investigation collected information from the states, including fingerprints, for those charged with sodomy, oral copulation, and lewd vagrancy and for those convicted of crimes against minors to create a "national bank of sex offenders and known homosexuals" (Eskridge 2008, 82). In 1951 and 1952, Eskridge writes, Congress attempted to create a national sex offender system (93). In 1947 California legislature "unanimously passed a law to require convicted sex offenders to register with the police in their home jurisdictions," and Chief Justice Earl Warren (the author of the 1954 *Brown* desegregation decision) successfully requested that this law be extended to include those convicted of "lewd vagrancy" explicitly to capture more homosexuals (Eskridge 2008, 92–93). This regulation of deviants was never race neutral. For example, "in the 1930s, when only six percent of its adult male population was nonwhite, twenty percent of New York City's sex offenders were black, as were twenty-one percent of those arrested for sodomy" (81).

According to Eskridge, policy makers continued to use incidents of child sexual violence to further target male homosexuals, or at the least men who had sex with other men. For example, in California, after the high-profile 1949 murder of an eight-year-old white girl, Linda Glucroft, by a man with a history of sexual violence against female children, then Governor Warren declared war on "sex fiends." However, the legal target of this war was men who had sex with other men. After Glucroft's death a cluster of laws targeted the sexual practices —and places—associated with men who have sex with men, including enhanced penalties for the crime of "loitering around a public toilet." The 1949 Miller Act explicitly sought to further criminalize men who have sex with men and to "strengthen the laws as they deal with sodomy and other perverted practices" (Eskridge, 89–92).

As cumbersome private records internal to law enforcement, these practices of documentation and surveillance shifted as the twentieth century advanced. By 1953 President Eisenhower barred homosexuals from holding federal employment (D'Emilio and Freedman 1988, 293). In the ensuing decades the landscape surrounding deviancy, sexuality, continued to transform. Many intertwined social and political movements pushed back on policing and criminalization, fought for visibility and recognition, and sought political power and civil rights. Lesbian and gay mobilizations pushed back on homophobia. Black power movements organized for the self-defense of black communities and for flourishing black futures. Feminist movements demanded equality and raised the visibility of sexual violence. Despite these varied justice movements, child sexual violence never adequately disengaged from associations with homophobia. As varied civil rights movements gained some formal recognition for marginalized groups, and sexual violence, particularly targeting women and children gained some prominence, policing emerged as the solution to ensure child sexual safety.

In Illinois, the 1986 Habitual Child Sex Offender Registration Law established the state's registry for those convicted of sexual offenses against children. In the subsequent thirty years, registration requirements in Illinois and across every state expanded to include a broader range of offenses, including, essentially, all sex offenses and crimes involving minors. Registries also increased the community notification components and the amount of information available to the public (the Illinois State Public Sex Offender website was up by 1999) and amplified the restrictions attached to registration.

Registries proliferated across the United States in the 1990s. In 1994, as part of the Federal Violent Crime Control and Law Enforcement Act, the Jacob Wetterling Crimes against Children and Sexually Violent Offender Registration Act required states to create sex offender registries for crime against children (Wright 2003). In 1996, in direct response to the abduction and murder of twelve-year-old Polly Klaas in 1992 and that of seven-year-old Megan Kanka in 1994 by men with prior convictions for sexual crimes, the federal government passed Megan's Law, establishing a national sex offender registry accessible to the public to circulate information about known sex offenders across the nation and to coordinate all the state registry systems (Wright 2003). In 2006, the Adam Walsh Child Protection and Safety Act, also known as the Sex Offender Registration and Notification Act (SORNA), established more stringent registry requirements, created a systemic classification system for all people convicted of sex offenses according to escalating levels of perceived danger—Tier 1, 2, or 3—requiring registration for a minimum of ten to fifteen years to life. SORNA required sex offenders to register in the jurisdictions where they work, live, and, if applicable, attend school and mandated that this information be available on the Internet.

The rapid implementation of these laws has been tested and supported in courts, and more draconian measures continue to appear. In Louisiana, effective August 1, 2012, all convicted sex offenders must list their criminal status on Facebook and other forms of social media (Martinez 2012). In 2011, Riverside County, California (following the lead of Orange County), banned all registered sex offenders from distributing candy, hanging up any Halloween decorations, or leaving any external lights lit on October 31 (Sewell 2011). Although Orange County repealed its law in 2013, the Riverside County law is still in place (Lovett 2013). In 2013, Los Angeles built a number of new "pocket parks" or tiny parks explicitly to force registered sex offenders to move out of neighborhoods (Jennings 2013). In 2012, New York's attorney general brokered an agreement with Sony and other top corporations that produce online gaming to ban registered sex offenders from participating in any online gaming (CBS 2012). The legal scholars Catherine Carpenter and Amy Beverlin (2012) chart ongoing and exponential growth in related legislation: "In 1994, when the Indiana General Assembly adopted Zachary's Law, the state's registration scheme (named in honor of ten-year-old Zachary Snider, who was molested and killed by a man with previous and related convictions), eight crimes triggered registration. In 2012, Zachary's Law listed forty offenses that trigger registration: twenty-one offenses trigger registration as a 'sex or violent offender' and an additional nineteen offenses trigger registration as a 'sex offender'" (1081–82). Carpenter and Beverlin state, "We have yet to reach peak proliferation of these laws," and identify a number of state proposals including "expanding the list of registerable offenses to include tongue kissing of a minor . . . breach of residency restrictions; and requiring weekly registration for homeless offenders" (1100).

The establishment and expansion of registries are part of a familiar reform narrative that promises safety but delivers more precarity and often, more violence. Or, grassroots and community organizing coalesces around experiences of harm, and the state responds with increased policing, more prisons, and additional punishing laws. Far from creating safety, criminalization deepens marginalized communities' vulnerability. In the violence against women movement, "we won the mainstream but lost the movement," writes sociologist Beth Richie in *Arrested Justice: Black Women, Male Violence, and the Build-Up of a Prison Nation*—a key text chronicling the shift from organizing to criminalization in the anti-violence movement. Registries might suggest that the problem of child sexual violence has been "won," but in reality, these laws do little to help vulnerable families, including children, do nothing to reduce or eradicate violence toward children, or to create needed public dialogues about the structural contexts that facilitate harm.

What's Wrong with Registries?

Masking Violence

Abduction and sexual assault by strangers are the least prevalent forms of sex crime. Available data clearly indicate that for all children under eighteen, strangers are consistently the least likely to be the perpetrators of sexual assaults, generally accounting for significantly less than 10 percent of them. According to a landmark 2000 study by the Bureau of Justice Statistics, which utilized sexual assault victimization data from a newly available database—the National Incident-Based Reporting System—strangers account for only 7 percent of sexual assaults against children (Bureau of Justice Statistics 2000). Marie Gottschalk summarizes the available research: "Friends, acquaintances, and family members are responsible for more than 90 percent of all sexual abuse of children" (2015, 124).[6] Registries operate on the premise that communities that are aware of who is a designated sexual predator will act correspondingly to protect/monitor their children. Yet, if there is an enemy, "the enemy is us" (Levine 2002). Registries are organized not to monitor family members or acquaintances—the most likely to harm or to abduct children—but to protect children from dangerous strangers. The circulation of photos and addresses of known sex offenders fosters the assumption that strangers pose the most significant threat to the safety of children. This is the dominant and mythic narrative of child sexual violence in the United States.

Mainstream media's representations of violence against children more frequently depict and sensationalize stranger assault cases, and the media are unlikely to attempt to be unbiased in their reporting of this topic (Best 1990; Rapping 2003). Kincaid offers a list of reasons for the explosion of panic in the 1980s and 1990s in the United States surrounding stranger child abuse and child abductions, among them that "it directs our attention away from more pressing ills, . . . it attacks working mothers most viciously . . . and it gives the police and policing agencies godlike power" (1998, 21). Or perhaps, as theorists such as Lauren Berlant suggest, the demonization of vulnerable populations who are already "too bruised by history" (as cited in Rhodes 2005, 402), such as sex offenders, signifies legitimate civic participation. Shunning the "worst of the worst" can be a pathway for our inclusion and acceptance.

Regardless, the consequences of this disproportionate representation are clear. The much more prevalent risk of violence within the family, a space that is conceptualized as both natural and safe, is erased or minimized. If violence to children is represented as the stranger, the nuclear and patriarchal family is preserved as a natural and safe institution. This template of the normal still persists, even as it is clearly not the norm demographically, and, as this discussion works to illustrate, it is often a violent space and institution for children and for women.

Community notification laws purport to protect children, but they do not address the core forms of violence, including sexual violence, that affect young people. The legal scholar Rose Corrigan analyzes Megan's Law in New Jersey and notes, "The Guidelines dwell at length on the harms done by strangers, though they rarely acknowledge that the types of assaults most feared by the public—the physically violent penetrative rape of a child by a stranger—are a tiny fraction of assaults" (2006, 291). In addition, Corrigan summarizes New Jersey's version of Megan's Law as erasing any institutional or systemic factors that shape or produce sexual violence and concurrently professionalize the work of advocacy. Corrigan suggests registries built on earlier gains of the feminist anti-rape movement. Yet, state laws, such as Megan's Law in New Jersey, do not include any analysis of power.

Failing Survivors

Registries are part of culture that posits that participation in the criminal justice realm is a positive experience for those who experience violence. Research by Kristin Bumiller (2008) and Beth Richie (2012) highlights that for many adult female survivors of sexual violence, participating in the criminal justice system fails to provide resolution and can increase the possibility of harm. Only a small percentage of sexual assault reports are prosecuted, and the person harmed must be willing to be persistent, as "discrediting victims is a significant factor despite rape law reforms" (Bumiller 2008, 11), or the "best defense in a rape trial is often the "indictment of the victim" (101). Many people, fearful of the forms of state intervention that can accompany reporting—including deportation, arrest, child seizure, and more—do not report acts of harm to law enforcement. Calling the police or reporting violence automatically engages a nexus of punitive systems that hold the potential for augmenting harm to the survivor (109). The survivors' needs or goals do not factor into how the case takes shape and moves forward; rather, their lives are open to assessment: "In rape prosecutions victims must be cooperative with law enforcement authorities and avoid any actions that might cause public scrutiny (such as being a welfare recipient, accessing emergency medical aid, and seeking personal profit)" (130).

While many social service agencies and support structures have been established for survivors of violence, these professionalized systems exercise deep "administrative power" (64) and remove agency and limit dignity. The lives of survivors who use these social services are professionally managed and under watch. "The increased surveillance of clients has also become a primary means to extend state control over citizens' lives" (65).

Many of those who experience sexual violence do not trust the criminal justice system to respond effectively. In 2013, Canada's Department of Justice issued a report, *Victims of Crime Research*, based on data collected from sexual abuse survivors across Canada. The conclusions are not surprising. The vast majority of those surveyed had little faith or trust in the Canadian police or the criminal justice system, specifically its ability to meaningfully address child sexual violence:

> Over two-thirds of those in the male sample (68%) and in the Northern sample (67%) and 64% in the female sample did not report the CSA [child sexual abuse] to the police or have another individual report the abuse. The findings were similar for survivors of ASA [adult sexual abuse]. In the male sample, 70% stated that they did not report the ASA, while 59% of those in the female sample and 56% of those in the Northern sample did not report the assault.

The most frequently reported reasons for not reporting CSA were because the participants thought that they would not be believed, they felt ashamed or embarrassed, they did not know they could report the abuse, and they had no family support. The reasons provided by survivors of ASA for not reporting the assault were similar to those of survivors of CSA. Other reasons cited by survivors of ASA included because they did not have any confidence in the criminal justice [system] and they were afraid of the offender. (Northcott 2013, 14)

While a response to survivors' not trusting law enforcement and judicial systems could be, and frequently is, to reform the system, given previous chapters' examples of criminal justice reform as carceral expansion, this move seems unlikely to yield desired results. Also, fundamentally strengthening law enforcement's abilities to respond to or engage with sexual violence, particularly child sexual violence, is not a preventive measure. This does not address how and why sexual violence persists.

Facilitating Carceral Expansion

Sex offender registries restrict employment, housing, and mobility, particularly in public spaces where children congregate. The restrictions are specific. In Florida's Miami-Dade County, the distance requirement is 2,500 feet, and many on the registry live under a causeway outside of city limits (Thompson 2007). In 2006, developers in Texas and Kansas marketed new housing developments as "sex offender free," requiring background checks for all potential purchasers. If someone who lives in the communities is convicted of a sex offense, they will be fined $1,500 a day until they leave (Koch 2006; Lohr 2006). In many jurisdictions people with sex offenses are specifically prohibited from participating in any activities related to Halloween. Through formal and private sector mobility and public space restrictions, these laws construct meanings about what kinds of public space are dangerous for children, where children are most at risk or vulnerable, and, by default, what kinds of spaces are safer or risk-free.

Registries also contribute to the privatization and the criminalization of public space. The sex offender is potentially lurking in every playground and school, and the drug seller is on every corner, thus necessitating surveillance cameras, metal detectors, background checks, private play lots, constant police presence, private security systems and forces, and more. Under the guise of protection, these punitive policies and institutions reconfigure space. While appearing neutral and in particular "color-blind," these technologies of surveillance participate in the privatization or demonization of public spaces, constraining those who do not have access to private resources and institutions.

With 70 percent of all reported sexual assaults against children committed in a residence—usually the victim's—this emphasis on public spaces, namely, parks and schools, is misplaced (Bureau of Justice Statistics 2000). In particular, schools have emerged as highly policed spaces in contemporary public policies. For example, almost every state has adopted drug-free zones around schools, and, as a 2006 Justice Policy Institute Report noted, these zones can overwhelm neighborhoods in urban areas, for example, "76 percent of Newark, and over half of Camden and Jersey City" (Greene, Pranis, and Ziedenberg 2006, 26). These zones amplify policing, and, notably, have not been successful in keeping drugs away from schools. By highlighting schools, these policies, not unlike the mobility restrictions in sex offender registries, create false perceptions of public safety.

Racially and economically homogeneous private schools, parks, and housing enclaves, often created through public infrastructure and funding, require and produce fear.[7] Privatizing public spaces and institutions has long required the production of identities seen as disposable or less than fully human, from the "welfare queen" to the "illegal alien" (Duggan 2003; Hancock 2004). From welfare to public education, demonizing recipients is one clear way to call into question the legitimacy of a public institution or program and to assert the importance of market-driven regulation. Inversely, protection is another way to reconfigure public entities. The public domains of parks, schools, mass transit, and the Internet are too dangerous for our most vulnerable; therefore, these domains must be under continuous surveillance and cannot be entrusted to inefficient public bureaucrats or entities. Only private companies can adequately manage security.

The fear of terrorism, of illegal aliens taking employment, of welfare freeloaders and prisoners using hard-earned tax dollars, of the child molestor teaching school—these feelings of disgust, fear, and anger produced by and through these identities become rationalizations to expand the punitive arm of the state. The state's response to the emotions is not to empower communities through local economic development or more public dollars and support for public education but to heighten individualist responses, to facilitate privatization and punitive state surveillance. The fearful feelings invite tough love, a defensive and protective "daddy" state, while the feelings of anger justify the dismantling of public programs.

The fears and feelings about sex offenders occur concurrently with the growth in the construction of supermax, or control-unit, prisons. A 2006 study by the Urban Institute charts the rarity of supermax prisons prior to 1986, yet by "2004, 44 states had supermax prisons" (Mears 2006, 1). These institutions, which keep men (and a few women) incarcerated in solitary confinement cells for twenty-two or twenty-three hours a day, were made possible through public discourses about the "worst of the worst." The public panic about sex offenders that grew in the 1990s cannot be seen in isolation from the explosion in construction of control units during that same decade. Registries and community notification laws are a central component of a larger carceral state that is also privatizing and reconfiguring public domains and impacting communities of color. The anxieties propagated by "sex offenders" also, as noted, enhance the policing of sexually marginalized people, increase the number of charges and convictions, and lengthen prison terms.

Expanding and Naturalizing Surveillance Technologies

Despite a lack of research demonstrating their efficacy, registries are part of an expanding field of private and government surveillance. States have developed telephone applications to facilitate immediate access to information about people on the registry. "The first incarnation of registration following the federal guidelines required that each registrant provide local law enforcement with their name, address, photograph, and fingerprints; in some states, the offender must also supply a biological specimen. Today, sex offenders may also be asked to supply driver's license numbers, dates and places of birth, dates and places of conviction, places of employment, passwords to social networking websites, and prior crimes. Some states also require offenders to provide DNA samples"

(Carpenter and Beverlin 2012, 1008). The North Carolina Department of Justice created an application that allows users to employ their phone to locate registered sex offenders—name, home and work address, photo, map—and conviction-related data (WRAL 2012). The private sector also continues to develop and offer multiple mobile telephone applications to search existing databases, to identify registered sex offenders, and to mine the maximum amount of available data about a person on the registry, map their location, and easily communicate these findings to other people. In early 2016 International Megan's Law passed requiring citizens convicted of sex offenses to carry passports that visibly mark their status as sex offenders (Neyfakh 2016).

This relentless focus on making information about those on registries publicly available continues to exacerbate a skewed landscape surrounding what it is meaningful or helpful for the public to know about their neighbors, teachers, or employees. The technologies developed to track and circulate information about those on the registry extend into other areas. In a 2011 op-ed in the *New York Times* on the increased push to track convicted sex offenders, the literary theorist Roger Lancaster asks readers to pay attention to the new technologies of surveillance, which prefigure regulation in other spheres: "Several states currently publish online listings of methamphetamine offenders, and other states are considering public registries for assorted crimes. Mimicking Megan's Law, Florida maintains a Web site that gives the personal details (including photo, name, age, address, offenses and periods of incarceration) of all prisoners released from custody. Some other states post similar public listings of paroled or recently released ex-convicts" (Lancaster 2011). Forms of electronic monitoring will not be confined to those convicted (or accused) of sexual violence against children.

These practices of surveillance and monitoring affect communities differentially. For example, background checks are routine for almost any employment position, effectively rendering those on the registry almost unemployable. These technologies—background checks, electronic monitoring, public crime notification systems—continue to play a pivotal role in bolstering demands for increased surveillance of public places, extensive postrelease requirements, and—at times—community notification. As notification technologies shift from print to online databases, offender information has begun to circulate increasingly rapidly and widely. Activists attempting to counter misinformation are often shut out from these platforms, and potential roles for a critical independent media are circumvented. The potential for broader-based community mobilizations is thus limited.

Flexibility of the Category

A patchwork of federal, state, and local laws determines who must register, and can include those convicted of sexting, possessing child pornography, soliciting prostitution, even public urination (Ackerman, Harris, Levenson, Zgoba 2011; Horowitz 2015). The language of a charge may not convey much about the risk someone poses, and many convictions reflect our attempts to untangle the unresolved thicket surrounding age, sex, and consent: Is a person convicted of "lewd and lascivious behavior," a charge still levied against men who engage in public sex with other men, a danger to others? Can a 16-year-old consent to any sexual activity? If a 14-year-old e-mails out naked photos of himself on a dare, is he distributing child pornography? While some convicted of sexual offenses have harmed others, particularly children, in awful and unimaginable ways, the category of "sex offenses" is used to further stigmatize and target vulnerable populations that are not harming others.

Sex workers in New Orleans (often transwomen and/or women of color) were charged with a statewide law that makes it a "crime against nature" to engage in "unnatural copulation" (committing acts of oral or anal sex). Conviction requires registration as a sex offender and to have "sex offender" stamped on their driver's license (Flaherty 2010). The deployment of these laws in New Orleans has little to do with public safety; rather, these laws are used to harass sex workers and to protect the interests of local businesses and homeowners. Flaherty (2011) documents that "almost 40 percent of those registered in Orleans Parish are there solely because they were accused of offering anal or oral sex for money. Seventy-five percent of those on the database for Crime Against Nature are women, and 80 percent are African American. Evidence gathered by advocates suggests a majority are poor or indigent." Sex workers in New Orleans, many mobilized through a local justice organization, Women with a Vision, partnered with legal advocates and successfully mounted a federal lawsuit challenging the statute (Flaherty 2011).

While police in New Orleans were classifying those convicted of sex work as "sex offenders," the Third U.S. District Court of Appeals in

Philadelphia ruled that a group of youths caught sexting (distribution of pornography) did not warrant felony charges (Rubinkam 2011). Both mainstream media coverage and prosecutors expressed significant concern for the futures of these young people and how a conviction and the subsequent requirement to register as a sex offender if convicted would negatively alter their lives permanently (Lewin 2010). For the sex workers in New Orleans, this was never the primary concern of the police, media, or the courts.

The criminalization of HIV nondisclosure in Canada and the United States also demonstrates the flexible application of the sex offender label. Over the past decade, a slate of charges—ranging from sexual assault to first-degree murder—have been brought against HIV-positive individuals for the failure to disclose their HIV status. These charges were overwhelmingly laid against immigrants, men of color, sex workers, and, increasingly, gay men. In 2015 college student Michael Johnson was convicted in Missouri of transmitting HIV and faces a minimum sentence of thirty years in prison (Schlinkmann 2015). The sexual practices of sex workers, teenagers, and people with HIV are all potentially subject to criminalization; therefore, they risk subsequent classification as sex offenders. This same disclosure rule is not required for any other disease that may be transmitted through sexual or other intimate contact.[8]

Trouble with Deviance

The push for the public registration of people with convictions for sex offenses evokes familiar queer histories. Many of the frameworks and strategies currently being used to detain, monitor, and punish people convicted of sex offenses are known by queer activists who have spent decades battling the policing and surveillance of street sex workers and of bars and clubs, bathhouses, and other queer public sexual cultures. Pre–Stonewall era gay (and lesbian) organizing included work that centered the intersections of prisons, policing, and queer lives. "Beginning in the early 1970s gay activists initiated a wide range of projects on behalf of prisoners they called "brothers" and "sisters," publishing newsletters, investigating and publicizing prison conditions, offering legal counseling, organizing prison ministries, sponsoring pen-pal and outreach projects, and assisting parolees" (Kunzel 2008, 12). Less visibly, people locked inside prisons also supported gay liberation movements and built formal and informal organizations. In 1977, members of the George Jackson Brigade in the penitentiary in Walla Walla, Washington, formed Men Against Sexism, the first organization for gay prisoners. As policing and punishment were central to queer lives, liberation movements forcefully centered prison justice–related analysis, service provisions, and organizing—with one exception. Kunzel notes that the issue of intergenerational sex, or men charged with or convicted of sex with minors, continually posed challenges for aspects of gay and lesbian organizing (2008, 24).

Yet by the 1980s most gay and lesbian movements had started to move toward legislative and other agendas, including gay marriage, and away from their earlier commitments to antiprison work. Kunzel quotes the gay activist leadership of David Frey to illustrate the rationale behind this shift: "Prison activism served a negative element in the debate [about gay and lesbian lives]" and "Gay Prison Activist is a role I see no future in" (Frey, as cited in Kunzel 2008, 29, 30). Resisting police brutality, pushing back against the criminalization of nonheteronormative sexualities, and fighting carceral expansion, formerly central to a queer liberation agenda, have widely disappeared from the agendas of mainstream LGBT organizations. This political shift has offered some privileges and resources to select nonheterosexuals and non-gender-conformers, while other marginalized groups have become increasingly isolated. When select white and affluent gays and lesbians were no longer the overt targets of policing, and queer organizational resources moved away from working against criminalization, queer and antiprison communities lost a formidable opponent to the naturalization of policing and criminalization. As public histories of queers resisting criminalization evaporated, our communities lost critical engagements with what constitutes "dangerous sexual behavior": in particular, how these designations are made, what claims of protection are articulated, and on whose behalf.

While current laws are not specifically designed to entrap consensual sodomy or to harass same-sex sexual practices, deviance is a social and legal framework used to control and marginalize (Best 2004). Deviance has included "interracial" marriage (and sex), illegal until overturned in 1967 by the *Loving v. State of Virginia* decision. Inversely, "normalcy" protected perpetrators and normalized violence; for example, it was legal for a husband to rape his wife until the 1970s (and as late as the 1990s in some states).[9] Deviance and child protection are still used against queers, as evidenced in domestic anti–gay marriage amendments and struggles surrounding same-sex parent or queer parent adoptions. (President Vladimir Putin's rationale in support of Russia's 2013 antigay laws was, in part, to "protect the children" [Lally 2014]). The 2006 Adam Walsh Act ensured that registration as a sex offender is retroactive (Ackerman, Harris, Levenson, Zgoba 2011). Even when laws are supposedly neutral, non-gender-conforming people, and/or those engaging in sexual activities with a person of the same sex, particularly young people of color, are disproportionately charged with a range of "quality of life" violations (Mogul, Ritchie, and Whitlock 2011; Spade 2011). Lewdness and indecent exposure charges are still levied against men who engage in consensual same-sex sexual acts in public spaces but are rarely used against public acts of heterosexuality (Eskridge 2008; Giordano 1999; Osborne 2005; Amnesty International 2006).

Associations between queers as deviant child molesters/sex offenders persist. Examples of the enmeshment of homophobia and child sexual abuse continue to recirculate. In 1994, in San Antonio, Texas, Elizabeth Ramirez, Anna Vasquez, Kristie Mayhugh, and Cassandra Rivera were arrested for the sexual assault of Ramirez's two young nieces, age seven and nine. Working-class Latinas with jobs at AutoZone and Arby's, all were friends, in their late teens or early twenties when arrested, and non-heterosexual: Cassandra and Anna were lovers and partners, and Kristie, a butch lesbian, had been the lover of Elizabeth, who was framed as the ringleader. All were convicted in a trial where the jury foreman was a minister who believed that homosexuality was a sin and wanted a life sentence. Elizabeth was sentenced to thirty-seven and a half years. Anna, Kristie, and Cassandra received fifteen-year sentences. Presenting no corroborating evidence and no previous histories of violence, the prosecution relied on "junk science" or the murky testimony of a pediatrician who claimed evidence of "healed trauma," plus the inconsistent testimony of Elizabeth's nieces. Racism, classism, and homophobia throughout the investigation and trial made it possible for the jury and the public to see these women as depraved and sexually violent (Chammah 2012, 2014). The convicted women were forgotten even by their lawyers; then, in 2010, a Canadian pen pal of Elizabeth's contacted the National Center for Research and Justice (NCRJ), a small and underfunded national organization that "educates and advocates for child-protective laws and criminal justice practices based on science, fairness, and good sense." In partnership with the Innocence Project of Texas, the NCRJ investigated evidence and leads that had gone unexplored by law enforcement in the 1990s: the father of Elizabeth's nieces, whom she had spurned and who had a history of vindictive threats; the dramatically inconsistent testimony of Elizabeth's nieces from complaint to jury trial; and the medical evidence, which was vague and also inconsistent. After a local paper carried a lengthy article about the problems with the case in 2010, one of Ramirez's nieces publicly recanted her allegations, and a very small movement to support the release of the "San Antonio Four" gained some momentum. In 2012 Anna was released on parole, and in 2013 Cassie, Kristie, and Elizabeth were also released. All registered sex offenders, they face a lifetime of surveillance in Texas (Chammah 2012, 2014).

Transgendered people, particularly those who are nonwhite and poor, are particularly vulnerable to criminalization. The frequency of incidents of transwomen stopped in public places by police and accused of solicitation while engaged in routine activities, identified by many activists as "walking while trans," is confirmed in *Injustice at Every Turn: A Report of the National Transgender Discrimination Survey* (Grant, Mottet, and Tanis 2011), which states that "29% of respondents reported police harassment or disrespect." Not only are transgendered people constructed as de facto sex workers by police but their status as "trans" is a potential crime in consensual sexual relationships. In the United Kingdom in 2013, twenty-five-year-old Chris Wilson, a transgender man, was convicted of a sexual offense, "obtaining sexual intimacy by fraud," because he failed to disclose to his female sexual partner that he was transgender (J. Morgan 2013). In 2012, twenty-year-old Gemma Barker was convicted of fraud (and assault) for "passing as a male" to secure sexual relationships with women. In conferring a thirty-month sentence, the judge stated that the acts were "deceptive and deceitful": "I have concluded that these offences are so serious that only a custodial sentence is appropriate" ("Staines Woman" 2012). These prosecutions and subsequent sentencing highlight the implicit assumption that trans bodies are inherently fraudulent/criminal and have no right to privacy (Sharpe 2014).

Linking the targeting of homosexuals in the past to contemporary sex offender registries is not a romantic appeal to celebrate outlaw sexualities. Queer people's histories of being labeled "sex offenders" do not guarantee an automatic political affinity with those who are currently being criminalized. However, while select queers are no longer explicitly targeted by public policies, new "sexual offender" legislation does increase queer vulnerability and exposure to imprisonment. Meanwhile, the most significant forms of sexual violence—intimate and familial violence—become obscured by the state's focus on stranger danger and "dangerous sexual offenders." Equally obscured are the endemic rates of sexual (and other forms of) violence that the incarcerated are subjected to within prisons. Most importantly, the state's response to "sex offenders" does not address persistent interpersonal sexual violence.

Registering Children

A shift toward criminalizing sexual activities perpetrated by minors—activities that may or may not be harmful—naturalizes linkages between age and consent, creating complex and uneven landscapes for youth to navigate sexuality; flattens the possibilities of child/youth sexual agency; and neatly masks the reality that criminalization is never neutral and instead disproportionately affects those who are most marginal. Yet the use of registries requires interrogation not simply as a failed public policy that does not address child sexual violence or create public safety but also for how registries produce meanings surrounding childhood and sexuality.

While these technologies were conceptualized and implemented to protect children from sexual violence, the same mechanisms are used to police the boundaries of childhood. Although the amount of national data about juveniles on sex offender registries is limited, Human Rights Watch's 2013 report *Raised on the Registry* and the U.S. Department of Justice's report *Juveniles Who Commit Sex Offenses against Minors* (Finkelhor, Ormrod, and Chaffin 2009), as well as a number of statewide reports, including one completed by the Illinois Juvenile Justice Commission in 2014, highlight an increase, as noted, in the production of preteen sex offenders. This section explores possible reasons for this increase.

Federal law requires registration for anyone, including juveniles, convicted of sexual offenses. How states have addressed juveniles convicted of sexual offenses and the federal requirement for registration varies. Some states have created registries specifically for juveniles (and when they age out they are placed on adult registries); some states include only older juveniles (generally those over the age of fourteen) on their juvenile registries; other states add only juveniles who were tried as adults to the adult registry (Illinois Juvenile Justice Commission 2014; Human Rights Watch 2013). Between 2012 and 2103 the U.S. General Accounting Office audited states and found that most were not in compliance with federal laws regarding registration and notification for registered sex offenders (Illinois Juvenile Justice Commission 2014).

While the increase of juveniles on the registry can be partially attributed to the expansion of laws that require registration, for many the status of not being an adult creates a host of additional forms of surveillance and policing. Across jurisdictions, a matrix of laws and agencies enforces and monitors the status of minors: parole and probation officers, youth and child welfare workers, truancy officers, and school social workers. The growth of juveniles on the registry is due in part to wider cultural support for the criminalization of sexual violence and deviancy but also in part to the specific vulnerability of nonadults within a carceral regime. Even reporting unwanted sexual contact with another young person can place minors in legal trouble, as they "may be charged with sex offenses based on their testimony about the fact that the incident occurred, if there is insufficient evidence to prove the use of force" (Illinois Juvenile Justice Commission 2014, 19).

The previously mentioned reports on juvenile sex offenders identify a wide range of activity that results in arrest, conviction, and registration, including consensual activity between two minors (or "near peers"), indecent exposure, and possession of child pornography. Research documents that preteen sexual offenses often involve family members (Illinois Juvenile Justice Commission 2014, 22–23).

While many youth, particularly those who are nonwhite and poor, are tried in adult court for crimes committed at age fifteen or sixteen, sexual offenses place younger youth outside of any protective logic associated with childhood. While diminished capacity is widely associated with children, sexual activity (that may or may not be harmful) suggests that children, even those as young as nine or ten years old, lose protective associations with childhood. The criminalization of sexual activities challenges a dominant and popular narrative of the child as innocent and not culpable.

For some, being a child creates a sexuality trap. Adolescence and childhood are temporal stages in preparation for adulthood. Yet, experience functions as a double bind. Remaining innocent, a key characteristic of childhood, requires the negation of the very experiences that define adulthood. Sexual practice and knowledge (acquired through force or not) appear to place one outside of childhood. Or as Kathryn Stockton writes: "Adults walk the line—the impossible line—of keeping the child at once what it is (what adults are not) and leading it toward what it cannot (at least as itself) ever be (what adults are)" (2009, 30–31). Identifying minors as culpable of sexual violence is further complicated by a cultural context that celebrates the child's value as a heterosexual object. As one example, in 2009, reports the journalist Mandy Morgan (2012), "Jours Après Lunes, a French clothing company, started a new line of children's 'loungerie'—thin, revealing undergarments, which are marketed for girls as young as 3 months old." These messages create a contradictory and potentially inflammable landscape: children must be asexual in a culture that (hetero)sexualizes the child.

The conviction of juveniles for sexual offenses also raises urgent questions about the naturalization of associations between age and consent. Consider this example from *Raised on the Registry:* "In 1997, Stella A., a 17-year-old high school student, was arrested and pled guilty to sodomy for performing consensual oral sex on a 15-year-old male classmate. Stella was placed on probation and required to register on the state's sex offender registry. Her photograph, address, and identifying information were publicly available for neighbors and the public to see" (Human Rights Watch 2013, 35). Stella's and her sexual partner's consent do not matter; instead, her acts are read as criminal, harm is made visible, and she is convicted and required to register. Psychological or developmental norms are produced as static and policed. For young people who are unable to consent, engaging in many sexual acts involves breaking the law. A minor circulating a nude selfie to a peer, something done by one in five teenagers as estimated by researchers, is potentially producing and circulating child pornography (Herman 2010). An adult engaging in this behavior with other consenting adults would not be committing a crime.

Young people both perpetrate and experience sexual violence, yet an exploration of the rise of young people convicted of sex offenses, in particular the increased representation of those under fourteen years of age, illustrates the inability of the carceral state to address harm. Concurrently, the placement of youth on the registry also illustrates the urgency of building public sites for dialogues about consent, vulnerability, age, agency, and sexuality. While the prevalent response to the growth of registries in general is silence, a few human rights organizations and the U.S. Department of Justice have tried to raise the visibility of youth on the registry. Their strategies are in tandem with mainstream juvenile justice reform, to position youth as exceptional. Yet, the criminalization of violations of age of consent laws not only participates in reifying biological or psychological assumptions about the nature of the relationship between age and consent but also suggests that criminalization is an effective tool to regulate vulnerability. While public reports such as *Raised on the Registry* seek to flag how youth are negatively affected by life on the registry, the uneven criminalization of youth is often erased.

Matthew Limon had just turned eighteen in 2002 when he was arrested in Kansas for performing consensual oral sex with a fourteen-year-old male. Limon was convicted of criminal sodomy and sentenced to seventeen years in prison. However, this sentence not overturned with the 2003 *Lawrence v. Texas* Supreme Court decision that decriminalized sodomy. Even though Kansas had a so-called Romeo and Juliet law, designed to make penalties less severe when the consensual sexual activity involves two teenagers, at the time Limon was convicted the law applied only to sexual encounters (including sodomy) involving a male and a female. Initially the Kansas Court of Appeals ruled against Limon, but in 2005 the Kansas Supreme Court finally overturned the discriminatory component of the Romeo and Juliet act and freed Limon (American Civil Liberties Union 2005).

In 2005 Genarlow Wilson, age seventeen, was arrested in Georgia for consensual oral sex with a fifteen-year-old female. While Georgia also had a Romeo and Juliet law in place that would have made this encounter a misdemeanor offense, the law did not apply to oral sex, only vaginal/penis intercourse (Dewan 2006). Convicted of aggravated child molestation and sentenced to ten years in prison, Wilson was released after a successful appeal to the Georgia Supreme Court in 2007 that did not overturn his sentence but declared the punishment disproportionate (Goodman 2007). Wendy Whittaker, seventeen years old when she had consensual oral sex with a fifteen-year-old male in Georgia, was convicted in 1998 of the crime of sodomy and subsequently placed on the sex offender registry. With the support of the Southern Center for Human Rights, Whittaker was able to remove her name from the registry in 2010 (Jones 2010).

In May 2013, in Florida, Sebastian River High School honor student and cheerleader Kaitlyn Hunt was charged with two counts of lewd and lascivious battery of a child. Hunt acknowledged having a consensual sexual relationship when seventeen years old with a fourteen-year-old female. In Florida, no person under the age of sixteen can consent to sexual activity. Charged just days after her eighteenth birthday, eventually Hunt pleaded no contest to charges including battery and interference with child custody and agreed to a deal that included four months in jail, house arrest for two years, and three years of probation and gave the state power to monitor her electronic communications (Harrison 2013).

While available reports document that these sexual encounters were consensual, the partners of Limon, Wilson, Whittaker, and Hunt were legally unable to consent. Considered fully culpable, Limon, Wilson, Whittaker, and Hunt did not benefit from any protective associations with childhood or adolescence and instead were charged with sexual offenses, convicted, and received significant punishment. In these scenarios age and the inability to consent trigger the production of *crime and harm*. Through this process consent emerges not as a fixed or a priori category tethered to age but as a structural and inflexible natural law.

As Limon, Hunt, Wilson, and Whittaker eventually secured some public attention and the interest of juvenile justice advocates, these are success stories. Undoubtedly, their relative youth functioned to enable access to even small measures of public (and judicial) support. Yet the four also offer examples of sexual activities between minors or near peers who were either nonwhite (Wilson), nonheterosexual (Limon and Hunt), or disrupting heterosexist scripts (Whittaker).

All child/youth-related sexual acts are not consensual or without harm. Instead, assessments of both harm and criminal activity are uneven. Social norms, tied to prevailing racialized and heterogendered scripts, shape how youth sexual activity is made visible and/or framed as criminal or injurious. Consider the high-profile media coverage surrounding the reported sexual assault of a sixteen-year-old girl by two sixteen-year-old members of a high school sports team in Steubenville, Ohio, in 2012 (Gabriel 2013). Townspeople, school officials, many parents, and local law enforcement were all too willing to discredit the survivor's experience, to reframe the assault as the consensual activity of wayward youth, and to collude to cover up what the survivor identified as violence. Dismissed as a loose girl, the initial narrative suggested that the sexual activity was consensual. Age is not the only factor determining criminalization. The futures of the male football players at Steubenville High mattered to the state and to the community. They retained some access to innocence despite their sexual experiences. Yet young people such as Wilson, Whittaker, Hunt, and Limon did not. Criminalization is offered as an effective tool to address youth sexual violence: all harmful sexual activity is criminalized, and all criminalized sexual activity is harmful. But criminalization flattens our understanding of youth sexuality and, concurrently, our collective understanding of harm and accountability.

In this political moment the strongest movement against public registries centers on the disproportionate number of young people who are convicted and required to register. While potentially helpful for some young people, campaigns that argue that juveniles should be shielded from requirements to register as sex offenders are missed opportunities to raise deeper and systematic questions (some of which are raised in this chapter). The expansion of criminalization to negotiate vulnerabilities does not invite a more rigorous investigation into the status of the child. While organizing that seeks to move young people off public registries may benefit a few individuals, these strategies risk failing to engage necessary and wider dialogues surrounding sexuality, youth, and harm that hold meaningful potential to reduce child sexual violence.

IV

After and Now

7

Not This

Building Futures Now

In 2007, I cotaught a social research class at the Multicultural Arts High School, located in the southwestern Chicago community of Little Village, also known as South Lawndale or "Mexico of the Midwest." This school was part of the Little Village High School complex, which was created in 2005 as a result of a protracted community struggle and housed four public schools. In 1997 the Little Village neighborhood was promised a new high school by Mayor Richard M. Daley, but although new schools were built in gentrifying, wealthier, and white neighborhoods across the city, this predominantly brown, black, and poor community with over-crowded schools did not get the promised new high school. Beginning on Mother's Day 2001, thirteen members of the Lawndale–Little Village community, primarily grandmothers, conducted a nineteen-day hunger strike to force administrators to approve and build the school (Stovall 2016).

Our research seminar–style class met every Wednesday morning in the library. My coteacher Therese Quinn and I designed the course to be an open-ended arts-based participatory research methods class. Students would identify questions they were interested in finding the answers to and use art to conduct an inquiry and to represent research findings. As the attention of the school and the surrounding community was focused on violence, not surprisingly the topic this class of sophomores and ju-niors selected to investigate was safety, particularly school safety. Collec-tively, we created a short survey to interview students about where they felt the most safe and the least safe in the school, and what students be-lieved could make the school safer. Interviewers took photos of locations interviewees identified as safe and unsafe. To the slight consternation of the school authorities, we also dispatched students during our class time to walk through the school when other students were in class to work on this project. Perhaps the project was popular largely because our students were permitted to walk around school during regularly scheduled class time.

We did not produce a particularly scientific or rigorous survey. In my notes, I cannot find a record of how many students we interviewed at a school that enrolled approximately 350 students. However, the findings were remarkably consistent. The surveyed students identified feeling unsafe in the spaces at the school that were not under surveillance: in the bathrooms and under the stairs. What might make students feel safer, beyond additional guards and more cameras, even under the stairs and in the bathrooms, was more police and functioning metal detectors.

These are young people intimately familiar with surveillance who experience the police as a daily and powerful negative force in their communities. A junior in our class, Brian, reported rather laconically to us in a Wednesday morning class that he did not do any work over the weekend because he was picked up the previous Friday and spent the weekend in jail. Brian was a goofy-looking, sweet-faced fifteen-year-old, and I looked forward to his loose participation in class. Brian's story was not unusual. Many youth in Little Village, a neighborhood dominated by blue-light surveillance cameras, are picked up by police, who had implemented a process called "carding." Police would stop youth in the neighborhood and fill out a card with information on them—name, birth date, telephone contact number, residence, and, if known, gang affiliation. This card would go on file and could subsequently count as police contact (Gorner 2013; Ramos 2013). Racial profiling by police in Chicago is neither new nor infrequent. In March 2015 the American Civil Liberties Union of Illinois released a report documenting that Chicago led the nation in the police use of racial profiling: "Black Chicagoans were subjected to 72% of all stops, yet constitute just 32% of the city's population" (American Civil Liberties Union of Illinois 2015, 3). Perhaps routine for communities of color, this practice is unthinkable for whiter and wealthier individuals.

Desires to be less vulnerable or to avoid harm are often channeled through the tools made available to imagine and understand security. In everyday exchanges and popular media representations, safety is generally defined as an increased police presence, more surveillance, or tougher punishments. Schools are safer with more armed security guards, or so goes the fact-free message in circulation. Yet this framework, as previous chapters support, is not backed by evidence.

Putting more police in schools does not reduce violence. Building more prisons does not act as a deterrent or reduce harm. Research highlights that tougher laws do not eradicate sexual trauma or necessarily meet the needs of those who experience violence. Capture by our prison nation increases people's risk of experiencing harm and facilitates premature death through substandard physical, dental, and mental health care while locked up. Being an "ex-offender" guarantees significant barriers to participating in every aspect of life. More prisons and more punitive laws generally mask sources of violence and distract us from building meaningful ways to address harm—to transform our communities.

Yet turning research on ineffective crime policies into action is challenging, as our current public safety system runs partially on affect. As the scholar Sara Ahmed writes: "Emotions *do things*, and they align individuals with communities—or bodily space with social space—through the very intensity of their attachments" (2004, 119, emphasis original). Decades of punitive policies in the United States have shaped differential affective investments in public safety. Police and prisons are offered as the solution to and the definition of safety. Even for some who live and survive as targets of state violence, policing and surveillance are the available mechanisms to make communities safer. People's moves to use or even to endorse the police and prisons cannot be dismissed as a form of false consciousness, ignorance, or conformity. We want to be and to feel safe.

A problematic concept, *safety* justified the lynching of black men to protect white women, ensured the removal of children from First Nations mothers, and still often sanctions formal and informal prohibitions against queers in jobs that involve children, to give a few examples. Such prohibitions are not merely remnants of a bygone era. In 2013 Towson University established a "White Student Union" to patrol the campus at night in response to safety concerns, or, as the organization states, "a spike in Black-on-White crime" (Wells 2013). And few forget the 2013 murder of a young African American man, Trayvon Martin, and the subsequent acquittal by an almost all-white jury of George Zimmerman, who was able to *stand his ground* because safety equals racial profiling. Dominant power structures use safety to prop up institutions and animate practices that actively harm select groups of people. Public safety is often predicated on, and subsequently reproduces, white supremacist capitalist heteropatriarchal systems. Yet, as highlighted by Brian and the other students at the Multicultural Arts High School, even if the very tools made available to even imagine safety make us profoundly unsafe, negotiating and reimagining what safety might look and feel like are complicated.

The historian Saidiya Hartman, in *Scenes of Subjection*, writes about the impossibility of using the concepts of agency and resistance in any analysis about black life under slavery. For Hartman, to use such concepts erases the political framework of slavery: "Within the enclosures of the avowedly total and reciprocal relations of master and slave in which the simplest expression of human feelings is impossible without reference to the other, the fetish or artifice of the slave's consent and agency effectively links the exercise of will and continued subjection" (1997, 53). For Hartman, the idea of using the language of consent or agency within this landscape potentially creates another form of domination.

I have turned to Hartman's work and my experience with the research project at the Multicultural Arts High School as I struggle with whether safety can be repopulated, reframed, reclaimed. Not only is the concept of safety imagined and operationalized in ways that make many profoundly insecure and at risk, but when communities organize to research, identify, and implement actions to increase their autonomy, self-determination, and overall well-being, these tactics are often absorbed and taken over by the state or other dominant, sometimes corporate, structures. As teacher and community groups organized the first standing-room-only workshop on restorative justice (RJ) at the Chicago Teachers Center in 2010, the language and the tools associated with restorative justice were being incorporated by Chicago's criminal juvenile justice system.

As Brian and his many comrades at the Multicultural Arts School identified, people want to feel safe. For some, safety is the desire to preserve privilege and power, and for others safety is the wish to not experience harm. Every day people encounter risk and want to not feel threatened or in jeopardy. Yet the responses available through mainstream media and our criminal justice frameworks to do something when violence goes down all sketch similar, and thin, possibilities of public safety. *Call the police. Dial 911. Don't get involved. Keep your mouth shut. Be still. Don't question the police. Don't look. Don't ask questions.*

Mimi Kim, cofounder of Creative Interventions, an Oakland-based organization that built and archived transformative justice (TJ) responses to harm, writes that many groups working alongside those who have experienced interpersonal harm take up the analysis, language, and conceptual frameworks the state has established. Kim writes that many antiviolence groups have taken "legitimate desires for safety and channeled them into interventions requiring shelter and arrest" (2012, 21). People want to feel safe, and these feelings have been effectively funneled into a landscape where police and prison expansion and more cameras under the stairways and in the bathrooms, however ineffective, are the dominant response. Eliminating the "cops in our heads and our hearts" as antiviolence organizer Paula X. Rojas writes, is potentially as challenging as removing those that line our schools and neighborhoods (Rojas 2007, 213).

Not This

For those who build safety outside of prisons and police, a challenge is often the difficulty of imagining other responses and an inability to recognize the current or past alternatives engaged by communities. The requirement for a solution shuts down critique and narrows any discussion. Often these roadblocks emerge as pressure to deal with the real issues in the constrained present. Building alternatives to our carceral regime, some argue, is too "pie in the sky" and is unable to offer a practical response to what to do in the present moment. *What can really be done to make the Multicultural Arts High School safer, now? As we cannot transform the community, more school security really is the next best strategy to implement. Additional surveillance cameras are the best response to a bad situation.* Responses in organizing and in scholarly contexts when *abolition* frameworks are introduced into conversations about prisons and policing include the following:

> *It is fine to keep dreaming, but we need something now.*
> *Well, I am not a utopian. I live in the real world.*
> *Let's be practical, really. Let's make this meeting achieve*
>   *something.*
> *I am with you but that will turn other people off.*
> *Sure, abolition for women and nonviolent offenders, but what*
>   *about the bad people?*

These responses continue to circulate in meetings, campaign planning sessions, and e-mail dialogues, and even during question-and-answer time at a range of public talks when abolition is raised. The perceived impossibility of any alternative is adroitly used not only to mask the ineffectiveness of the current system but to halt attempts at imagining or practicing other pathways.

Building for abolition does not mean a world free of violence. Rather, it acknowledges that prisons and policing are not a just, efficient, or moral solution to the problems that shape violence and lack in communities. As social assistance programs are eliminated or reduced and as the options poor people possess to cope with untenable situations are criminalized, the majority of those in prisons and jails *are* poor people marked by white supremacy. Locking more people up attempts to disappear from public view the negligence and failures of the state to provide high-quality public education, health care, a minimum wage that is a living wage, and more. Policing and imprisonment have never had a neutral or benign function in the United States. Policing reform, for example, often spurred by media scrutiny on an act of police violence, have functioned to expand the scope and the resources attached to policing, and has also worked to obscure that violence is the norm, not an aberration, of policing (Herzing 2015). As many activists and scholars have noted, abolition does not mean that people will not do "bad things" but that our carceral state does little to reduce the occurrence of violence and harm and does nothing to alter the social or political conditions that potentially facilitate interpersonal violence. In short, an abolition politic excavates core or root causes of violence masked by the carceral regime.

An abolition politic also underscores that our prison-industrial complex is not a broken system but is functioning precisely as designed and is intimately linked to white supremacy. We have imagined, built, implemented, and affirmed carceral systems that disproportionately target communities of color. We have built prisons and detention centers; passed regressive, uneven, and punishing drug laws; trained police to racially profile and to stop and frisk; and empowered employers and landlords to discriminate against people with convictions and arrest records. The placement of police officers in urban schools results in high arrest rates for youth of color and no decrease in school-based crime or violence. Abolition frames the through-line of white supremacy and demands another future because of abolition's referent: slavery.

Yet these prevalent responses to abolition—to be more pragmatic *or real*—are not unfamiliar. Abolitionists fighting to end slavery, disability justice workers demanding access, queers organizing to decriminalize sodomy and end police brutality, frequently trigger the responses: *We*

*can't go too far too fast, don't make yourself a target, we need to wait, we
must move slowly, don't be too visible, don't make them angry, we can't ask
for that right now* . . . Liberation under oppression is unthinkable by
design.

Our prison nation alters time, uses time against us. A part of the work
of abolition is a refusal of this punishing clock, a historically queer tactic.
In *Cruising Utopia*, José Esteban Muñoz (2009) writes that "the future is
queerness's domain . . . Queerness is that thing that lets us feel that this
world is not enough, that indeed something is missing" (1). Queers (and
other marginal communities) have historically worked to imagine and live
outside of a condemning present. Requiring more than a radical imagination, abolition asks us to live as if we were already beyond this punishing time.

This is risky. Demands for the radical redistribution of power and
resources by oppressed communities are met with accommodation or
co-optation and also by direct and lethal forms of state violence. Those
marked as less than fully human who question existing power structures, including how resources are allocated, are highly vulnerable targets for law enforcement and everyday people who feel justified to enact
their perception of the state's agenda. Over decades during the twentieth
century, the U.S. Counter Intelligence Program (COINTELPRO) covertly
sought to infiltrate, entrap, and eliminate racial and economic justice organizations and movements.[1] COINTELPRO deployed all available types
of force, including assassination, arrest, and imprisonment. Anti-
immigrant border vigilantes calling themselves the Minutemen, often
armed, patrol the border between the United States and Mexico and
forcibly halt people they identify as unlawful migrants. Although not
law enforcement officers, the Minutemen feel empowered to act as
agents of the state. COINTELPRO sought to arrest movements for self-
determination that challenged racial and gendered ideological norms
and the Minutemen aim to halt people's attempts to seek refuge and
flourishing futures. Our imaginative and material possibilities for resistance are constrained by these forms of violent backlash.

The prevalence of the push to be practical illuminates the power of an
abolition framework in this political moment. Making the claim that
something is broken or unjust does not require a fix for the question. As
Elizabeth Povinelli writes, "*Not this* makes a difference even if it does not
produce a prepositional otherwise" (2011, 191). The ability to offer a neat

resolution is not a prerequisite for critique or analysis. Povinelli cites the feminist activist Valerie Solanas's SCUM manifesto to exemplify how the latter's manifesto interrupts the banal everyday status quo forms of institutionalized patriarchal violence. *Not this* reorients the terrain and forces other imaginative possibilities. *Not this*, a tool of the marginal, firmly interrupts business as usual. For Povinelli, *not this* makes "the world unready-at-hand for those whom it has worked smoothly—so smoothly that there seems little difference between the world as a normative projection and the world as it is a differential lived" (192). The fierceness of *not this* holds such potential to momentarily interrupt the daily grind, the everyday business as usual forms of harm. The persistent request *to be pragmatic, to ask for less, to slow down, to wait, to be practical* is a part of the slow time of what Povinelli identifies as late liberalism. Asking those harmed to wait, and to then wait more for ends that are inadequate, is characteristic, Povinelli writes, of this punishing time.

Although an abolition framework, as well as other forms of analysis and critique, does not require a response, and although a part of the power is in the interruption, the refusal, many people imagine, create, and build interventions. While some organizing targets policing, jails, criminal justice laws, and immigration detention centers, equally valuable local and ad hoc initiatives move beyond these sites to examine the scaffolding and ideologies that make the idea of prison necessary, even imaginable. "What is, so to speak, the object of abolition? Not so much the abolition of prisons but the abolition of a society that could have prisons, that could have slavery, that could have the wage, and therefore not abolition as the elimination of anything but abolition as the founding of a new society" (Moten and Harney 2004, 114). Across the United States, ad hoc formations and organized groups are both stating *not this* to the carceral regime and visualizing and practicing how public safety could be otherwise. Messy and fraught, these emergent practices and projects and imaginings create a cluster of possibility: another present to seed new futures.

Building Otherwise/Alternatives

As noted, a growing number of small, often ad hoc, organizations, collectives, and groups are trying to build of community, to reclaim or redefine safety, and to carve out possibilities for responding to harm and violence that do not involve the police. This is not new work within the United States or across the globe. Many could never rely on the police or the state to ensure their safety and developed ways to address harm and modes of accountability. Some of these responses were (and are) no more just or transformative than policing or other punitive state responses. Building alternatives is both reactive (that is, struggling to create and proliferate more "in the moment" tools to enable other responses to harm beyond engaging the prison nation) and preventive (that is, attempting to shift climate, context, and communities that produce and naturalize forms of violence). Even in the current conditions that define safety for us as law and order and make it difficult to suggest solutions other than calling the police, vibrant local scenes involving community organizations and digital cultures—tweeting, Facebook, and tumblr—document ongoing attempts to provoke imagination and engage possibilities. Over the past fifteen years, a number of formal organizations have sprung up, among them Sista to Sista (New York), Empowering Communities, Ending Violence (Chicago), Creative Interventions, the Storytelling and Organizing Project (Oakland), Philly Stands UP (Philadelphia), the Young Women's Empowerment Project (Chicago), Audre Lorde Project (New York), Communities Against Rape and Abuse (Seattle), and more. Many of these organizations self-identify as abolitionist, as engaged in practicing transformative justice, and/or as building alternatives to incarceration. Others are committed to practicing forms of community accountability.

These organizations, many with few or no paid staff, are location- and context-specific.[2] Many identify as being centered on and led by those who are queer and/or by people of color. I use queer here to signify both nonnormative sexualities and gender expressions but also to flag the liberatory, anti-assimilative nature of the politics of the organizations. Centering the leadership of those who have experienced harm, grounded in a transformative and anti-oppressive political vision, these organizations imagine and negotiate alternatives and support community-led transformation. This is slow work. For example, generationFIVE is an organization committed to eradicating childhood sexual violence in five generations without state intervention. For generationFIVE, the work is deliberate and germinal. The expectation at the outset is that these changes will take five generations. The phenomenal writing that emerged in recent years to document this labor has created a rich and critically reflective landscape for transformative justice.[3]

I continue to participate in organizations and ad hoc mobilizations that have included a number of Chicago gatherings on engaging transformative justice, for example at DePaul University in 2009 and at the University of Illinois–Chicago in 2013. My experience with both the crisis/reactive initiatives and the wider preventive paradigm-shifting work is complex, heartbreaking, and ongoing. Two hesitant TJ processes come immediately to mind: A colleague/comrade reached out after experiencing a sexual assault and wanted a nonpolice intervention to hold the perpetrator accountable. Those of us that responded to this request for a TJ process were fumbled and slow. We were effective at supporting the survivor, but less effective in figuring out how to hold the perpetrator accountable. When a student at my university was harmed by another student and initiated a TJ process, and subsequently asked to be more central to the process of building accountability for the one who had perpetrated the harm, the process veered toward shaming and collapsed. In both of these cases, an organization or an ad hoc group of people formed to try to build other responses at the request of the person who had experienced harm. While the outcomes were mixed, and while sharing details publicly even years later to facilitate learning is challenging, even the tentative and collective responses we formulated in each of these two incidents reframed the roles of bystanders, gathered people together to talk about collective responses, and built capacities to imagine something different. Things shifted. People moved.

These practices interrupt traditional and linear notions of progress and success and failure. In *The Queer Art of Failure,* the cultural studies critic Judith (Jack) Halberstam (2011) works to dislodge the pervasive progress narrative central to contemporary understandings of U.S. life. Beyond attempting to dispose of the "success/failure" binary, Halberstam argues in favor of inhabiting and exploring failure: "Under certain circumstances, failing, losing, forgetting, unmaking, undoing, unbecoming, not knowing may in fact offer more creative, more cooperative, more surprising ways of being in the world" (2011, 2). It is not hard to see what the trouble with success might be for queers (or others) whose bodies and life paths are incompatible with so-called normal life. For many, failing at what normative culture has marked as success seems not only more life-generating and pleasurable but the only possible pathway. Similarly, for this work the success and failure dynamic can be another trap. *See, we tried this alternative and it failed!* Thinking and organizing beyond the success/failure binary when possible is instructive.

Much of this work is also ad hoc, undertaken by everyday people on their blocks, and is not archived or documented. Several years ago, my household decided that we would no longer be silent witnesses to an ongoing "domestic disturbance." For two summers, we watched the police roll up to the house two doors south of our building to respond to verbal and sometimes physical altercations between a heterosexual couple with alcohol and drug problems. Like everyone else on the block, we sat in our backyard and ignored their fights. No one wanted to get involved. *It was a private matter. They are always high or drunk, and clearly crazy. Hell, we might have gotten hurt ourselves.* After enough yelling, someone on the block might finally call the police, and one or both of the people might be picked up, but they would return days later. After deciding to not look away, my household strategized and formulated a loose plan that was neither radical nor labor-intensive. We introduced ourselves to this couple who lived two doors south and made a point to have repeated conversations about mundane topics in moments when no one appeared in crisis or high or drunk. We talked about the weather, food, life. We found out that one of them had chronic and debilitating health problems. We talked to other neighbors about what was going on and about how to reduce the police presence, which no one in the neighborhood wanted. We moved from hanging out in the backyard to also sitting on our front stoop and talking to the people that walked by. When we heard yelling and what might be violence, at least two of us walked over and said, "Hi. Is everyone okay?" Our actions changed the neighborhood in small ways. People on the block talked to one another more. We shared information about other issues on our block: elderly neighbors that needed help, annoying dog owners that did not pick up dog poop, bad landlords. One of the two individuals moved away for a spell, and on their return it was quieter. The police visits were reduced to a trickle. Perhaps the violence was driven inside, into the basement or behind locked doors and windows. Perhaps our friendliness was interpreted as social shaming. Perhaps we simply masked the problem. Yet this experience did give us a new way of thinking about our block, about the work of community, the relationships between neighbors, and the idea that a bystander is never neutral but rather plays an integral role.

Transformative justice as a framework is often in an uncomfortable alliance with the more established and recognized practice of restorative justice. As defined by the Chicago organization Community Justice for Youth Institute (n.d.), a restorative justice model is based on "a theory of justice that emphasizes repairing the harm caused by crime and conflict." The overall goals of RJ practices are to try to heal the whole community from an incident in which people were harmed and, ideally, to help prevent the same sort of harm from happening again. TJ, built in part through the perceived limitations of RJ, argues that the conditions that made harm imaginable and possible must be transformed, not restored, in order to build strong and just communities capable of addressing harm. TJ questions whether harm can ever truly be healed or the victim restored in a context where structural inequality is the pervasive norm. An inherently flexible approach, TJ is structured less as a single model and more as a political outlook driven by values of prison-industrial complex abolition, harm reduction (the goal of reducing harm caused to an individual or community by an action regardless of whether that action can be completely stopped or prevented), and holistic healing. TJ has often taken root within organizing focusing on sexual and gendered violence. If transformative responses to sexual violence can be built, then responses to other forms of harm must be feasible.

Many TJ and RJ organizations offer popular education–style workshops on varied components of transformative justice. While the language used is often a training discourse, the aims are to shift paradigms. The goal of TJ is not to create another checklist or rubric of approved practices or patented techniques that can be learned in an hourlong workshop but to change modes of association. Through public workshops or small popular education sessions, participants are offered strategies to explore some of the practices, politics, and feelings associated with TJ. For example, a generationFIVE workshop in 2010 at the U.S. Social Forum attracted approximately seventy-five people. Participants started by standing with eyes closed and breathing, and then discussed learned and embodied responses to risk. This workshop was difficult for me. While so much of the work I do is all about people and our bodies, this labor is simultaneously deeply disconnected from any kind of embodied practice. Standing with a group of people, practicing my breath, and paying attention to my body was challenging. *What does breathing have to do with justice?* For many TJ practitioners, creating community and building alternatives to police and prisons start with the body and retooling feelings of community and our individual response to risk or threat.

Despite a focus on the body and on a radical political imagination, TJ does not naïvely engage romantic assumptions about community or that transformative justice is the response to violence. This movement is relatively self-reflexive, and continues to name ongoing challenges for TJ (Chen, Dulani, and Piepzna-Samarasinha 2011). Many groups struggle to have a consistent on-the-ground presence. TJ and RJ work is frequently highly gendered with the Challenging Male Supremacy Project as a noted organizational exception.[4] Some TJ initiatives dependent on mercurial forms of foundation funding or small government grants that are tied to service delivery, whereas others have resisted these funding sources. While an organization with no paid staff can potentially produce flexible analysis and support creative interventions, few resources can also create instability and burnout. In a moment when people are keenly looking for alternatives, identifying any organization as *the* (or even *an*) example of a site where transformative justice is working or a success—such as I do in this chapter—can also create a pressured context.

This chapter started with the question of reclaiming public safety. While it is potentially an impossible task, people are repopulating this term. Imagining and trying other responses to violence and harm, of struggling to shift cultures to preventively address some of the harm and lack that lead to violence—these are cracks that create possibilities, openings, for other ways of thinking beyond the current public safety paradigm. Therefore, the struggle of transformative justice is not simply to retake public safety but to begin the work of dismantling the old framework. Pollyannaish? Naïvely optimistic? Utopian? Yes, although I would prefer curious and invested. While Lauren Berlant (2011) has warned that this focus on possibility may be a dangerously cruel form of optimism or hope as "an attachment to a significantly problematic object" (24), committing to imagination and engagement seems like the only livable path.

In some moments imaginative possibilities appear to proliferate. Gatherings such as the U.S. Social Forum, Free Minds Free People, and the Allied Media Conference routinely showcase intimate and transformative work by a wide range of ad hoc and local organizations: attempts to subvert jury duty; tactics to interrupt the recruitment of teenagers into police and military work; projects by cisgendered men who have perpetrated harm and violence that work with similar men; road maps for accountability mechanisms that aim to meet the needs of survivors while aiming to transform both the conditions that made harm feasible and the individual(s) who perpetrated this harm. While a familiar refrain is that there is no alternative other than to respond to violence through policing or incarceration, everywhere people invent, remember, and try to make other ways.

Yet, even from within this ripe landscape of emerging transformative justice practices, we still struggle for what to do when harm happens. These groups and practices do not provide linear, neat narratives of successful alternatives to calling the police. While this is not a requirement for engagement or critique, the expectation of being able to solve the problem creates a messiness, an ambiguity, that is often hard to hold. The stakes are so very high for this work. As the antiviolence organizer and scholar Mimi Kim writes, our capacity to meet the needs of people in deep crisis is thin. Kim notes that many in the antiviolence community still advise people in immediate crisis to call the police, even if we know that this intervention could potentially augment the harm that is happening: "Despite our growing recognition of the political and material problems embedded in the criminal legal response, our answering machines still tell women to call 911 in case of emergency. We still instruct women—whether undocumented immigrants, queer, transgendered, fearful of the police due to targeted brutality, or otherwise unwilling to subject themselves or their abusers to this system—to call the police" (M. Kim 2009, 213). Kim's invocation that many in crisis resort to using a state-supported and -controlled institution, the police, invites more precision and thought about the role of the state. What role could or even should the state play in transformative justice projects for the long haul? Is the state only or always negative?

State Formation

State refers to politically organized physical space or terrain led by a form of government that possesses powers such as the right to collect taxes and that can offer services for the collective: schools, access to water and garbage collection, police and military forces, hospitals. Never static, these services and entities form part of the public sphere. Yet, under neoliberal readjustment, the contours of the state are frequently not easily recognizable. As public funding is withdrawn (if it was ever provided) from state-run services, private dollars flow in to fill the gap. *Shadow state* refers to philanthropic foundations, nonprofit organizations, for-profit entities, and other nongovernmental forces that essentially fulfill functions that were once at least nominally identified as the purview of the state (Wolch 1990; Gilmore 2009). This constellation of nongovernmental organizations the shadow state, delivers services, but generally does not press back on the state or challenge structures that require or produce inequities. Organizations that work to meet the needs of the "deserving poor," for example, form networks of power and function as a reminder that decentralization, key to neoliberal policies, does not mean withdrawal; rather, the state's relationships and abilities to negotiate power, to "govern from a distance," shift and potentially expand (Rose 1999).

For example, across the United States, governmental funding for public schools has stagnated or shrunk. Starting in 1991, states passed legislation that permitted the establishment of charter schools run by private or nonprofit actors supported by a limited amount of public funds. Today, across all urban contexts, charter schools are identified as public and receive state dollars but operate outside of most forms of governmental regulation and oversight. Overwhelmingly, these schools enroll low-income students of color. As some charter schools are heavily funded by philanthropic sources which also play key leadership roles, including the Gates Foundation and the Broad Foundations, can these charter schools still be defined as public? Inversely, public revenues support a range of private for-profit organizations and services. In Chicago: public funds are used through tax increment financing (TIF) to support the development of private and for-profit entities. Is the local franchise sandwich shop in my neighborhood, built and opened with TIF funds, a publicly supported private enterprise?

Within this neoliberal landscape, the contours of the state, never a static singular entity, continue to shift. As the theorists Fred Moten and Stefano Harney suggest, the boundaries of the state are negotiated and actively produced by our labor: "Not only is [the state] not a monolith but it's very, very thoroughly aerated. There are all kinds of little holes and tunnels and ditches and highways and byways through the state that are being produced and maintained constantly by the people who are also at the same time doing this labor that ends in the production of the state. So, what is it that these folks are producing?" (Harney and Moten 2013, 144–45). In our RJ and TJ work, what are we producing? What larger structures do the tunnels and holes we are making reinforce or weaken?

Questions about the role of the state emerged concretely for me when I had the opportunity to travel to Norway in the late summer of 2013 to attend a Critical Criminology conference. Many of the participants were from Scandinavian countries, and while deconstructing the myth of "Scandinavian exceptionalism" or that this bloc of nations was better, and while deeply critical their own nations' prison systems—including a resurgence of a punitive and racialized approach to immigration—these scholars also described programs that sought to build viable responses to interpersonal violence that did not trigger punishment and policing. Christina Ericson, a Swedish researcher, described her work assessing a state-run program deliberately organized outside of the criminal–legal sphere. This project aimed to support survivors of intimate partner violence when the person who perpetrated the harm voluntarily agreed to participate in therapeutic treatment. Although I did not see this project working on the ground, this initiative appeared to center some of the values of transformative justice. The survivor should have control over the process. Not all survivors want to leave. People can change. Police and criminalization are neither the only nor the best responses and should never be the first line of intervention. Support services must be separated from punitive and policing entities. People who have experienced harm can make decisions about what they need. Cautiously optimistic, Ericson offered an example of a state-supported response to intimate partner violence that centered core TJ values and practices (Ericson 2013).

In the United States, working with the state feels much more tricky and less possible in this political moment. U.S.-based TJ projects emerged in part because of the abject failure of the state either to address the root causes of interpersonal violence or to acknowledge how state responses— policing and criminalization—actually increase harm and instability.[5] TJ frameworks emerged in part as a critique of and response to the institutionalization of RJ. While sometimes not formally acknowledged, TJ organizations frame building safety as outside of state-based institutions. The Safe OUTside the System Collective, part of the New York–based community organization the Audre Lorde Project, explicitly acknowledges its work as outside of state systems: "The Safe OUTside the System

(SOS) Collective is an anti-violence program led by and for Lesbian, Gay, Bisexual, Two Spirit, Trans, and Gender Non Conforming people of color. We are devoted to challenging hate and police violence by using community-based strategies rather than relying on the police."[6] The SOS Collective emerged because state responses to harm reproduced racialized forms of heteropatriarchy and increased communities' experiences of harm and vulnerability.

These two examples, a Swedish model where the state supports and enacts TJ principles and U.S.-based TJ programs that are explicitly anti-state, raise fundamental questions about the role and the nature of the state in building more just communities. Some U.S. groups that seek to build alternative responses to violence have elected to work with the state and often identify their work as "restorative justice" (not transformative justice). One example of a program that builds alternative frameworks to harm but is also funded by and integrated with the state is the Arizona-based program RESTORE: Responsibility and Equity for Sexual Transgressions Offering a Restorative Experience. Framed as a restorative justice initiative, RESTORE is a collaborative effort among law enforcement, public health agencies, sexual assault services, and prosecutors that seeks to "facilitate a victim-centered, community driven resolution of selected individual sex crimes that creates and carries out a plan for accountability, healing and public safety" (Koss 2009, 218–19). Funded by the Centers for Disease Control, RESTORE demonstrates that "carefully reasoned, safe and respectful alternatives can be offered for sexual assault if we collaborate, consult and listen to the needs of our constituencies" (Koss 2009, 219).

While data available on the program come from collaborating entities, not from survivors, the framework laid out by RESTORE centers language familiar to those working in TJ communities. Participation in RESTORE is voluntary: a survivor must decide to pursue this process, and the perpetrator, or "responsible party," must agree to participate. The RESTORE framework has seemingly anticipated the majority of the barriers that would stop either survivors or perpetrators from participating. Concern that the survivor might feel pressure to forgive is structurally responded to with a process whereby the responsible party provides an apology at the closure of the process, but there is not an expectation that the survivor will forgive. Throughout the process, the survivor is provided with multiple opportunities to speak or to designate someone to speak.

For the perpetrator of harm, the concerns are also anticipated. The fear of excessive or counterproductive shaming is addressed through advanced preparation, and the process is framed to work to eliminate these outcomes (Koss 2009, 223, 225).

Even though data is partial, RESTORE, while not providing the response but potential imaginative other possibilities, offers an example of an antiviolence project explicitly partnered with the state. With an increased rhetoric of the "end of mass incarceration" and a growing interest in alternatives to incarceration (for some), including restorative responses, the state's tentative willingness to support alternatives is unsurprising. Questions remain: Are these alternatives policing and incarceration under new guises?

For me, working with the state is not completely off the table for several reasons. First, the state is not inherently good, neutral, or bad. Antiprison organizers have pushed back on the carceral state, but our strategies indicate that we have not fully abandoned all facets or forms of democratic governance. The popular slogan "Schools, not jails," or the work of organizations such as Californians United for a Responsible Budget (CURB) that struggle to realign California's budget from incarceration to public services such as providing quality and accessible public education and health care, highlight that abolitionists' goals include the eradication of the carceral regime.

Second, gauging the borders of the state, or an ability to be outside, seems not possible. While many TJ groups that I have flagged in this chapter receive zero funding and operate as autonomous entities or gather resources only directly from members, other groups have been able to form partnerships with foundations and philanthropic entities and have been able to hire staff members and develop materials and resources. Is funding from sources such as the Soros Foundation or the Gates Foundation better or less politically charged than funding from the Federal Bureau of Prisons? Is a grant from the Chicago Foundation for Women less constraining or problematic than resources from the U.S. Department of Health and Human Services? Each comes with differing lines of accountability and differing modes of performance and an agreement—tacit or not—to legitimate particular paradigms. As some groups develop organizational systems—*a board of directors or a collective? Staff personnel manuals and bylaws?*—funding is not the only way TJ and RJ movements are tied to the state or to capitalism. While in many contexts the state and the market are twinned structures with conjoined aims, they are not the same entity. Whether this distinction has any value left beyond rhetoric, I am not certain. Yet, while I act as if a distinction between capitalism and the state should matter, an outside to either of these systems, some days, seems inconceivable.

And finally, even in the short term, I argue that we cannot fully reject the state because this apparatus traps many we love. Working-class children attend public schools. Homeschooling, private school, or unschooling is a financial or structural impossibility. Community-based holistic health care is not uniformly available. The neighbors I love cannot provide chemotherapy. Food stamps, subsidized housing—for too many there is no community to provide these services. People are already court-involved, systems-controlled. For many, the possibility of movement outside the state is a luxury. Or, as is starkly visible in the field of public education, without some idea of a state, in our current landscape, there is only the market. I want our collective wealth to provide high-quality free postsecondary education, health care for all, housing, and art—not pay for military interventions and policing. Imagine what could be done with the resources spent on maintaining our military infrastructure. With over 1.68 million men and women in military service, eleven hundred bases across the globe, and only six thousand Foreign Service officers and two thousand U.S. Agency for International Development workers, the military *is* U.S. international aid, diplomacy, and foreign relations. The military has more members in bands than the State Department has Foreign Service officers (González, Gusterson, and Price 2009). Imagine what communities could do with these resources.

Putting aside the too significant question of whether (and how) to recognize a carceral state and that even community-developed initiatives to support the welfare of all people are often coercive and punitive, this discussion of the state aims to raise fundamental questions about our ongoing TJ and RJ practices. Is our work to continue to build multiple local SOS collectives—organizations to create responses to harm and violence outside of the system? Are our practices to build a noncoercive welfare state? Or to continue to operate (as we understand it) outside of state formations? And what is outside the system? Also, if, as is the case, our language and our work will be co-opted to other ends, how prepared are we to continue? Yet, is our use of community any less problematic (or fictive) than the state? How can we practice and build collectivity outside of the old model of borders, citizenship, and belonging? Although asking questions does not require knowing the responses, with pleasure I commit to imagining and building communities not bound by policed borders, together.

Acknowledgments

Over the past few years I have had the opportunity to collaborate, research, or coauthor with a cadre of generous and generative people, including Bill Ayers, Liat Ben-Moshe, Michelle Boyd, Owen Daniel-McCarter, Daysi Diaz-Strong, Christina Gomez, Gillian Harkins, Jane Hereth, Jessi Jackson, Mariame Kaba, Kevin Kumashiro, Crystal Laura, Jodi Lawston, Maria Luna Duarte, Liam Michaud, Ray Noll, Josh Pavan, Sarah Ross, Cassandra Shaylor, Dave Stovall, Lewis Wallace, Maisha Winn, and my longtime collaborator Therese Quinn, who is such a fierce Scorpio. Their smart ideas are laced throughout this book, but all errors are mine.

My thinking and acting continue to be sharpened by other forms of collectivity, including being a part of a number of organizations: Critical Resistance, whose members include Shana Agid, Rose Braz, Rachel Herzing, Priya Kandaswamy, Jenna Loyd, and Ari Wohlfeiler; the Prison Neighborhood Arts Project, specifically Damon Locks and Jill Petty; the Sister Jean Hughes Adult High School, including Itzamna Arista, Lasana Kazembe, and Ajitha Reddy; and many other organizations, including Education for Liberation, Project 8, Chicagoland Researchers and Advocates for Transformative Education (CReATE), and the (anti) PIC Teaching Collective. I also work alongside and am shaped by many local and national organizations/mobilizations, including Against Equality, Black and Pink, Black Youth Project 100, Blocks Together, Caucus of Rank and File Educators, Creative Interventions, generationFIVE, Chicago Freedom School, Illinois Safe Schools Alliance, INCITE! Women of Color Against Violence, Prisoner Correspondence Project, Project NIA, Teachers for Social Justice, Transformative Justice Law Project, and the Young Women's Empowerment Project.

I presented public talks that contributed to the development of the ideas in this book at SUNY–Buffalo, Mills College, St. Mary's College, Butler University, Indiana University, the YMCA / United First Methodist Church and University of Illinois in Urbana–Champaign, the University of Colorado–Boulder, the University of California–Berkeley, the University of Illinois–Chicago, Monash University, the University of Minnesota, the New School for Social Research, the University College of London, and the Centre for Crime and Justice Studies at the Open University. The invitation to participate in a number of focused convenings—including Feminists in Game Studies (FiGs), Queer Dreams and Non-Profit Blues, and Engendering Feminisms—enhanced this work and offered me the opportunity to engage with people and movements. I am indebted to the collective labor and thought behind countless community events, from Atlanta to Zion (Illinois), which continue to shape my practice and thinking, including: workshops, rallies, tech-ins, actions, marches, advances (and retreats), round tables, exhibits, and so much more.

A 2009–2010 Lillian Robinson Fellowship at the Simone de Beauvoir Institute at Concordia University planted the seeds for this book. Most invaluable writing started with a 2011–2012 residency with the Institute for Research on Race and Public Policy at the University of Illinois–Chicago. The support and vision of the institute, including Director Beth Richie and Michelle Boyd, Francesca Gaiba, Rhoda Gutierrez, and Ileana Jimenez, and Delania Washington also offered me the opportunity to experience radical intellectual community. Thank you. Anna Mae Duane generously invited me to work with a crew of historians at the 2013 Small Bonds: Enslaved Children, Past and Present Colloquium at the University of Connecticut, Storrs. The 2014 Gender and Incarceration Think Tank at the Institute for Research on Race and Public Policy brought together a smart crew of abolitionists. A 2015–2016 fellowship from the Soros Foundation provided the opportunity to work with Judith Levine.

Sisters Inside and Flat Out in Australia have permanently altered my decolonial feminist landscape. Deep appreciation to Phoebe Barton (and Jessie Boylan), Annie Braybrook, Bree Carlton, Amanda George, Annie Nash, Kim Pate, Emma Russell—all the folks associated with Flat Out and Sisters—and powerhouse Debbie Kilroy. Their generosity and labor is invaluable and transformative.

In addition to all the previously mentioned people, throughout the long writing process I benefited from feedback on chapters and conversations with Ken Addison, Subini Annamma, Ann Aviles, Brooke Beloso, Leslie Bloom, Karma Chavez, Ryan Conrad, Angela Davis, Gina Dent, Bernadine Dohrn, David Feiner, Gabi Fitz, Laura Fugikawa, Brian Galaviz, Julia Gutierrez, Fong Hermes, José Herrera, Francisco Ibáñez-Carrasco, Alice Kim,

Patricia Krueger-Henney, Kristin Li, Pauline Lipman, Heather Middlemass, Tawana Pope, Gloria Ortiz, Yasmin Nair, Dylan Rodríguez, Karen Reyes, Fran Royster, Ann Russo, Roberto Sanabria, Laurie Schaffner, Damien Sojoyner, Dean Spade, Eric Stanley, Emily Thuma, Sabina Vaught, Durene Wheeler, and Connie Wun.

Appreciation to Northeastern Illinois University, particularly to the students, faculty, and staff in the Women's and Gender Studies Program, the Educational Inquiry and Curriculum Studies Department, the Sociology and Justice Studies Departments, the Latino and Latin American Studies Program, and all my comrades in my labor union, University Professional of Illinois, Local 4100. Jason Wiedemann and Erin Warholm at the University of Minnesota Press supported and shaped this project as did the editing staff, including Barbara Goodhouse and Maura Neville.

Tim Barnett, Tyler Steinkamp, Mollie Dowling, Nicole McClelland, and particularly the lovely Laurie Fuller make life full, playful, and queer. Denise, Elena, Stacia, Heather, and Holly Middlemass are the best relations. This project is for Sister Jean Hughes, who lived for the revolution, and for Berlynn Devi Sharma, who will too.

Notes

Introduction

1. I use *queer* in multiple ways throughout this book—as an adjective and as a noun that can, and here does, refer to sexualities and gender identities that challenge normative, binary categories. To this end I include Q for "queer" with LGBT and often use the term queer as shorthand for LGBTQ letters. I also invoke the radical form of queer as a verb, or a stance that assumes and honors human complexities and demands action toward ending oppressive social systems that limit our gendered, sexual, and creative lives.

2. Research by Himmelstein and Bruckner follows a decade of work by advocacy organizations including the Gay, Lesbian and Straight Educators Network (GLSEN) that clearly outlines how LGBTQ and non-gender-conforming youth are also disproportionately targeted for suspension and expulsions and denied the right to an education (for example, see Diaz and Kosciw 2009).

3. See, for example, the impact of the 2012 *Miller v. Alabama* Supreme Court decision, which ruled unconstitutional sentences of life without parole for people convicted of crimes committed while juveniles (Clark 2012), and the Obama administration's 2012 memorandum, titled *Deferred Action for Childhood Arrivals,* which gave some undocumented youth residing in the United States temporary relief from the threat of deportation (Napolitano 2012).

1. Magical Age

1. See chapter 6, "Registering Sex, Rethinking Safety," for a more robust discussion and critique of sex offender registries.

2. Chapter 6, "Registering Sex, Rethinking Safety," offers examples of these tensions.

3. Between 2011 and 2013, twenty-three states did engage in promising measures to reduce the number of youth tried in adult courts or serving time in adult prisons (Juvenile Law Center 2013).

4. Among the first to be prosecuted under the Mann Act, in 1913, was the African American boxer Jack Johnson, who was convicted of "trafficking a

prostitute" from Pittsburgh to Chicago. Critics (and later historians) argued that this prosecution was white and that the woman who was identified as the prostitute was his girlfriend (Luker 1998).

5. Starting in the 1670s, according to Anna Mae Duane (2010), the Virginia legislators established laws requiring that the age of all indentured people arriving without identification papers at the colony must be determined before they received their terms of service. Yet this law applied only to Christians, therefore refusing any age differentiation for nonwhite young people and effectively denying them emergent privileges attached to childhood (131–32).

2. The Trouble with the Child in the Carceral State

1. See chapter 6, "Registering Sex, Rethinking Safety," for more detailed analysis of sex offender registries and community notification laws.

2. The Jacob Wetterling Act and the Adam Walsh Act, both named after white boys, are notable exceptions. The literary theorist Roger Lancaster (2011) points out that while the naming of these laws can appear more populist or democratic than laws that are not directly tied to a specific case or a victim, the personification functions to shut down dissent.

3. A tool available to women to participate in the wider public sphere, maternalism can also be used to trivialize their political work or to reproduce narrow heterogendered and racialized forms of motherhood or family. The political scientist Ange-Marie Hancock (2004) examined the history of women's roles in the development of social welfare programs in the United States and concluded that white women (and to a lesser extent bourgeois black women) used their social and political position as mothers to advocate for social welfare programs for "lesser" but still "worthy" women. This strategy has resulted in longer-term political and social costs: paternalism and the reinforcement of a racialized and gendered nation-state.

4. In 2013, the Walking Free Foundation published the first-ever Global Slavery Index (http://www.globalslaveryindex.org/about/) in an attempt to produce consistent empirical data to document and to subsequently eradicate modern day slavery.

5. Andrea Smith argues that resistant organizing and analysis by people of color to white supremacy can erase important distinctions between how forms of white supremacy are lived in the United States. Smith develops a three-pronged analysis of white supremacy in the United States: slaveability or anti-black racism, anchoring capitalism; genocide, which anchors colonialism; and orientalism, anchoring war (A. Smith 2006).

3. Beyond Reform

1. See the 2013 State of Illinois efficiencies fact sheet: http://ftpcontent4.world now.com/kfvs12/news/FINAL%20Efficiencies%20Fact%20Sheet%20-%20FY2013 %20Budget.pdf.

2. See the Rebalancing Initiative: http://cgfa.ilga.gov/upload/GovernorsD DandMHCRebalancingInitiative.pdf.

3. These discriminatory practices of classification did not (and still do not) go unchallenged. For example, *Larry P. v. Riles* (1972, 1979, 1984, 1986) began as a class action suit in 1971 against the San Francisco Unified School District because African Americans made up 28.5 percent of the total student population and 66 percent of the students were placed in classes for the "Educable Mentally Retarded" (Russo and Talbert-Johnson 1997, 139). The case finally went to trial in 1977, and Judge Robert Peckham subsequently ruled that standardized intelligence tests are biased and track black children into educational dead ends (139). Yet, these select legal wins have not arrested the overrepresentation of students of color, particularly those who are black, First Nations, and Latino, in classifications where they are not only segregated but frequently receive schooling that is not a track to postsecondary education or employment.

4. In 1988, William Horton, who was rearrested in Massachusetts while released on a weekend furlough program, was used by Republicans to discredit the 1988 Democratic presidential candidate, Michael Dukakis.

5. Perhaps these alternatives to incarceration are "kinder, gentler, cages" (Braz 2006), but they are still prisons. People are not at these facilities voluntarily. Many in women's prisons in California oppose the implementation of these community-based alternatives to incarceration (Braz 2006).

6. The Sybil Brand Institute, the former jail for women in Los Angeles, created a "Daddy Tank," where the conditions were "three to four times worse" than in the rest of the jail (Kunzel 2008, 15–16). The "Daddy Tank" segregated women on the basis of their gender appearance and/or behavior: "short hair cuts or no make-up, those wearing trousers with flys [*sic*], jockey shorts, Tshirts or turned up socks, those who spread their legs when they sit, and those who hold a cigarette between thumb and forefinger" (Kunzel 2008, 15).

7. The first recommendation of a 2007 report on the status of transgender people in New York's prisons for those the state considers men, *It Is a War in Here*, produced by the Sylvia Rivera Project, an organization focused on supporting the self-determination and gender liberation of all people, pushed for decarceration and for the system to address the reasons for the high rates of imprisonment faced by transgender communities: "Adopt measures that will reduce the criminalization and imprisonment of transgender, intersex, and gender non-conforming people in recognition of the extreme danger this population

faces while imprisoned" (Sylvia Rivera Law Project 2007, 34). The recommendations forefront the self-determination of transgender people and the demand for clear policies from punitive systems, and do not include a request for transgender prisons or jails or even cells specifically marked for transgender people.

8. In a punishing twist, at CCJ people have to apply to be a part of this pride group, and CCJ officials determine who counts as LGBTQ enough to participate (personal conversation, Ray Noll 2014).

4. Restorative Justice Is Not Enough

1. Lockwood is a pseudonym. The other names of schools throughout the chapter are not. This chapter is based on an article coauthored with Lewis Wallace, Jane Hereth, and Mariame Kaba. Mariame Kaba is the founder and director of Project NIA, an organization dedicated to developing community-based alternatives to youth incarceration. Lewis Wallace is a journalist. Jane Hereth is a social worker. I am one of the founders of the Sister Jean Hughes Adult High School, a diploma-granting institution for formerly incarcerated individuals, and am a faculty member at a local university. All four authors are members of the Chicago Anti Prison–Industrial Complex Teaching Collective, which has created and facilitates introductory workshops and distributes free materials about the prison–industrial complex.

2. An established term within restorative justice movements, peace room refers to a permanently or temporarily allocated space that functions as a designated location for people to congregate to collectively share experiences, build community, and create possibilities for resolution.

3. The Dyett High School informal report was compiled by high school staff and shared with authors in 2008. Fenger data shared as part of a PowerPoint presentation at a Chicago Restorative Justice gathering facilitated by Judge Sophia Hall on March 1, 2012.

4. An exception to this could be the 2010 CPS initiative Culture of Calm, which directed millions of dollars of funding into a year of antiviolence programs across the school district, a small percentage of which went to local RJ partners. In 2011, the city renewed the funding in an attempt to extend the positive effects of the program, which appeared to have helped reduce violence and increase school attendance. This program was triggered by the high-profile death of Derrion Albert (Ahmed-Ullah 2011a).

5. We use parent to represent the range of adults who function as primary caregivers in communities, including grandparents, aunts, uncles, guardians, and older siblings.

6. The High HOPES Campaign involves many of the same organizations that worked on earlier campaigns to have RJ added to the school discipline code.

7. For example, as of 2015 the Community Justice for Youth Institute provides RJ training for students, parents, teachers, and administrators, as well as for community members hoping to implement restorative practices with youth in settings outside of schools. Alternatives, Inc., an organization serving youth on the north side of Chicago, has been training schools and youth across the city in RJ practices since 1996. They operate a summer internship program, bringing peer mediators and peer jury members from around the city together for skill sharing, leadership development, and relationship building. Alternatives, Inc. also uses restorative practices to mediate conflict within their afterschool programs for youth (Community Justice for Youth Institute n.d.).

8. See also the work of Jean Anyon, *Radical Possibilities* (2005).

9. Related to Traub's analysis, schools are sites vulnerable to persistent and often unchecked reform initiatives. As Charles Payne (1997) noted, good ideas can fail in part because schools have been forced to adopt so many reform initiatives over the years that educators find themselves resistant (often with good reasons) to being subjected to the latest foolproof program guaranteed to transform their practice.

10. *The Black Power Mixed Tape 1967–1975* (2011), directed by Göran Olsson.

11. At Lockwood some students chose to go to the traditional detention room because they thought they might be left alone there.

12. *Shadow state* describes the constellation of foundations, nonprofit organizations, for-profit entities, and other nongovernmental forces that engage in providing a range of needed services (Wolch 1990; Gilmore 2009).

13. Organizations we have encountered nationwide that are affiliated with transformative justice and community accountability include Philly Stands Up! (http://phillystandsup.wordpress.com), Communities United Against Violence (http://www.cuav.org), Communities Against Rape and Abuse (http://cara-seattle.blogspot.com), Support New York (http://supportny.org), and many others cited in *The Revolution Starts at Home* (Chen, Dulani, and Piepzna-Samarasinha 2011).

5. Life and Death

1. See Sylvia Wynter's dialogue with Katherine McKittrick in *Sylvia Wynter: On Being Human as Praxis* (McKittrick 2015) for a related discussion where Wynter outlines an ecumenically human origin story that includes a redefinition of the human as hybrid.

2. A body of research suggests the limits of the biomedical model of illness to understand mental health. This chapter does not engage this debate. For further reading, see Franz Fannon's *The Wretched of the Earth* (translation 1963), Erving Goffman's *Stigma: Notes on the Management of Spoiled Identity* (1963), Dorothy Smith's *Women Look at Psychiatry* (1975), Michel Foucault's *Discipline and*

Punishment (1977), and Jonathan Metzl's *The Protest Psychosis: How Schizophrenia Became a Black Disease* (2010).

3. See, for example, Emily Thuma (2014), "'Prison/Psychiatric State': Coalition Politics and Opposition to Institutional Violence in the Feminist 1970s," *Feminist Formations* 26, no. 2, for a detailed discussion of feminist antiviolence organizing that linked antiprison and antipsychiatry struggles.

4. The report states: "In this study, Black women received the fewest number of responses to their résumés, and they were the only group to have the same positive response rate from potential employers, regardless of incarceration history. In focus groups, Black women tended to pinpoint racial discrimination as a barrier to employment prior to and following their period of incarceration. It is possible that a public perception of their culpability—where a criminal record may serve as a proxy for race—tends to impact African Americans more than their counterparts of other ethnic and racial groups" (Morris, Sumner, and Borja 2008, 27).

6. Registering Sex, Rethinking Safety

1. Again, I deliberately use *child, youth, minor,* and *juvenile* somewhat interchangeably. Innocence is a core characteristic of these identities, an association that grows more tenuous with age and experience.

2. Research documents that adults arrested for perpetrating child sexual violence are likely to have experienced sexual violence as a child (Glasser et al. 2001; Bentovim and Williams 1998; Simons, Wurtele, and Durham 2008).

3. Never monolithic, community groups and movements are composed of individuals who often challenge their organizations' mandates; and the "on the ground" work of an organization can look very different from its stated mission. Yet, the National Organization for Women (NOW) (http://www.now.org/), National Coalition Against Domestic Violence (http://www.ncadv.org), V-DAY (http://newsite.vday.org/), and the Human Rights Campaign (http://www.hrc.org/) offer no public materials to challenge registries and community notification laws. A number of organizations have emerged to challenge registries over the past decade—including Women Against Registries (https://www.womenagainstregistry.org/), Reform Sex Offender Laws, Inc. (http://nationalrsol.org/), and National Center for Reason and Justice (http://www.ncrj.org/), yet these organizations do not center antiprison, LGBTQ, or feminist values.

4. See also Humphreys (1970) for a description of the use of police and state resources to monitor and entrap men who had sex with other men in public spaces through the use of hidden cameras, decoys, and other mechanisms of surveillance (83–93).

5. Margot Canaday writes that tracking lesbians (except for those perceived to be engaged in sex work) held less interest for the state, as "male perverts mattered so much more to the state because male citizens did" (13).

6. People convicted of sex offenses are much less likely than convicted non–sex offenders to be rearrested. A Department of Justice study published in 2012 identified the recidivism rate for sex offenders as about 5 percent within five years of being released from custody (Zgoba et al. 2012). Yet, other research does suggests that people convicted of sex offenses are about "four times more likely than non-sex offenders to be arrested for another sex crime after their discharge from prison" (Bureau of Justice Statistics 2003, 1). Of the 9,691 male sex offenders released from prisons in fifteen states in 1994, 5.3 percent were rearrested for a new sex crime within three years of release (Bureau of Justice Statistics 2003, 1). Those convicted as juveniles for sexual offenses have the lowest recidivism rates (Illinois Juvenile Justice Commission 2014).

7. For research on the growth in gated communities, see, for example, the work of the cultural geographer Setha Low (2004, 2005, 2008).

8. The Supreme Court of Canada, in the 2012 Mabior decision, ruled that individuals who know they are HIV-positive can be subjected to criminal prosecution for aggravated sexual assault (with the potential for the maximum sentence of life in prison, including sex offender status) if they do not disclose their HIV status prior to sex. While organizations worked to intervene in this case and presented evidence that would push the court to lower the threshold of what the courts would understand as criminalizable HIV transmission, the courts did not respond to this scientific evidence. With the Mabior decision, the law now appears to require all people with HIV to disclose their status prior to sex regardless of the risk (Makin 2012).

9. For example, until 1993, according to North Carolina law, "a person may not be prosecuted under this article if the victim is the person's legal spouse at the time of the commission of the alleged rape or sexual offense unless the parties are living separate and apart" (National Center for Victims of Crime 2004).

7. Not This

1. For more information on COINTELPRO, see the documentary *COINTEL-PRO 101*, from the Freedom Archives: http://www.freedomarchives.org/Cointel pro.html.

2. Many of the organizations I reference have already been written about in a range of formal and ad hoc publications, including Ching-In Chen, Jai Dulani, and Leah Lakshmi Piepzna-Samarasinha, eds., *The Revolution Starts at Home: Confronting Intimate Violence within Activist Communities* (2011); INCITE! Women

of Color Against Violence, ed., *The Revolution Will Not Be Funded* (2007); *The Abolitionist* (Spring 2012, edited by members of a collective linked to Critical Resistance); Ana Clarissa Rojas Duranzo, Alisa Bierria, and Mimi Kim, eds., "Community Accountability: Emerging Movements to Transform Violence," special issue, *Social Justice: A Journal of Crime Conflict and World Order* 37, no. 4 (2011–2012); and James Ptacek, ed., *Restorative Justice and Violence against Women* (2010).

3. generationFIVE: http://www.generationfive.org/.

4. See Gaurav Jashnani, R. J. Maccani, and Alan Greig (from the Challenging Male Supremacy Project) (2011), "What Does It Feel Like When Change Finally Comes? Male Supremacy, Accountability, and Transformative Justice."

5. At the Critical Criminology conference, Sarah Lamble, a scholar working in the United Kingdom who was on the same panel as Christina Ericson, presented her work on emerging transformative justice initiatives across the United States. Lamble outlined central TJ principles as identified by projects across the United States, particularly the Oakland-based project Creative Interventions and the Storytelling and Organizing Project (STOP) (Lamble 2013).

6. See the Audre Lorde Project's website for an extended description of the work of the Safe OUTside the System Collective: http://alp.org/community/sos.

Bibliography

"Accuracy in Criminal Background Checks." 2012. Editorial. *New York Times.*

Acey, Camille. 2000. "This Is an Illogical Statement: Dangerous Trends in Anti-Prison Activism." *Social Justice Journal* 27, no. 3: 206–11.

Ackerman, Alissa R., Andrew Harris, Jill Levenson, and Kristen Zgoba. 2011. "Who are the people in your neighborhood? A descriptive analysis of individuals on public sex offender registries." *International Journal of Law and Psychiatry* 34: 149–59.

Adams, David Wallace. 1988. "Fundamental Considerations: The Deep Meaning of Native American Schooling, 1880–1900." *Harvard Educational Review* 58, no. 1: 1–28.

Advancement Project. 2010. "Test, Punish, and Push Out: How 'Zero Tolerance' and High-Stakes Testing Funnel Youth into the School-to-Prison Pipeline." March. http://b.3cdn.net/advancement/d05cb2181a4545db07_r2im6caqe.pdf.

Agan, Amanda. 2011. "Sex Offender Registries: Fear Without Function?" *The Journal of Law & Economics* 54 (1): 207–39.

Agustín, Laura María. 2007. *Sex at the Margins: Migration, Labour Markets and the Rescue Industry.* London: Zed Books.

Ahmed, Sarah. 2004. *The Cultural Politics of an Emotion.* London, UK: Routledge.

Ahmed-Ullah, Noreen. 2010. "In CPS, Library Void Goes beyond One Sit-In." *Chicago Tribune,* October 26.

———. 2011a. "Chicago Public Schools Officials Eyeing Updated Security Cameras for 14 High Schools." *Chicago Tribune,* July 24.

———. 2011b. "More Tolerance in New CPS Code of Conduct." *Chicago Tribune,* July 28.

———. 2011c. "Programs for At-Risk Students' Safety at Risk." *Chicago Tribune,* June 9.

Ahmed-Ullah, Noreen, John Chase, and Bob Secter. 2013. "CPS Approves Largest School Closure in Chicago's History." *Chicago Tribune,* May 23.

Alexander, Michelle. 2010. *The New Jim Crow: Mass Incarceration in the Age of Colorblindness.* New York: New Press.

Allard, Patricia. 2002. "Life Sentences: Denying Welfare Benefits to Women Convicted of Drug Offenses." *Sentencing Project.* February, http://www.sentencingproject.org/doc/publications/women_lifesentences.pdf.

Alternatives, Inc. n.d. *"What Is Restorative Justice?"* http://www.alternativesyouth.org/restorative_justice/what-restorative-justice.

American Bar Association Juvenile Justice Center. 2004. "Cruel and Unusual Punishment: The Juvenile Death Penalty; Adolescence, Brain Development and Legal Culpability." January. http://www.abanet.org/crimjust/juvjus/Adolescence.pdf.

American Civil Liberties Union. 2005. "ACLU Applauds Unanimous Kansas Supreme Court Decision Reversing Conviction of Gay Teen Unfairly Punished under "Romeo and Juliet" Law." https://www.aclu.org/news/aclu-applauds-unanimous-kansas-supreme-court-decision-reversing-conviction-gay-teen-unfairly.

American Civil Liberties Union of Illinois. 2015. *Stop and Frisk in Chicago.* March. http://www.aclu-il.org/wp-content/uploads/2015/03/ACLU_StopandFrisk_6.pdf.

American Federation of Teachers. n.d. "Academic Staffing Crisis." http://www.aft.org/issues/highered/acadstaffing.cfm.

Amnesty International. 2006. "Stonewalled: Still Demanding Respect." Amnesty International. http://www.amnesty.org/en/library/asset/AMR51/001/2006/en/f420c754-d46f-11dd-8743-d305bea2b2c7/amr510012006en.pdf.

Anderson, James D. 1988. *The Education of Blacks in the South, 1860–1935.* Chapel Hill: University of North Carolina Press.

Anyon, Jean. 2005. *Radical Possibilities.* New York: Routledge.

Ariès, Philippe. 1962. *Centuries of Childhood: A Social History of Family Life.* New York: Random House.

Armstrong, Cheryl. 2012. "Heartbreaking School Bully Complaints." *Courthouse News Service,* June 5. http://www.courthousenews.com/2012/06/05/47115.htm.

Arnett, Jeffrey Jensen. 2000. "Emerging Adulthood: A Theory of Development from the Late Teens through the Twenties." *American Psychologist* 55, no. 5: 469–80.

Arts Alliance Illinois. 2005. Arts at the Core: Every School, Every Student. Illinois Arts Education Initiative. http://www.artsalliance.org/arts-education/resources/research.

Ashley, Jessica, and Kimberly Burke. 2009. *Implementing Restorative Justice: A Guide for Schools.* Illinois Criminal Justice Information Authority. http://www.icjia.state.il.us/public/pdf/BARJ/SCHOOL%20BARJ%20GUIDEBOOOK.pdf.

Austin, Roy L., Jr. 2013. "Investigation of the Escambia County Jail." *U.S. Department of Justice.* May 22, http://www.justice.gov/iso/opa/resources/7492013522113545964446.pdf.

Ayers, William. 1998. *A Kind and Just Parent: The Children of Juvenile Court.* Boston: Beacon Press.

Ayers, William, Bernadine Dohrn, and Rick Ayers, eds. 2001. *Zero Tolerance: Resisting the Drive for Punishment in Our Schools.* New York: New Press.

Bagget, Charles, Kellie Magnuson, Margaret Hughes, Martine Caverl, Nelida Torres, Ora Schub, and Robert Spicer. 2007. "AREA Dialogue: Schoolhouse to Jailhouse Pipeline." *AREA Chicago*. http://www.areachicago.org/p/issues/issue -4/schoolhouse-jailhouse-pipeline/.

Ballout, Dana. 2013. "Chicago's Mental Health Clinic Closings: 20 Months Later." *Al Jazeera*. December 26, http://america.aljazeera.com/watch/shows /the-stream/multimedia/chicago-mental-healthclosings20monthsafter.html.

Barkley Brown, Elsa. 1992. "What Has Happened Here: The Politics of Difference in Women's History and Feminist Politics." *Feminist Studies* 18, no. 2 (Summer): 295–312.

Barnes, Robert. 2012. "Supreme Court Says States May Not Impose Mandatory Life Sentences on Juvenile Murderers." *Washington Post*, June 25.

———. 2013. "Supreme Court Says Law Can't Dictate Anti-AIDS Groups' Speech." *Washington Post*, June 20.

Beckett, Katherine, and Naomi Murakawa. 2012. "Mapping the Shadow Carceral State: Toward an Institutionally Capacious Approach to Punishment." *Theoretical Criminology* 16, no. 2: 221–44.

Beitsch, Rebecca. 2015. "States Rethink Restrictions on Food Stamps, Welfare for Drug Felons." Pew Charitable Trust. July 30. http://www.pewtrusts.org/en /research-and-analysis/blogs/stateline/2015/07/30/states-rethink-restrictions -on-food-stamps-welfare-for-drug-felons.

Ben-Moshe, Liat. 2013. Disabling Incarceration: Connecting Disability to Divergent Confinements in the USA. *Critical Sociology* 39, no. 3: 385–403.

Bentovim, Arnon and Bryn Williams. 1998. "Children and Adolescents: Victims Who Become Perpetrators." *Advances in Psychiatric Treatment* 4, no. 2: 101–7.

Berger, Joseph. 2009. "Despite Law, Few Trafficking Arrests." *New York Times*, December 3.

Berlant, Lauren. 2011. *Cruel Optimism*. Durham, NC: Duke University Press.

———. 2004. *Compassion: The Culture and Politics of an Emotion*. New York: Routledge.

Bernstein, Elizabeth. 2010. "Militarized Humanitarianism Meets Carceral Feminism: The Politics of Sex, Rights, and Freedom in Contemporary Antitrafficking Campaigns." *Signs: Journal of Women in Culture and Society* 36, no. 1: 45–71.

Bernstein, Robin. 2011. *Racial Innocence: Performing American Childhood from Slavery to Civil Rights*. New York: New York University Press.

Best, Joel. 1990. *Threatened Children: Rhetoric and Concern about Child-Victims*. Chicago: University of Chicago Press.

———. 2004. *Deviance: Career of a Concept*. Belmont, Calif.: Wadsworth.

Black, M.C., K.C. Basile, M.J. Breiding, S.G. Smith, M.L. Walters, M.T. Merrick, J. Chen, and M.R. Stevens, 2011. *The National Intimate Partner and Sexual*

Violence Survey (NISVS): 2010 Summary Report. Atlanta, GA: National Center for Injury Prevention and Control, Centers for Disease Control and Prevention.

The Black Power Mixtape 1967–1975. 2011. DVD. Directed by Göran Olsson. Sweden: Story ABT.

Bloom, Barbara, Barbara Owen, and Stephanie Covington. 2004. "Women Offenders and the Gendered Effects of Public Policy." *Review of Policy Research* 21, no. 1 : 1–24.

"Boy, 13, Accused of Killing 2-Year-Old Brother Is Youngest Florida Inmate Awaiting Trial." 2012. *New York Daily News,* September 16.

Braddock, D., R. Hemp, M. C. Rizzolo, L. Haffer, S. Tanis, and J. Wu. 2011. *The State of the States in Developmental Disabilities.* Boulder: University of Colorado, Department of Psychiatry and Coleman Institute for Cognitive Disabilities.

Braz, Rose. 2006. "Kinder, Gentler, Gender Responsive Cages." *Women, Girls and Criminal Justice,* October/November: 87–91.

Brewer, Holly. 2005. *Birth or Consent: Children, Law, and the Anglo-American Revolution in Authority.* Chapel Hill: University of North Carolina Press.

Briggs, Laura. 1998. "Discourses of 'Forced Sterilization' in Puerto Rico." *Differences* 10, no. 2: 30–66.

Bronner, Ethan. 2012. "Sentencing Ruling Reflects Rethinking on Juvenile Justice." *New York Times,* June 26.

Brown, Emma. 2013. "DC to Close 15 Underenrolled Schools." *Washington Post,* January 17.

Brown, Mark. 2012. "Ace Pianist—Once an Undocumented Korean Immigrant—Is the Original Dreamer." *Chicago Sun Times,* August 3.

Brown, Patricia Leigh. 2013. "Opening Up, Students Transform a Vicious Circle." *New York Times,* April 3.

Browne, Angela, Brenda Miller, and Eugene Maguin. 1999. "Prevalence and Severity of Lifetime Physical and Sexual Victimization among Incarcerated Women." *International Journal of Law and Psychiatry* 22, nos. 3–4: 301–22.

Browne, Judith A. 2003. "Derailed: The School to Jailhouse Track." *Advancement Project.* http://b.3cdn.net/advancement/c509d077028b4d0544_mlbrq3seg.pdf.

Bumiller, Kristin. 2008. *In an Abusive State: How Neoliberalism Appropriated the Feminist Movement against Sexual Violence.* Durham, N.C.: Duke University Press.

Bump, Phillip. 2015. "Hillary Clinton Hopes to Undo the Mass Incarceration System Bill Clinton Helped Build." *Washington Post,* April 29.

Bureau of Justice Statistics. 2000. "Sexual Assault of Young Children as Reported to Law Enforcement: Victim, Incident, and Offender Characteristics in 2000." July. http://www.bjs.gov/content/pub/pdf/saycrle.pdf.

———. 2003. "Recidivism of Sex Offenders Released from Prison in 1994." November. http://www.bjs.gov/content/pub/pdf/rsorp94.pdf.

———. 2012. "One in 34 U.S. Adults under Correctional Supervision in 2011, Lowest Rate since 2000." November 29. http://www.bjs.gov/content/pub/press /cpus11ppus11pr.cfm.

———. 2014. "In 2013 the State Prison Population Rose for the First Time since 2009." Press release, Bureau of Justice Statistics. September 16. http://www.bjs .gov/content/pub/press/p13pr.cfm.

———. 2014. "Recidivism Of Prisoners Released In 30 States In 2005: Patterns From 2005 to 2010." April 22. http://www.bjs.gov/index.cfm?ty=pbdetail&iid =4986.

Canaday, Margot. 2009. *The Straight State: Sexuality and Citizenship in Twentieth Century America*. Princeton, N.J.: Princeton University Press.

Cannold, Julie. 2012. "Teen Says Bullies Beat Him, Sues New York Schools." *CNN*, June 21. http://www.cnn.com/2012/06/20/justice/new-york-bullying-attack-blind/.

Caputo, Angela. 2010. "Seventeen." *Chicago Reporter*, August 31.

———. 2013. "Cell Blocks." *Chicago Reporter*, March 1.

Carpenter, Catherine, and A. Beverlin. 2012. "The Evolution of Unconstitutionality in Sex Offender Registration Laws." *Hastings Law Review Journal* 63: 1071–1133.

Cathcart, Rebecca. 2008. "Boy's Killing, Labeled a Hate Crime, Stuns a Town." *New York Times*, February 23.

CBS. 2012. "New York Moves to Ban Sex Offenders from Online Gaming Networks." http://newyork.cbslocal.com/2012/04/05/new-york-moves-to-ban-sex -offenders-from-online-gaming-networks.

CBS Chicago News. 2012. "Village of Crete Calls Off Plans for Immigrant Detention Center." June 12. http://chicago.cbslocal.com/2012/06/12/village-of-crete -calls-off-plans-for-immigrant-detention-center/.

Chachkevitch, Alexandra. 2012. "Door Shutting on Residents of Last Unrenovated Cabrini-Green Row Houses." *Chicago Tribune*, February 16.

Chammah, Maurice. 2012. "A Growing Battle for Exoneration." *Texas Tribune*, November 17.

———. 2014. "The Mystery of the San Antonio Four." *Texas Observer*, January 2.

Chapkis, Wendy. 2003. "Trafficking, Migration, and the Law: Protecting Innocents, Punishing Immigrants." *Gender and Society* 17, no. 6: 923–37.

Chen, Ching-In, Jai Dulani, and Leah Lakshmi Piepzna-Samarasinha, eds. 2011. *The Revolution Starts at Home: Confronting Intimate Violence within Activist Communities*. Boston: South End Press.

"Chicago Homicides Outnumber U.S. Troop Killings in Afghanistan." 2012. *Huffington Post*, June 16. http://www.huffingtonpost.com/2012/06/16/chicago -homicide-rate-wor_n_1602692.html.

Child Trends. 2015. "All 51 States Have a Bullying Law. Now What?" *Child Trends*, April 27. http://www.childtrends.org/all-50-states-now-have-a-bullying-law -now-what/.

Christie, Nils. 2000. *Crime Control as Industry: Towards Gulags, Western Style.* 3rd ed. London: Routledge.

Clark, Maggie. 2012. "States Reconsider Juvenile Life Sentences." *Pew Charitable Trusts,* July 27. http://www.pewtrusts.org/en/research-and-analysis/blogs/stateline/2012/07/27/states-reconsider-juvenile-life-sentences.

Clausen, Jan. 1992. "The End of History." *Feminist Studies* 18, no. 2 (Summer): 421–29.

Coates, Tah-Nehisi. 2013. "The Gangs of Chicago." *The Atlantic,* December 18.

Cohen, Cathy. 2005. "Punks, Bulldaggers, and Welfare Queens: The Radical Potential of Queer Politics?" In *Black Queer Studies,* edited by E. Patrick Johnson and Mae G. Henderson. Durham, N.C.: Duke University Press.

———. 2012. "Death and Rebirth of a Movement: Queering Critical Ethnic Studies." *Social Justice* 37, no. 4: 126–32.

Cohen, Patricia. 2010. "Long Road to Adulthood Is Growing Even Longer." *New York Times,* June 11.

Coley, Richard J., and Paul E. Barton. 2006. "Locked Up and Locked Out: An Educational Perspective on the U.S. Prison Population." Educational Testing Service, February. http://files.eric.ed.gov/fulltext/ED496101.pdf.

"Commons Approves Bill to Lower Gay Age of Consent." 2000. *The Guardian,* February 11. http://www.theguardian.com/politics/2000/feb/11/uk.politicalnews1.

Community Justice for Youth Institute [CJYI]. n.d. *CJYI and Restorative Justice.* http://cjyi.org/cjyi-services.

Correctional Association of New York. 2009. "Education from the Inside, Out: The Multiple Benefits of College Programs in Prison." January. http://www.correctionalassociation.org/wp-content/uploads/2012/05/Higher_Education_Full_Report_2009.pdf.

Corrigan, Rose. 2006. "Making Meaning of Megan's Law." *Law and Social Inquiry* 31: 267–312.

"CPS Discipline Code Revised—Slightly." 2005. *Community Media Workshop,* August 24. http://www.newstips.org/2005/08/cps-discipline-code-revised-slightly/.

CR 10 Publications Collective. 2008. Introduction to *Abolition Now! 10 Years of Strategy and Struggle against the Prison Industrial Complex.* Oakland, Calif.: AK Press.

Crenshaw, Kimberlé Williams. 1994. "Mapping the Margins: Intersectionality, Identity Politics, and Violence against Women of Color." In *The Public Nature of Private Violence,* edited by Martha A. Fineman and Roxanne Mykitiuk. New York: Routledge.

———. 2015. "Black Girls Matter: Pushed Out, Overpoliced and Underprotected." African American Policy Forum. www.atlanticphilanthropies.org/sites/default/files/uploads/BlackGirlsMatter_Report.pdf.

Critical Resistance. 2012. *The Abolitionist.* Spring. http://www.criticalresistance.org/.

———. n.d. "Not So Common Language." http://www.criticalresistance.org/.

Dai, Serena. 2010. "Quinn Names Acting Director for Corrections Dept." *Chicago Tribune*, September 3.

Dardick, Hal. 2000. "Jury to Exert Peer Pressure." *Chicago Tribune*, November 29.

Davey, Monica. 2006. "Iowa's Residency Rules Drive Sex Offenders Underground." *New York Times*, March 15.

———. 2010. "Safety Is Issue as Budget Cuts Free Prisoners." *New York Times*, March 4.

———. 2013. "Chicago Killings Fall, as Officials Praise Progress." *New York Times*, December 31.

Davey, Monica, and Abby Goodnough. 2007. "Doubts Rise as States Hold Sex Offenders after Prison." *New York Times*, March 4.

Davies, Nick. 2009. "Inquiry Fails to Find Single Trafficker Who Forced Anybody into Prostitution." *The Guardian*, October 19.

Davis, Angela. 1996. "Incarcerated Women: Transformative Strategies." *Black Renaissance / Renaissance Noir* 1, no. 1: 20–34.

———. 2000. *States of Confinement: Policing, Detention and Prison.* Edited by Joy James. New York: St. Martin's Press.

———. 2003. *Are Prisons Obsolete?* New York: Seven Stories Press.

———. 2005. *Abolition Democracy: Prisons, Democracy, and Empire.* New York: Seven Stories Press.

———. 2010. *Narrative of the Life of Frederick Douglass, an American Slave, Written by Himself: A New Critical Education.* San Francisco: City Lights Books.

Davis, Lennard J., ed. 2010. *The Disability Studies Reader.* New York: Routledge.

Debonis, Mike. 2014. "'Ban the Box' Bill Gets D.C. Council's Tentative Approval after Years of Debate." *Washington Post,* June 3.

D'Emilio, John, and Estelle Freedman. 1988. *Intimate Matters: A History of Sexuality in America.* New York: HarperCollins.

DePrang, Emily. 2012. "Life on the List." *Texas Observer,* May 31.

"Derrion Albert's Death May Be Rooted in School Closures." 2009. *NBC Chicago,* October 7. http://www.nbcchicago.com/news/local/holder-arne-duncan -fenger-city-hall-daley-63642507.html.

Devereaux, Ryan. 2012. "Scrutiny Mounts as NYPD 'Stop-and-Frisk' Searches Hit Record High." *The Guardian,* February 14. http://www.theguardian.com /world/2012/feb/14/nypd-stop-frisk-record-high.

Dewan, Shaila. 2006. "Georgia Man Fights Conviction as Molester." *New York Times,* December 19. http://www.nytimes.com/2006/12/19/us/19georgia.html?_r=0.

Diaz, Elizabeth M. and Joseph G. Kosciw. 2009. *Shared Differences: The Experiences of Lesbian, Gay, Bisexual, and Transgender Students of Color in Our Nation's Schools.* New York: GLSEN.

Díaz-Cotto, Juanita. 2006. *Chicana Lives and Criminal Justice: Voices from El Barrio.* Austin: University of Texas Press.

Dilulio, John J. 1995. "The Coming of the Super-Predators." *Weekly Standard,* November 27.

Dobbs, David. 2011. "Beautiful Brains." *National Geographic.*

Dohrn, Bernadine. 2000. "Look Out, Kid, It Is Something You Did: The Criminalization of Children." In *The Public Assault on America's Children: Poverty, Violence, and Juvenile Injustice,* edited by Valerie Polakow. New York: Teachers College Press.

Duane, Anna Mae. 2010. *Suffering Childhood in Early America: Violence, Race, and the Making of the Child Victim.* Athens: University of Georgia Press.

Dumke, Mick, and Ben Joravsky. 2011. "The Grass Gap." *Chicago Reader.* http://www.chicagoreader.com/chicago/chicago-marijuana-arrest-statistics/Content?oid=4198958.

Duncan, Garrett A. 2000. "Urban Pedagogies and the Celling of Adolescents of Color." *Social Justice: A Journal of Crime Conflict and World Order* 27: 29–42.

Durazo, Ana Clarissa Rojas, Alisa Bierria, and Mimi Kim, eds. 2012. "Community Accountability: Emerging Movements to Transform Violence." Special issue of *Social Justice: A Journal of Crime Conflict and World Order* 37, no. 4.

Eby, Charlotte. 2005. "Court Upholds Housing Restrictions for Sex Offenders." *Sioux City Journal,* July 30.

Edelman, Lee. 2004. *No Future: Queer Theory and the Death Drive.* Durham, N.C.: Duke University Press.

Edholm, Charlton. 1899. *Traffic in Girls and Work of Rescue Mission.* Chicago: Charlton Edholm.

Education Law Center. 2013. "Bullying." March 1. http://www.edlawcenter.org/issues/bullying.html.

Eisenman, Stephen. 2010. "The Scandal That Wasn't or How Not to Reform the Prison System in Illinois. *Monthly Review.* September 15. http://mrzine.monthlyreview.org/2010/eisenman150910.html.

Emmer, Pascal, Adrian Lowe, and R. Barrett Marshall. 2011. "This Is a Prison, Glitter Is Not Allowed: Experiences of Trans and Gender Variant People in Pennsylvania's Prison Systems." *The Hearts on a Wire Collective.* http://www.scribd.com/doc/56677078/This-is-a-Prison-Glitter-is-Not-Allowed.

"End Mass Incarceration Now." 2014. *New York Times,* May 24.

Ericson, Christina. 2013. Panelist. "Critical Criminology in a Changing World—Tradition and Innovation," European Group for the Study of Deviance and Social Control Annual Meeting. Oslo, Norway, August 29–September 1.

Erikson, Kurt. 2013. "Dwight Prison Plan Advancing." *Quad City Times,* June 12.

Erisman, Wendy, and Jeanne Bayer Contardo. 2005. "Learning to Reduce Recidivism." *Institute for Higher Education Policy,* November. http://www.ihep.org /assets/files/publications/g-l/LearningReduceRecidivism.pdf.

Escobar, Martha. 2010. "Understanding the Roots of Latina Migrants' Captivity." *Social Justice* 35, no. 2: 7–20.

Eskridge, William. 2008. *Dishonorable Passions: Sodomy Laws in America, 1861–2003.* New York: Viking Books.

Espiritu, Yen Le. 1992. *Asian American Panethnicity: Bridging Institutions and Identities.* Philadelphia: Temple University Press.

Evans, Linda. 2004. "Playing Global Cop: U.S. Militarism and the Prison Industrial Complex." In *Global Lockdown: Race, Gender, and the Prison-Industrial Complex,* edited by Julia Sudbury. New York: Routledge.

Faith, Karlene, and Anne Near. 2005. *13 Women: Parables from Prison.* Vancouver: Douglas and McIntyre.

Fanon, Franz. 1963. *The Wretched of the Earth.* Trans. Constance Farrington. New York: Grove Press.

Fay, Kay. 2014. "Likely Cuomo Challengers Sound Off on Prison College Plan." *Legislative Gazette,* March 3. http://www.legislativegazette.com/Articles-Top -Stories-c-2014–03–03–87026.113122-Likely-Cuomo-challengers-sound-off-on -prison-college-plan.html.

Feel Tank Chicago. 2008. Manifesto. http://www.feeltankchicago.net/.

Feld, Barry. 1999. *Bad Kids: Race and the Transformation of the Juvenile Court.* New York: Oxford University Press.

Ferri, Beth and David Connor. 2004. "Special Education and the Subverting of Brown." *Journal of Gender, Race, & Justice.* 8, no. 1: 57–74.

Feuer, Alan. 2005. "Pataki Uses State Law to Hold Sex Offenders after Prison." *New York Times,* October 4.

Fine, Michelle, and Sara McClelland. 2006. "Sexuality Education and Desire: Still Missing after All These Years." *Harvard Educational Review* 76, no. 3: 297–338.

Fine, Michelle, Maria Elena Torre, Kathy Boudin, Iris Bowen, Judith Clark, Donna Hylton, Migdalia Martinez, "Missy," Rosemarie A. Roberts, Pamela Smart, and Debora Upegui. 2001. "Changing Minds: The Impact of College in Prison." *Prison Policy,* September. http://www.prisonpolicy.org/scans/changing _minds.pdf.

Finkelhor, David, Richard Ormrod, and Mark Chaffin. 2009. *Juveniles Who Commit Sex Offenses against Minors.* U.S. Department of Justice, Office of Justice Programs, Office of Juvenile Justice and Delinquency Prevention. https://www.ncjrs.gov/pdffiles1/ojjdp/227763.pdf.

Flaherty, Jordan. 2010. "Her Crime? Sex Work in New Orleans." *Colorlines.* January 13. http://www.colorlines.com/articles/her-crime-sex-work-new-orleans.

————. 2011. "Federal Civil Rights Suit Challenges Louisiana's Felony Sex Work Law." *Colorlines*, March 17. http://www.colorlines.com/articles/federal-civil-rights-suit-challenges-louisianas-felony-sex-work-law.

"F.O.R.C.E. Fighting to Overcome Records and Create Equality." n.d. Community Renewal Society. http://www.communityrenewalsociety.org/force-fighting-overcome-records-and-create-equality.

Ford, Glen. 2012. "Black Teachers Fired en Masse." *Black Agenda Report*, February 22. http://blackagendareport.com/content/black-teachers-fired-en-masse.

Foucault, Michel. 1977. *Discipline and Punish: The Birth of the Prison*. Translated by Alan Sheridan, London: Allen Lane, Penguin.

————. 1988. "Technologies of the Self." A seminar with Michel Foucault at the University of Vermont, October 1982. In *Technologies of the Self: A Seminar with Michel Foucault*, edited by L. H. Martin, H. Gutman, and P. H. Hutton. Amherst: University of Massachusetts Press.

————. 1993. "Alternatives à la prison: Diffusion ou décroissance du contrôle social?" *Criminologie* 26, no. 1: 13–34.

Fraser, Joelle. 2003. "An American Seduction: Portrait of a Prison Town." In *Prison Nation: The Warehousing of America's Poor*, edited by Tara Herivel and Paul Wright. New York: Routledge.

Fraser, Nancy. 1997. *Justice Interruptus: Critical Reflections on the "Postsocialist" Condition*. New York: Routledge.

Freedman, Estelle B. 1981. *Their Sisters Keepers: Women's Prison Reform in America, 1830—1930*. Ann Arbor: University of Michigan Press.

"Frequently Asked Questions." n.d. *Global Slavery Index 2013*. http://www.globalslaveryindex.org/faq/.

Friedman, Matt. 2010. "NJ Assembly, Senate Pass 'Anti-Bullying Bill of Rights' in Wake of Tyler Clementi's Death." *NJ.com*, November 22. http://www.nj.com/news/index.ssf/2010/11/nj_assembly_passes_anti-bullyi.html.

"Friends Say Classmate Killed Self after Bullying on Sexuality." 2011. WSNV, December 7. http://www.wsmv.com/story/16213348/friends-say-classmate-killed-self-after-bullying-on-sexuality.

Frost, Natasha, Judith Greene, and Kevin Pranis. 2008. "The Punitiveness Report, Part I: Growth Trends and Recent Research." Women's Prison Association. http://www.wpaonline.org/institute/hardhit/part1.htm#_ftnref25.

Gabriel, Trip. 2013. "Inquiry in Cover-Up of Ohio Rape Yields Indictment of Four Adults." *New York Times*, November 25. http://www.nytimes.com/2013/11/26/us/steubenville-school-superintendent-indicted-in-rape-case.html?_r=0.

Garcia, Monique. 2009. "Gov. Pat Quinn Admits Mistake on Early-Release of Prisoners, Blames Corrections Chief." *Chicago Tribune*, December 31.

————. 2012. "Guards' Union, Quinn Fight over Prison Closures." *Chicago Tribune*, August 27.

Garcia, Monique, and David Heinzmann. 2010. "Early-Release Program 'Ill Conceived,' Panel Say." *Chicago Tribune*, August 13.

Garda, Robert. 2005. "The New IDEA: Shifting Educational Paradigms to Achieve Racial Equality in Special Education." *College of Law Alabama Law Review* 56, no. 4: 1071–134.

Garland-Thomson, Rosemarie. 2002. "Integrating Disability, Transforming Feminist Theory." *NWSA Journal* 14, no. 3: 1–32.

Gender JUST. 2010. *Gender JUST Statement on Recent Suicides.* October 19. http://queertoday.ning.com/profiles/blogs/gender-just-statement-on.

generationFIVE. 2007. "Towards Transformative Justice." http://www.generation five.org/downloads/G5_Toward_Transformative_Justice.pdf.

———. n.d. "Our Approach." http://www.generationfive.org/index.asp?sec=3& pg=48.

Gilliam, Walter S. 2005. "Prekindergarteners Left Behind: Expulsion Rates in State PreKindergarten Programs." Foundation for Child Development, May 1. http://fcd-us.org/sites/default/files/Expulsion/Completereport.pdf.

Gilmore, Ruth Wilson. 2007. *Golden Gulag: Prisons, Surplus, Crisis, and Opposition in Globalizing California.* Berkeley: University of California Press.

———. 2009. "In the Shadow of the Shadow State." In *The Revolution Will Not Be Funded: Beyond the Non-profit Industrial Complex,* edited by INCITE! Women of Color Against Violence. New York: South End Press.

Gingrich, Newt, and Pat Nolan. 2011. "Prison Reform: A Smart Way for States to Save Money and Lives." *Washington Post*, January 7.

Giordano, Scott A. 1999. "Lawyers: Sex Offender Registry Still Unfairly Targets Gay Men and Victimless Crimes." *Bay Windows*, September 30.

Gira-Grant, Melissa. 2014. "The Price of a Sex Slave Rescue Fantasy." *New York Times*, May 29.

Glasser, M., I. Kolvin, D. Campbell, A. Glasser, I. Leitch, and S. Farrelly. 2001. "Cycle of Child Sexual Abuse: Links between Being a Victim and Becoming a Perpetrator." *British Journal of Psychiatry* 179, no. 6: 482–94.

Glaze, Lauren, Danielle Kaeble, Todd Minton, and Anastasios Tsoutis. 2015. *Correctional Populations in the United States, 2014. Bureau of Justice Statistics Bulletin.* U.S. Department of Justice. December 29. http://www.bjs.gov/content /pub/pdf/cpus14.pdf.

Goetz, Edward. 2013. *New Deal Ruins: Race, Economic Justice, and Public Housing Policy.* Ithaca, N.Y.: Cornell University Press.

Goffman, Erving. 1963. *Stigma: Notes on the Management of Spoiled Identity.* New York: Prentice-Hall.

Goldberg, Michelle. 2014. "Why Marriage Won't Solve Poverty." *The Nation.* January 15.

Golgowski, Nina. 2014. "Transgender Teen Bullied at School Faces Criminal Charges for Fight Which Only Suspended Other Girls." *New York Daily News,* January 9.

Gonnerman, Jennifer. 2004. "Million-Dollar Blocks." *Village Voice,* November 9.

González, Roberto, Hugh Gusterson, and David Price. 2009. "Introduction: War, Culture and Counterinsurgency." In *The Counter-counterinsurgency Manual,* edited by Network of Concerned Anthropologists. Chicago: Prickly Paradigm Press.

Goode, Erica. 2013. "U.S. Prison Populations Decline, Reflecting New Approach to Crime." *New York Times,* July 25.

Goodman, Brenda. 2007. "Georgia Court Frees Man Convicted in Sex Case." *New York Times,* October 27.

Gorgol, Laura E., and Brian A. Sponsler. 2011. "Unlocking Potential: Results of a National Survey of Postsecondary Education in State Prisons." Institute for Higher Education Policy, May. http://www.ihep.org/assets/files/publications /s-z/Unlocking_Potential-PSCE_FINAL_REPORT_May_2011.pdf.

Gorner, Jeremy. 2013. "Police Stops Raise Suspicions." *Chicago Tribune.* January 4.

Gottschalk, Marie. 2015. *Caught: The Prison State and the Lockdown of American Politics.* Princeton, N.J.: Princeton University Press.

Gould, Jens Erik. 2011. "Seth's Law: Can a Bullied Boy Leave California a Legal Legacy?" *Time,* August 5.

Grant, Jamie, Lisa Mottet, and Justin Tanis. 2011. *Injustice at Every Turn: A Report of the National Transgender Discrimination Survey.* http://www.thetaskforce .org/downloads/reports/reports/ntds_summary.pdf.

Greene, Judith, Kevin Pranis, and Jason Ziedenberg. 2006. "Disparity by Design: How Drug-Free Zone Laws Impact Racial Disparity–and Fail to Protect Youth." *Justice Policy Institute Report.* http://www.justicepolicy.org/reports /SchoolZonesReport306.pdf.

Greenfeld, Lawrence, and Steven K. Smith. 1999. "American Indians and Crime." *U.S. Department of Justice—Bureau of Justice Statistics,* February. http:// www.bjs.gov/content/pub/pdf/aic.pdf.

Greenhouse, Linda. 2007. "Justices Limit the Use of Race in School Plans for Integration." *New York Times,* June 29.

Gregory, Anne, Russell J. Skiba, and Pedro A. Noguera. 2010. "The Achievement Gap and the Discipline Gap: Two Sides of the Same Coin?" *Educational Researcher* 39, no. 1: 59–68.

Griffin, Patrick, Sean Addie, Benjamin Adams, and Kathy Firestine. 2011. *Trying Juveniles as Adults: An Analysis of State Transfer Laws and Reporting.* U.S. Department of Justice, National Center for Juvenile Justice. http://www.ncjj .org/pdf/Transfer_232434.pdf.

Gustafson, Kaaryn. 2011. *Cheating Welfare: Public Assistance and the Criminalization of Poverty.* New York: New York University Press.

Haig-Brown, Celia. 1988. *Resistance and Renewal: Surviving the Indian Residential School*. Vancouver: Arsenal Pulp Press.

Halberstam, Judith. 2011. *The Queer Art of Failure*. Durham, N.C.: Duke University Press.

Hancock, Ange-Marie. 2004. *The Politics of Disgust: The Public Identity of the Welfare Queen*. New York: New York University Press.

Haney, Lynne. 2010. *Offending Women: Power, Punishment, and the Regulation of Desire*. Berkeley: University of California Press.

Harkins, Gillian. 2009. *Everybody's Family Romance: Reading Incest in Neoliberal America*. Minneapolis: University of Minnesota Press.

Harkins, Gillian, and Erica Meiners. 2014. "Beyond Crisis: College in Prison through the Abolition Undercommons." "Theory" section of *Lateral: Cultural Studies Association Journal (3)*. Spring. http://csalateral.org/issue3/theory/harkins-meiners.

Harlow, Caroline Wolf. 2003. "Education and Correctional Populations." U.S. Department of Justice—Bureau of Justice Statistics, January. http://www.bjs.gov/content/pub/pdf/ecp.pdf.

Harney, Stefano and Fred Moten. 2013. *The Undercommons: Fugitive Planning & Black Study*. Brooklyn, N.Y.: Autonomedia.

"Harper High School, Part One." 2013. *This American Life*, no. 487. Originally aired February 15. http://www.thisamericanlife.org/radio-archives/episode/487/harper-high-school-part-one.

Harris, Angela. 2011. "Heteropatriarchy Kills: Challenging Gender Violence in a Prison Nation." *Washington University Journal of Law and Policy* 37, no. 13.

Harris, Rebecca, and Dona Fernandes. 2013. "Timeline: The School Closings Debate." *Catalyst Chicago*, February 28. http://www.catalyst-chicago.org/notebook/2013/02/28/20852/timeline-school-closings-debate.

Harrison, Carlos. 2013. "Florida Student, 18, Arrested for Sex with Teammate, 14." *New York Times*, May 21.

Harris-Perry, Melissa. 2011. *Sister Citizen: Shame, Stereotypes, and Black Women in America*. New Haven, Conn.: Yale University Press.

Harry, Beth, and Janette Klingner. 2005. *Why Are There So Many Minority Students in Special Education? Understanding Race and Disability in Schools*. New York: Teachers College Press.

Hartman, Saidiya V. 1997. *Scenes of Subjection: Terror, Slavery, and Self-Making in Nineteenth-Century America*. New York: Oxford University Press.

———. 2007. *Lose Your Mother: A Journey Along the Atlantic Slave Route*. New York: Farrar, Straus and Giroux.

Hebdige, Dick. 1988. *Hiding in The Light: On Images and Things*. London: Routledge.

Heffernan, Shannon. 2013. "CTA Expands Employment Program for People Exiting Prison." WBEZ, March 6. http://www.wbez.org/news/cta-expands -employment-program-people-exiting-prison-105942.

Henig, Robin Marantz. 2010. "What Is It about 20-Somethings?" *New York Times*, August 18.

Herbert, Bob. 2007. "6-Year-Olds under Arrest." *New York Times*, April 8.

———. 2010. "Too Long Ignored." *New York Times*, August 20.

Herman, Joshua. 2010. "Sexting: It's No Joke, It's a Crime." *Illinois Bar Journal* 98, no. 4: 192.

Herzing, Rachel. 2015. "Big Dreams and Bold Steps Towards a Police Free Future." *Truthout*. September 16. http://www.truth-out.org/opinion/item/32813 -big-dreams-and-bold-steps-toward-a-police-free-future.

High HOPES Campaign. 2012. "From Policy to Standard Practice: Restorative Justice in Chicago Public Schools." Community Renewal Society, February. http://www.box.com/s/86i7djik1i72p47tnlnf.

Himmelstein, Katherine, and Hannah Bruckner. 2011. "Criminal-Justice and School Sanctions against Non-heterosexual Youth: A National Longitudinal Study." *Pediatrics* 12, no. 1: 48–57.

Horowitz, Emily. 2015. *Protecting Our Kids: How Sex Offender Laws Are Failing Us*. Santa Barbara, Calif.: Praeger.

Horwitz, Sari. 2014. "State Takes Steps to Reduce Sexual Assault in Prisons." *Washington Post*, May 28.

Hu, Winnie. 2011. "Bullying Law Puts New Jersey Schools on Spot." *New York Times*, August 30.

Human Rights Watch. 2003. "Ill-Equipped: U.S. Prisons and Offenders with Mental Illness." http://www.hrw.org/reports/2003/usa1003/usa1003.pdf.

———. 2013. *Raised on the Registry: The Irreparable Harm of Placing Children on Sex Offender Registries in the US*. Human Rights Watch. http://www.hrw.org /sites/default/files/reports/us0513_ForUpload_1.pdf.

Humphreys, Laud. 1970. *Tearoom Trade: Impersonal Sex in Public Spaces*. Chicago: Aldine.

Hunt, Kasie. 2014. "Bill Clinton: Prison Sentences to Take Center Stage in 2016." MSNBC News, October 8. http://www.msnbc.com/msnbc/bill-clinton-prison -sentences-take-center-stage-2016.

Hussain, Rummana. 2013. "Convicted Serial Rapist Sentenced to 75 Years for Sexual Assaults." *Chicago Sun Times*, December 4.

Illinois Department of Corrections Facilities Information. 2011. http://www.idoc .state.il.us/subsections/facilities/information.asp?instchoice=mpb.

Illinois Department of Juvenile Justice. 2009. "Illinois Juvenile Justice Commission Annual Report to the Governor and General Assembly for Calendar

Years 2007 and 2008." Illinois Department of Human Services, February 10. http://www.dhs.state.il.us/page.aspx?item=43000.

Illinois Juvenile Justice Commission. 2014. *Improving Illinois' Response to Sexual Offenses Committed by Youth: Recommendations for Law, Policy and Practice.* Illinois Juvenile Justice Commission. http://ijjc.illinois.gov/sites/ijjc.illinois .gov/files/assets/IJJC%20-%20Improving%20Illinois%27%20Response%20to %20Sexual%20Offenses%20Committed%20by%20Youth%20-%20No%20Ap pendices%20updated.pdf.

INCITE! Women of Color Against Violence. 2003. "Community Accountability Working Document." http://www.incite-national.org/index.php?s=93.

———. 2006. *Color of Violence: The INCITE! Anthology.* Boston: South End Press.

INCITE! Women of Color Against Violence and Critical Resistance. 2008. "The Critical Resistance and INCITE! Statement on Gender Violence and the Prison Industrial Complex." In CR10 Publication Collective (Ed.), *Abolition Now! Ten Years of Strategy and Struggle Against the Prison Industrial Complex,* 15–20. Oakland, Calif.: AK Press.

Institute for Metropolitan Affairs, Daniel Clark, Jennifer Janichek, and Kathleen Kane-Willis. 2006. *Intersecting Voices: Impacts of Illinois' Drug Policies.* Illinois Consortium on Drug Policies. http://www.roosevelt.edu/ima/pdfs/intersecting Voices.pdf.

Irvine, Martha. 2003. "Adult at 18? Who Are You Kidding? The Age Is Now 26." *Los Angeles Times,* October 26.

Isensee, Laura. 2014. "Feds Investigate Racial Complaint against School Closures." *Houston Public Media,* July 17. http://www.houstonpublicmedia. org/news/feds-investigate-racial-complaint/.

James, Joy. 2005. *The New Abolitionists: (Neo) Slave Narratives and Contemporary Prison Writings.* Albany: State University of New York Press.

Jarrett, Valerie and Broderick Johnson. 2014. "My Brother's Keeper: A New White House Initiative to Empower Boys and Young Men of Color." White House Blog Post. February 27. https://www.whitehouse.gov/blog/2014/02/27 /my-brother-s-keeper-new-white-house-initiative-empower-boys-and-young -men-color.

Jashnani, Gaurav, R. J. Maccani, and Alan Greig, 2011. "What Does It Feel Like When Change Finally Comes?" In *The Revolution Starts at Home! Confronting Intimate Violence within Activist Communities,* edited by Ching-In Chen, Jai Dulani, and Leah Lakshmi Piepzna-Samarasinha, 217–36. Boston: South End Press.

Jenkins, Phillip. 1998. *Moral Panic: Changing Conceptions of the Child Molester.* New Haven, Conn.: Yale University Press.

Jennings, Angel. 2013. "L.A. sees parks as a weapon against sex offenders." *LA Times*. February 28.

John Howard Association. 2010. "Summary: Too Many, Too Long: Monitoring Tour of Dwight Correctional Center Report." John Howard Association.

Johnson, Paula. 2003. *Inner Lives: Voices of African American Women in Prison*. New York: New York University Press.

Jones, Walter. 2010. "Judge Removes Harlem Woman from Sex Offender List." *Augusta Chronicle*, September 18. http://chronicle.augusta.com/latest-news /2010-09-18/woman-ga-sex-registry.

Justice Policy Institute. 2002. "Cellblocks or Classrooms? The Funding of Higher Education and Corrections and Its Impact on African American Men." http://www. justicepolicy.org/images/upload/0209_REP_CellblocksClassrooms_BBAC.pdf.

Kaba, Mariame, and Frank Edwards. 2012. "Policing Chicago Public Schools: A Gateway to the School-to-Prison Pipeline." Project NIA, January. https:// policeinschools.wordpress.com/.

Kaplan, Thomas. 2012. "New York Has Some Prisons to Sell You." *New York Times*, May 27.

———. 2014. "Cuomo Drops Plan to Use State Money to Pay for College Classes for Inmates." *New York Times*, April 2.

Karp, Sarah. 2009. "Duncan Says Turnarounds Not to Blame for School Violence." *Catalyst Chicago*, October 7. http://www.catalyst-chicago.org/notebook /2009/10/07/duncan-says-turnarounds-not-blame-school-violence.

Katz, Cindi. 2008. "Childhood as Spectacle: Relays of Anxiety and the Reconfiguration of the Child." *Cultural Geographies* 15, no. 1: 5–17.

Kelley, Robin. 2002. *Freedom Dreams*. Boston: Beacon Press.

Kelly, Esteban Lance. 2012. "Philly Stands Up: Inside the Politics and Poetics of Transformative Justice and Community." *Social Justice* 37, no. 4: 44–57.

Kempadoo, Kamala. 2005. "Introduction: From Moral Panic to Global Justice: Changing Perspectives on Trafficking." In *Trafficking and Prostitution Reconsidered: New Perspectives on Migration, Sex Work, and Human Rights*, edited by K. Kempadoo, J. Sanghera, and B. Pattanaik. Boulder, Colo.: Paradigm.

Keung, Nicholas. 2009. "'Status Indians' Face Threat of Extinction." *Star Canada*, May 10.

Kilgore, James. 2014. "The Spread of Electronic Monitoring: No Quick Fix for Mass Incarceration." *Truth-Out*, July 20. http://truth-out.org/news/item/25232 -the-spread-of-electronic-monitoring-no-quick-fix-for-mass-incarceration.

Kim, Catherine, Daniel Losen, and Damon Hewitt. 2010. *The School to Prison Pipeline: Structuring Legal Reform*. New York: New York University Press.

Kim, Jeanne. 2013. "Gun Rights, Gun Control and a Local Push to Tax Guns and Their Ammo." *Chicago Bureau*. January 16. http://www.chicago-bureau.org /gun-rights-gun-control-and-a-local-push-to-tax-guns-and-their-ammo/.

Kim, Mimi. 2009. "Alternative interventions to intimate violence: Defining political and pragmatic challenges." In *Restorative Justice and Violence against Women* edited by James Ptacek, 193–217. New York: Oxford University Press.

———. 2012. "Moving beyond critique: Creative Interventions and reconstructions of community accountability." *Social Justice,* 37, no. 4, 14–35.

Kincaid, James. 1992. *Child-Loving: The Erotic Child and Victorian Culture.* New York: Routledge.

———. 1998. *Erotic Innocence: The Culture of Child Molesting.* Durham, N.C.: Duke University Press.

Knox, Richard. 2010. "The Teen Brain: It's Just Not Grown Up Yet." NPR, March 1. http://www.npr.org/templates/story/story.php?storyId=124119468.

Koch, Wendy. 2006. "Development Bars Sex Offenders." *USA Today,* June 15.

Kosciw, Joseph, Emily Greytak, Elizabeth Diaz, and Mark Bartkiewicz. 2010. *The 2005 National School Climate Survey: The Experience of Lesbian, Gay, Bisexual, and Transgendered Students in Our Nation's Schools.* New York: GLSEN.

Koss, Mary. 2009. "Restorative Justice for Acquaintance Rape and Misdemeanor Sex Crimes. " In *Restorative Justice and Violence Against Women,* edited by James Ptacek (pp. 193–217). New York: Oxford University Press.

Krisberg, Barry. 2005. *Redeeming Our Children.* Thousand Oaks, Calif.: Sage.

———. 2007. "And Justice for Some: Differential Treatment of Youth of Color in the Justice System." National Center on Crime and Delinquency, January.

Kristof, Nicholas. 2013. "Slavery Isn't a Thing of the Past." *New York Times,* November 6.

Kumashiro, Kevin K. 2008. *The Seduction of Common Sense: How the Right Has Framed the Debate on America's Schools.* New York: Teachers College Press.

Kunzel, Regina. 2008. "Lessons in Being Gay: Queer Encounters in Gay and Lesbian Prison Activism." *Radical History Review* 100: 11–37.

Lally, Kathy. 2014. "Putin: Gay People Will Be Safe at Olympics if They 'Leave Kids Alone.'" *Washington Post,* January 17.

Lamble, Sarah. 2013. Panelist. "Critical Criminology in a Changing World—Tradition and Innovation," European Group for the Study of Deviance and Social Control Annual Meeting. Oslo, Norway, August 29–September 1.

Lancaster, Roger. 2011. *Sex Panic and the Punitive State.* Berkeley: University of California Press.

Lane, Charles. 2005. "5–4 Supreme Court Abolishes Juvenile Executions." *Washington Post,* March 2.

Lanza-Kaduce, Lonn, Charles E. Frazier, Jodi Lane, and Donna M. Bishop. 2002. "Juvenile Transfer to Criminal Court Study." Florida Department of Juvenile Justice, January 8. http://www.prisonpolicy.org/scans/juveniletransfers.pdf.

Laura, Crystal. 2014. *Being Bad: My Baby Brother and the School-to-Prison Pipeline*. New York: Teachers College Press.

La Vigne, Nancy G., Cynthia A. Mamalian, Jeremy Travis, and Christy Visher. 2003. "A Portrait of Prisoner Re-entry in Illinois." *Urban Institute Report*, April 17. http://www.urban.org/url.cfm?ID=410662.

La Vigne, Nancy G., Christy Visher, and Jennifer L. Castro. 2004. "Chicago Prisoners' Experiences Returning Home." *Urban Institute Report*, December. http://www.urban.org/UploadedPDF/311115_ChicagoPrisoners.pdf.

Lawston, Jodie, and Ashley Lucas. 2011. *Razor Wire Women: Prisoners, Activists, Scholars, and Artists*. New York: SUNY Press.

Legal Action Center. 2004. *After Prison: Roadblocks to Reentry*. http://www.lac.org/roadblocks-to-reentry/upload/lacreport/LAC_PrintReport.pdf.

Lemire, Elise. 2002. *Miscegenation: Making Race in America*. Philadelphia: University of Pennsylvania Press.

Levine, Judith. 2002. *Harmful to Minors: The Perils of Protecting Children from Sex*. Minneapolis: University of Minnesota Press.

Lewin, Tamar. 2010. "Rethinking Sex Offender Laws for Youth Texting." *New York Times*, March 20.

Lewis, Karen. 2013. "Shifting the Mark: Why School Closings Are Wrong." *Chicago Tribune*, March 29.

Lipman, Pauline. 2003. *High Stakes Education: Inequality, Globalization, and Urban School Reform*. New York: RoutledgeFalmer.

Lipman, Pauline, Kelly Vaughan, and Rhoda Ray Gutierrez. 2014. "Root Shock: Parents' Perspectives on School Closings in Chicago." Collaborative for Equity and Justice in Education, June. http://ceje.uic.edu/wp-content/uploads/2014/06/Root-Shock-Report-Compressed.pdf.

Liptak, Adam. 2010. "Justices Limit Life Sentences for Juveniles." *New York Times*, May 17.

Lochner, Lance, and Enrico Moretti. 2004. "The Effect of Education on Crime: Evidence from Prison Inmates, Arrests, and Self-Reports." *American Economic Review* 94, no. 1: 155–89.

"Locked In: The Costly Criminalisation of the Mentally Ill." 2013. *The Economist*, August 3. http://www.economist.com/news/united-states/21582535-costly-criminalisation-mentally-ill-locked?fsrc=scn/tw_ec/locked_in.

Logan, Wayne. 2009. *Knowledge as Power: Criminal Registration and Community Notification Laws in America*. Stanford, Calif.: Stanford University Press.

Lohr, Kathy. 2006. "Sex Offenders Screened Out of Some Neighborhoods." NPR, October 10. http://www.npr.org/templates/story/story.php?storyId=6231080.

Long, Ray, and Monique Garcia. 2012. "Quinn Moving Forward on Prison Closures." *Chicago Tribune*, June 19.

Lopez, Mark Hugo, and Michael T. Light. 2009. "A Rising Share: Hispanics and Federal Crime." Pew Hispanic Center, February 18. http://pewhispanic.org /files/reports/104.pdf.

Lorde, Audre. 1984. *Sister Outsider: Essays and Speeches.* Trumansburg, N.Y.: Crossing Press.

Losen, Daniel J. 2011. "Discipline Policies, Successful Schools, and Racial Justice." Boulder, Colo.: National Education Policy Center. http://nepc.colorado .edu/publication/discipline-policies.

Losen, Daniel J., and Gary Orfield, eds. 2002. *Racial Inequality in Special Education.* Cambridge, Mass.: Harvard Education Press.

Losen, Daniel J., and Russell Skiba. 2010. "Suspended Education: Urban Middle Schools in Crisis." Southern Poverty Law Center. http://www.splcenter.org /sites/default/files/downloads/publication/Suspended_Education.pdf.

Lovett, Ian. 2013. "Restricted Group Speaks Up, Saying Sex Crime Measures Go Too Far." *New York Times,* October 1.

Low, Setha. 2004. *Behind the Gates: Life, Security, and the Pursuit of Happiness in Fortress America.* New York: Routledge.

———. 2005. "How Private Interests Take Over Public Space: Zoning, Taxes, and Incorporation of Gated Communities." In *The Politics of Public Space,* edited by Setha Low and Neil Smith. New York: Routledge.

———. 2008. "The Fortification of Residential Neighborhoods and the New Emotions of Home." Special issue, M. Van der Land and L. Reinders, eds., *Housing, Theory, and Society* 25, no. 1: 47–65.

Lowe, Kenneth, and Kurt Erickson. 2013. "Dwight Prison Set to Close March 31; Mayor Calls News 'Devastating.'" *Pantagraph News,* March 6. http://www .pantagraph.com/news/local/dwight-prison-set-to-close-march-mayor-calls -news-devastating/article_947e2f02–86b5–11e2-b23b-0019bb2963f4.html.

Luker, Kristin. 1998. "Sex, Social Hygiene, and the State: The Double-Edged Sword of Social Reform." *Theory and Society* 27: 601–34.

Lutton, Linda. 2013. "Few Chicago School Closings Will Move Kids to Top-Performing Schools." WBEZ, May 19. http://www.wbez.org/news/few-chi cago-school-closings-will-move-kids-top-performing-schools-107261.

Lyderson, Kari, and Carlos Javier Ortiz. 2012. "More Young People Are Killed in Chicago Than Any Other American City." *Chicago Reporter,* January 25.

"Lynching and the Death Penalty." 2012. Symposium at the University of Texas School of Law, March 23–24.

Maidenberg, Micah. 2009. "Anderson Situation Reverberates: Local Parolee Program Named in Civil Suit." *Chicago Journal,* December 9.

Main, Frank, and Rummana Hussain. 2011. "Sex Assault Victim: What Happened . . . Was Completely Preventable." *Chicago Sun Times,* December 3.

Maki, John. 2013. "JHA's Statement on Dwight's Proposed Closure: Without a Plan to Safely Reduce Illinois' Prison Population, Closing Dwight Will Make a Bad Problem Worse." John Howard Association of Illinois. http://www.thejha.org/dwightclosure.

Makin, Kirk. 2012. "Where the Supreme Court Went Wrong on HIV Disclosure." *Globe and Mail*, October 12. http://www.theglobeandmail.com/news/national/where-the-supreme-court-went-wrong-on-hiv-disclosure/article4610682/.

Manly, George, and Chesly Wright. 1955. "Education Prepares Convicts for Future Freedom: Stateville and Joliet." *Chicago Daily Tribune*, July 9.

Marcum, Diana. 2010. "Standing Up for a Dream: With a Vote Due Soon on the Legislation, Undocumented Students Are Shedding Their Secrecy and Speaking Out." *Los Angeles Times*, November 28.

Marks, Kathy. 2013. "Australia Takes Symbolic Step to Recognising Aboriginal Rights." *The Independent*, February 13.

Marlan, Tori. 2005. "Prisoner of the Past." *Chicago Reader*, April 7.

Martinez, Michael. 2012. "New La. Law: Sex Offenders Must List Status on Facebook, Other Social Media." *CNN*, June 21. http://www.cnn.com/2012/06/20/tech/louisiana-sex-offenders-social-media/.

Mauer, Marc, and Meda Chesney-Lind, eds. 2003. *Invisible Punishment: The Collateral Consequences of Mass Imprisonment*. New York: New Press.

McBride, Dwight. 2001. *Impossible Witnesses: Truth, Abolitionism, and Slave Testimony*. New York: New York University Press.

McClain, Dani. 2014. "'Black Women, Like Black Men, Scar': Conversation on My Brother's Keeper Heats Up." *The Nation*, June 18.

McCready, Lance. 2010. *Making Space for Diverse Masculinities: Difference, Intersectionality, and Engagement in an Urban High School*. New York: Peter Lang.

McCreery, Patrick. 2008. "Save Our Children / Let Us Marry: Gay Activists Appropriate the Rhetoric of Child Protectionism." *Radical History Review* 100: 186–207.

McKinley, Jesse and James McKinley Jr. 2016. "Cuomo Proposes Higher-Education Initiative in New York Prisons." *New York Times*, January 10.

McKittrick, Katherine (Ed). 2015. *Sylvia Wynter: On Being Human as Praxis*. Durham, N.C.: Duke University Press.

McNally, Joel. 2003. "A Ghetto Within a Ghetto." *Rethinking Schools Online* 17, no. 3. http://www.rethinkingschools.org/restrict.asp?path=archive/17_03/ghet173.shtml.

Mears, Daniel P. 2006. "Evaluating the Effectiveness of Supermax Prisons." Urban Institute, March. http://www.urban.org/uploadedPDF/411326_supermax_prisons.pdf.

Meiners, Erica. 2007. *Right to Be Hostile: Schools, Prisons, and the Making of Public Enemies*. New York: Routledge.

Meiners, Erica, and Therese Quinn. 2009. "Doing and Feeling Research in Public: Queer Organizing for Public Education and Justice." *International Journal of Qualitative Studies in Education* 23, no. 2: 147–64.

Meisner, Jason, and Steve Schmadeke. 2014. "Lawsuit Accuses Cook County of Allowing 'Sadistic Culture' at Jail." *Chicago Tribune,* February 27.

Meissner, Doris, Donald M. Kerwin, Muzaffar Chishti, and Claire Bergeron. 2013. "Immigration Enforcement in the United States: The Rise of a Formidable Machinery." *Migration Policy Institute,* January. http://carnegie.org /fileadmin/Media/Image_Galleries/immigration_enforcement_in__us_MPI _report.pdf.

Metzl, Jonathan. 2010. *The Protest Psychosis: How Schizophrenia Became a Black Disease.* Boston, MA.: Beacon Press.

Mihalopoulos, Dan. 2013. "Toni Preckwinkle Rips Emanuel, Says CPS Closure Plan 'Weakens Our Public Schools.'" *Chicago Sun-Times,* May 16.

Miller, Lisa. 2013. "Cyberbullying Law Shields Teachers from Student Tormentors." NPR, February 19. http://www.npr.org/2013/02/19/172329526/cyber -bulling-law-shields-teachers-from-student-tormentors.

Mogul, Joey, Andrea Ritchie, and Kay Whitlock. 2011. *Queer (In)Justice: The Criminalization of LGBT People in the United States.* Boston: Beacon Press.

Morgan, Joe. 2013. "Man 'Guilty' of Fraud for Not Telling Girlfriend He Was Trans." *Gay Star News,* March 7. http://www.gaystarnews.com/article/man -%E2%80%98guilty%E2%80%99-fraud-not-telling-girlfriend-he-was-trans 070313.

Morgan, Mandy. 2012. "Toddlers and Tears: The Sexualization of Young Girls." *Desert News,* November 17. http://www.deseretnews.com/article/865567072 /Toddlers-and-Tears-The-sexualization-of-young-girls.html?pg=all.

Morris, Monique W., Michael Sumner, and Jessica Z. Borja. 2008. "A Higher Hurdle: Barriers to Employment for Formerly Incarcerated Women." *Berkeley Law,* December. http://www.law.berkeley.edu/files/A_Higher_Hurdle _December_2008(1).pdf.

Morrison, Toni. 1994. Afterword to *The Bluest Eye.* New York: Penguin.

Moser, Whet. 2011. "Innocent until Proven Guilty? Not in Public Housing." *Chicago Magazine,* September 6.

Moten, Fred and Stefano Harney. 2004. "The University and the Undercommons: Seven Theses." *Social Text* 79, no. 22: 101–15.

Muhammad, Charlene. 2014. "Punishing Bullies or Targeting Black Youth?" *Final Call,* May 22. http://www.finalcall.com/artman/publish/National_News _2/article_101450.shtml.

Muhammad, Khalil Gibran. 2010. *The Condemnation of Blackness: Race, Crime, and the Making of Modern Urban America.* Cambridge, Mass.: Harvard University Press.

Muñoz, José Esteban. 2009. *Cruising Utopia: The Then and There of Queer Futurity*. New York: New York University Press.

Murakawa, Naomi. 2015. *The First Civil Right: How Liberals Built Prison America*. Oxford: Oxford University Press.

Murakawa, Naomi, and Katherine Beckett. 2010. "The Penology of Racial Innocence." *Law and Society Review* 44, no. 3/4: 695–730.

"Murderers Released: Illinois Prisoners Freed in Budget Shortfall." 2010. *Huffington Post*, March 18. http://www.huffingtonpost.com/2010/01/06/murderers -released-illino_n_413172.html.

Muwakkil, Salim. 2016. "Not Your Grandfather's Black Freedom Movement: An Interview with BYP100's Charlene Carruthers." *In These Times*. February 8. http://inthesetimes.com/article/18755/charlene-carruthers-on-byp200-Laquan -McDonald-and-police-violence.

Na, Chongmin, and Denise G. Gottfredson. 2011. "Police Officers in Schools: Effects on School Crime and the Processing of Offending Behaviors." *Justice Quarterly*, October: 1–32. doi:10.1080/07418825.2011.615754.

Nair, Yasmin. 2013. "Bars for Life: LGBTQs and Sex Offender Registries." *Windy City Times*, May 8. http://www.windycitymediagroup.com/lgbt/Bars-For-Life -LGBTQs-and-sex-offender-registries/42714.html.

Napolitano, Janet. 2012. "Exercising Prosecutorial Discretion with Respect to Individuals Who Came to the United States as Children." Department of Homeland Security Memorandum. June 12. http://www.dhs.gov/xlibrary /assets/s1-exercising-prosecutorial-discretion-individuals-who-came-to-us-as -children.pdf.

National Center for Victims of Crime. 2004. "Spousal Rape Laws: 20 Years Later." http://www.ncvc.org/ncvc/main.aspx?dbName=DocumentViewer&D ocumentID=32701.

National Employment Law Project. 2012. "The Low-Wage Recovery and Growing Inequality." National Employment Law Project Data Brief. August. http:// www.nelp.org/content/uploads/2015/03/LowWageRecovery2012.pdf.

Neyfakh, Leon. 2016. "Obama Just Signed a Really Bad Criminal Justice Law." *Slate*. February 9. http://www.slate.com/articles/news_and_politics/crime/2016 /02/the_international_megan_s_law_obama_just_signed_is_bad_law.html.

Ngai, Mae M. 2004. *Impossible Subjects: Illegal Aliens and the Making of Modern America*. Princeton, N.J.: Princeton University Press.

Nix, Naomi. 2012. "Crete Withdraws from Detention Center Consideration." *Chicago Tribune*, June 12.

Noll, Ray. 2013. "Queer Rehab at Cook County Jail." Paper presented at the symposium "Asylums and Prisons: Deinstitutionalization and Decarceration," University of Chicago, May 3.

Norris, D. W. 2011. "Panel Hears from Murphysboro on IYC Closing." *The Southern*, October 12.

Northcott, Melissa. 2013. "A Survey of Victims of Sexual Violence." *The Victims of Crime Research Digest 6. Government of Canada.* http://www.justice.gc.ca/eng/rp-pr/cj-jp/victim/rd6-rr6/rd6-rr6.pdf.

Novak, Daniel. 1978. *The Wheel of Servitude: Black Forced Labor after Slavery.* Lexington: University Press of Kentucky.

NPC Research. 2013. "Testing the Cost Savings of Judicial Diversion. Final Report." March. http://www.npcresearch.com/Files/NY_Judicial_Diversion_Cost_Study_Report_0313.pdf.

Oakes, Jeannie. 1985. *Keeping Track: How Schools Structure Inequality.* Birmingham: Vail-Ballou Press.

Ocasio, Linda. 2013. "Sex and Labor Trafficking in the U.S.: A Q & A on the 21st Century Slave Trade. *The Star Ledger.* March 3. http://blog.nj.com/njv_editorial_page/2013/03/sex_and_labor_trafficking_in_t.html.

O'Connor, John. 2009. "AP Report: Illinois Prisons Shave Terms, Secretly Release Inmates." *State Journal–Register,* December 13.

Olivo, Antonio. 2010. "Chicago Students Step Up Debate on Immigration Reform." *Chicago Tribune,* January 18.

Olkon, Sara. 2008. "Ida B. Wells Complex Set to Close, but Some Residents Aren't Ready to Leave." *Chicago Tribune,* August 11.

O'Neil, Kevin. 2013. "CTA and Rail Union Agree to Reinstate Apprentice Program for Car Cleaners." *Chicago Now,* February 16. http://www.chicagonow.com/cta-tattler/2014/02/cta-and-rail-union-agree-to-reinstate-apprentice-program-for-car-cleaners/.

O'Neill, Helen. 2012. "Children of Undocumented Families 'Outing' Their Illegal Status." *Chicago Sun Times,* June 3.

Osborne, Duncan. 2005. "Disparate Results in NJ Lewdness Arrests." *Gay City News,* July 14. http://gaycitynews.com/gcn_428/disparatesresults.html.

Page, Joshua. 2004. "Eliminating the Enemy: The Import of Denying Prisoners Access to Higher Education in Clinton's America." *Punishment and Society* 6, no. 4: 357–78.

Parents Organized to Win, Educate and Renew—Policy Action Council [POWER-PAC] Elementary Justice Committee. 2010. "Parent-to-Parent Guide: Restorative Justice in Chicago Public Schools." *Community Organizing and Family Issues.* http://cofionline.org/files/parenttoparent.pdf.

Pascoe, C. J. 2007. *Dude, You're a Fag: Masculinity and Sexuality in High School.* Berkeley: University of California Press.

Patterson, Orlando. 1982. *Slavery and Social Death: A Comparative Study.* Cambridge, Mass.: Harvard University Press.

Payne, Charles M. 1997. "'I Don't Want Your Nasty Pot of Gold': Urban School Climate and Public Policy." Working paper, Institute for Policy Research, Northwestern University. http://www.eric.ed.gov/PDFS/ED412313.pdf.

"Pepsi to Pay $3.13 Million and Make Major Policy Changes to Resolve EEOC Finding of Nationwide Hiring Discrimination Against African Americans." 2012. United States Equal Opportunity Commission Press Release. January 1. http://www.eeoc.gov/eeoc/newsroom/release/1-11-12a.cfm.

Petit, Becky, and Bruce Western. 2004. "Mass Imprisonment and the Life Course: Race and Class Inequality in U.S. Incarceration." *American Sociological Review* 69, no. 2: 151–69.

Petteruti, Amanda, Nastassia Walsh, and Tracy Velázquez. 2009. "The Costs of Confinement: Why Good Juvenile Justice Policies Make Good Fiscal Sense." *Justice Policy Institute* 256. May. http://www.justicepolicy.org/images/upload /09_05_REP_CostsOfConfinement_JJ_PS.pdf.

Pew Center on the States. 2009. *One in 31: The Long Reach of American Corrections.* Washington, DC: The Pew Charitable Trusts. http://www.pewtrusts.org/~/media /legacy/uploadedfiles/pcs_assets/2009/pspp1in31reportfinalweb32609pdf.pdf.

Pfleger, Michael L. 2013. "When Your Own Union Is against You." *Chicago Tribune,* December 12.

Phillips, Anna. 2011. "City Reports More Suspensions, but Serious Crimes Declined." *New York Times,* November 1.

Pliley, Jessica. 2014. *Policing Sexuality: The Mann Act and the Making of the FBI.* Cambridge, Mass.: Harvard University Press.

Porter, Nicole D. 2012. "On the Chopping Block 2012: State Prison Closings." The Sentencing Project, December. http://sentencingproject.org/doc/publications /On%20the%20Chopping%20Block%202012.pdf.

Povinelli, Elizabeth. 2011. *Economies of Abandonment: Social Belonging and Endurance in Late Liberalism.* Durham, N.C.: Duke University Press.

Praetorious, Dean. 2011. "Jamey Rodemeyer, 14-Year-Old Boy, Commits Suicide after Gay Bullying; Parents Carry on Message." *Huffington Post,* September 20. http://www.huffingtonpost.com/2011/09/20/jamey-rodemeyer-suicide-gay -bullying_n_972023.html.

Precious Knowledge. 2011. DVD. Directed by Ari Palos and produced by Eren Isabel McGinnis. Dos Vatos Productions.

Ptacek, James, ed. 2010. *Restorative Justice and Violence against Women.* Oxford: Oxford University Press.

Quinn, Therese and Meiners, Erica. 2009. *Flaunt It! Queers Organizing for Public Education and Justice.* New York: Peter Lang.

Quinones, Sam. 2012. "LAPD Plans Separate Jail for Transgender Suspects." *Los Angeles Times,* April 15.

Ramos, Elliott. 2013. "Poor Data Keeps Chicago's Stop and Frisk Hidden from Scrutiny." WBEZ, September 12. http://www.chicagopublicradio.org/news /poor-data-keeps-chicagos-stop-and-frisk-hidden-scrutiny-108670.

Rape Abuse Incest National Network. n.d. "Sexual Assault Statistics." https:// rainn.org/statistics.

Rapping, Elayne. 2003. *Law and Justice as Seen on TV.* New York: New York University Press.

Rashbaum, William K. 2013. "With Special Courts, State Aims to Steer Women away from Sex Trade." *New York Times,* September 25.

"Reducing Youth Incarceration in the United States." 2013. Annie E. Casey Foundation, February 5. http://www.aecf.org/resources/reducing-youth-incar ceration-in-the-united-states/.

Reid, Kim and Knight, Michelle. 2006. "Disability Justifies Exclusion of Minority Students: A Critical History Grounded in Disability Studies." *Educational Researcher* 35, no. 6: 18–23.

Reynolds, Tina. 2010. "A Formerly Incarcerated Woman Takes on Policy." *Dialectical Anthropology* 34, no. 4: 453–55.

Rezin, Ashlee. 2013. "Local ICE Raid Ramps Up Efforts to Stop Deportations during Immigration Debate." *Progress Illinois,* June 17. http://www.progress illinois.com/posts/content/2013/06/14/local-ice-raid-prompts-activists-push -end-deportations-during-immigration-d.

Rhodes, Lorna. 2005. "Changing the Subject: Conversation in Supermax." *Cultural Anthropology* 20: 388–411.

Richie, Beth. 1996. *Compelled to Crime: The Gender Entrapment of Battered Black Women.* New York: Routledge.

———. 2012. *Arrested Justice: Black Women, Male Violence, and the Build-Up of a Prison Nation.* New York: New York University Press.

Right on Crime. n.d. *Reform in Action: State Initiatives.* http://www.righton crime.com/reform-in-action/state-initiatives/.

Roberts, Dorothy. 1997. *Killing the Black Body: Race, Reproduction, and the Meaning of Liberty.* New York: Vintage Books.

———. 2002. *Shattered Bonds: The Color of Child Welfare.* New York: Basic Civitas Books.

———. 2003. "Child Welfare and Civil Rights." *University of Illinois Law Review* 1: 171–82.

———. 2011. *Fatal Invention: How Science, Politics, and Big Business Re-create Race in the Twenty-First Century.* New York: New Press.

Rodríguez, Dylan. 2008. "'I Would Wish Death on You . . .': Race, Gender, and Immigration in the Globality of the U.S. Prison Regime." *Scholar and Feminist Online* 6, no. 3.

Rojas, Paula. 2007. "Are the Cops in Our Heads and Hearts?" From *The Revolution Will Not Be Funded, Beyond the Non-Profit Industrial Complex,* edited by INCITE! Women of Color Against Violence, 197–214. Boston, Mass.: South End Press.

Rondeaux, Candace. 2006. "Can Castration Be a Solution for Sex Offenders? Man Who Mutilated Himself in Jail Thinks So, but Debate on Its Effectiveness Continues in Va., Elsewhere." *Washington Post,* July 5.

Rose, Nikolas. 1999. *Powers of Freedom: Reframing Political Thought.* New York: Cambridge University Press.

Rosenberg, Robin. 2013. "There Is No Defense for Afluenza." *Slate,* December 17. http://www.slate.com/articles/health_and_science/medical_examiner/2013 /12/ethan_couch_affluenza_defense_critique_of_the_psychology_of_no_con sequences.html.

Russo, Charles and Carolyn Talbert-Johnson. 1997. "The Overrepresentation of African American Children in Special Education: The Resegregation of Educational Programming?" *Education and Urban Society* 9, no. 2: 136–47.

San Miguel, Guadalupe, Jr. 1997. "Roused from Our Slumbers." In *Latinos and Education: A Critical Reader,* edited by Antonia Darder, Rodolfo D. Torres, and Henry Gutierrez. New York: Routledge.

Saulny, Susan. 2009. "Attorney General, in Chicago, Pledges Youth Violence Effort." *New York Times,* October 7.

Savage, Charlie. 2013. "Justice Dept. Seeks to Curtail Stiff Drug Sentences." *New York Times,* August 12.

Schaffner, Laurie. 2002. "An Age of Reason: Paradoxes in the U.S. Legal Constructions of Adulthood." *International Journal of Children's Rights* 10: 201–32.

———. 2006. *Girls in Trouble with the Law.* Camden, N.J.: Rutgers University Press.

Schlikerman, Becky, and Fran Spielman. 2013. "Shuttered CPS Elementary to Be Home of Chicago High School for the Arts: Sources." *Chicago Sun-Times,* November 3.

Schlinkmann, Mark. 2015. "Ex-College Wrestler Gets 30 Years in HIV Case in St. Charles County." *St. Louis Dispatch.* July 13. http://www.stltoday.com /news/local/crime-and-courts/ex-college-wrestler-gets-years-in-hiv-case-in -st/article_c3123243-b8d3-58c9-97df-e2c5a504902a.html.

Schmadeke, Steve and Todd Lighty. 2015. "Cook County Jury Awards $18 Million to Three Rape Victims." *Chicago Tribune.* July. http://www.chicagotribune. com/news/local/breaking/ct-multimillion-verdict-halfway-house-met-2015 0716-story.html.

Schmich, Mary. 2011. "CTA Job May Carry Apprentice to Next Stop." *Chicago Tribune,* December 16.

Schoettler, Jim. 2013. "Cristian Fernandez Pleads Guilty to Manslaughter in Death of Half Brother." *Florida Times Union*, February 8.

Schultz, Brian. 2008. *Spectacular Things Happen Along the Way: Lessons from an Urban Classroom*. New York: Teachers College Press.

Schutz, Paris. 2013. "CTA's Ex-Offenders Program Ending." *Chicago Tonight*, WTTW, December 17. http://chicagotonight.wttw.com/2013/12/17/ctas-ex -offenders-program-ending.

Schwartzapfel, Beth. 2015. "Obama Is Reinstating Pell Grants for Prisoners." *The Marshall Project*. July 30. https://www.themarshallproject.org/2015/07/30 /obama-is-reinstating-pell-grants-for-prisoners#.HYYyTsNWu.

Schwarz, Alan. 2011. "School Discipline Study Raises Fresh Questions." *New York Times*, July 19.

"Search for Sex Offenders: There's an App for that." 2012. *WRAL.com*. http:// www.wral.com/news/local/story/10693554/.

The Sentencing Project. 2002. "Mentally Ill Offenders in the Criminal Justice System: An Analysis and Prescription." http://www.sentencingproject.org /doc/publications/sl_mentallyilloffenders.pdf.

———. 2008. "Reducing Racial Disparity in the Criminal Justice System: A Manual for Practitioners and Policymakers." http://www.sentencingproject.org /doc/publications/rd_reducingracialdisparity.pdf.

Sewell, Abby. 2011. "Halloween Night Restrictions are Added for Sex Offenders." *LA Times*, November 11.

Sharpe, Alex. 2014. "Criminalising Sexual Intimacy: Transgender Defendants and the Legal Construction of Non-Consent." *Criminal Law Review*, 207–23.

Shipps, Dorothy. 2006. *Chicago School Reform, Corporate Style: Chicago, 1880–2000*. Lawrence: University Press of Kansas.

Silliman, Jael, and Anannya Bhattacharjee. 2002. *Policing the National Body: Race, Gender, and Criminalization*. Cambridge, Mass.: South End Press.

Simkins, Sandra, Amy E. Hirsh, Erin McNamara Horvat, and Marjorie B. Moss. 2004. "The School to Prison Pipeline for Girls: The Role of Physical and Sexual Abuse." *Children's Legal Rights Journal* 24, no. 4: 56–72.

Simmons, Lizbet. 2009. "End of the Line: Tracing Racial Inequality from School to Prison." *Race/Ethnicity: Multidisciplinary Global Perspectives* 2, no. 2: 215–41.

Simon, Jonathan. 2000. "Megan's Law: Crime and Democracy in Late Modern America." *Law and Social Inquiry* 25: 1111–50.

———. 2007. *Governing through Crime: How the War on Crime Transformed American Democracy and Created a Culture of Fear*. New York: Oxford University Press.

Simons, D., S. Wurtele, and R. Durham. 2008. "Developmental Experiences of Child Sexual Abusers and Rapists." *Child Abuse and Neglect* 32: 549–60. New York: New Press.

Skiba, Russell J., Robert S. Michael, and Abra Carroll Nardo. 2002. "The Color of Discipline: Sources of Racial and Gender Disproportionality in School Punishment." *Urban Review* 34, no. 2: 317–42.

Slife, Erica, and Duaa Eldeib. 2011. "New Goal for Juvenile Center: Clear It Out." *Chicago Tribune,* December 9.

Smith, Andrea. 2005. *Conquest: Sexual Violence and American Indian Genocide.* Cambridge, Mass.: South End Press.

———. 2006. "Heteropatriarchy and the Three Pillars of White Supremacy." In *Color of Violence: The INCITE! Anthology,* edited by INCITE! Women of Color Against Violence, 66-74. Boston: South End Press.

Smith, Dorothy. 1975. *Women Look at Psychiatry.* Vancouver, B.C.: Press Gang Publishers.

Smith, Nat, and Eric A. Stanley. 2011. *Captive Genders: Trans Embodiment and the Prison Industrial Complex.* Oakland: AK Press.

Smith, Robin M., and Nirmala Erevelles. 2004. "Toward an Enabling Education: The Difference That Disability Makes." *Educational Researcher* 23, no. 8: 31–36.

Snyder, Sharon and David Mitchell. 2006. *Cultural Locations of Disability.* Chicago: University of Chicago Press.

Soderlund, Gretchen. 2005. "Running from the Rescuers: New U.S. Crusades against Sex Trafficking and the Rhetoric of Abolition." *NWSA Journal* 17, no. 3: 54–87.

Sojoyner, Damien. 2010. "Enclosures Abound: Black Cultural Autonomy, Prison Regime and Public Education." *Race Ethnicity and Education* 13, no. 3: 349–65.

———. 2013. "Black Radicals Make for Bad Citizens: Undoing the Myth of the School to Prison Pipeline." *Berkeley Review of Education* 4, no. 2: 241–63.

SOS Collective. 2010. "Safe OUTside the System: The SOS Collective." http://alp .org/ community/sos+safe+outside+the+system.

Soung, Patricia. 2011. "Social and Biological Constructions of Youth: Implications for Juvenile Justice and Racial Equity." *Northwestern Journal of Law and Social Policy* 6, no. 2: 428–44.

Spade, Dean. 2011. *Normal Life: Administrative Violence, Critical Trans Politics, and the Limits of Law.* Brooklyn, N.Y.: South End Press.

"SPLC Files Federal Lawsuit over Inadequate Medical, Mental Health Care in Alabama Prisons." 2014. Southern Poverty Law Center, June 17. http://www .splcenter.org/get-informed/news/splc-files-federal-lawsuit-over-inadequate -medical-mental-health-care-in-alabama-p.

"Staines Woman Dressed as Boy Jailed for Sex Assaults." 2012. BBC, March 5. http://www.bbc.co.uk/news/uk-england-surrey-17256641.

"Statewide Ban the Box: Reducing Unfair Barriers to Employment of People with Criminal Records." 2013. National Employment Law Project, November. http:// www.nelp.org/page/-/SCLP/ModelStateHiringInitiatives.pdf?nocdn=1.

Steelwater, Eliza. 2003. *The Hangman's Knot: Lynching, Legal Execution, and America's Struggle with the Death Penalty.* Oxford: Westview Press.

Steinmetz, Katy, 2015. "States Battle Over Bathroom Access for Transgender People." *Time.* March 6. http://time.com/3734714/transgender-bathroom -bills-lgbt-discrimination/.

Stern, Alexandra Minna. 2005. *Eugenic Nation: Faults and Frontiers of Better Breeding in Modern America.* Berkeley: University California Press.

Steurer, Stephen J., and Linda Smith. 2003. "Education Reduces Crime: Three State Recidivism Study." Correctional Education Association, February. http: //www.ceanational.org/PDFs/EdReducesCrime.pdf.

Stinson, Jeffrey. 2014. "More States and Cities Ban Employers from Using Criminal History to Block Hiring." *Buffalo News,* June 16.

Stockton, Kathryn. 2009. *The Queer Child: or, Growing Sideways in the Twentieth Century.* Durham, N.C.: Duke University Press.

Stoler, Laura Ann. 1995. *Race and the Education of Desire: Foucault's History of Sexuality and the Colonial Order of Things.* Durham, N.C.: Duke University Press.

Stovall, David. 2016. *Born Out of Struggle: Critical Race Theory, School Creation, and the Politics of Interruption.* Albany, N.Y.: SUNY Press.

Strom, Stephanie. 2010. "Mississippi A.C.L.U. Rejects $20,000 for Alternate Prom." *New York Times,* March 31.

Sudbury, Julia. 2004. *Global Lockdown: Race, Gender, and the Prison–Industrial Complex.* New York: Routledge.

———. 2011. "From Women Prisoners to People in Women's Prisons: Challenging the Gender Binary in Antiprison Work." In *Razor Wire Women: Prisoners, Activists, Scholars, and Artists,* edited by Jodie Michelle Lawston and Ashley E. Lucas. Albany: State University of New York Press.

Sylvia Rivera Law Project. 2007. *"It is a War in Here": A Report on the Treatment of Transgender and Intersex People in New York State Men's Prisons.* Sylvia Rivera Law Project. http://srlp.org/files/warinhere.pdf.

Terrell, Kellee. 2012. "Deadly Distinction: Chicago Has the Highest Murder Rate in the U.S." *BET,* February 1. http://www.bet.com/news/health/2012/02/01 /chicago-has-highest-murder-rate-in-the-u-s.html.

Thompkins, Douglas E. 2010. "The Expanding Prisoner Reentry Industry." *Dialectical Anthropology* 34, no. 4: 589–604.

Thompkins, Douglas E., Ric Curtis, and Travis Wendel. 2010. "Forum: The Prison Reentry Industry." *Dialectical Anthropology* 34, no. 4: 427–29.

Thompson, Isaiah. 2007. "Swept under the Bridge: Sex Offenders Are Ordered to Sleep Near a Center for Abused Kids." *Miami New Times,* March 8.

Thrupkaew, Noy. 2012. "A Misguided Moral Crusade." *New York Times,* September 22.

Thuma, Emily. 2014. "'Prison/Psychiatric State': Coalition Politics and Opposition to Institutional Violence in the Feminist 1970s." *Feminist Formations* 26, no. 2: 26–51.

Transformative Justice Law Project. n.d. "Who We Are?" http://tjlp.org/about /our-values/.

Transforming Conflict. n.d. "Restorative Approaches and Practices." http://www .transformingconflict.org/Restorative_Approaches_and_Practices.php.

Traub, James. 2000. "What No School Can Do." *New York Times*, January 16.

Tullis, Paul. 2013. "Can Forgiveness Play a Role in Criminal Justice?" *New York Times Magazine*, January 4.

Twohey, Megan. 2009. "St. Leonard Closes Doors to Sex Offenders: Julius Anderson Incidents Led Halfway House to Change." *Chicago Tribune*, December 6.

Uggen, Christopher, Sarah Shannon, and Jeff Manza. 2012. *State-Level Estimates of Felon Disenfranchisement in the United States, 2010.* Washington, D.C.: The Sentencing Project. http://sentencingproject.org/doc/publications/fd_State _Level_Estimates_of_Felon_Disen_2010.pdf.

U.S. Department of Education. "Civil Rights Data Collection." http://orcdata .ed.gov.

Ustinova, Anatasia. 2012. "Charter-School Growth Fuels Chicago Teacher Fears." *Bloomberg Businessweek*, September 13. http://www.bloomberg.com /news/2012–09–13/charter-school-growth-fuels-chicago-teacher-fears.html.

Valbrun, Marjorie. 2011. "States: Food Stamp, Welfare Bans for Drug Felons Counterproductive." *America's Wire*, April 9. http://newamericamedia.org/2011 /04/states-food-stamp-welfare-bans-for-drug-felons-counterproductive.php.

Vance, Carole S. 2011. "Thinking Trafficking, Thinking Sex." *GLQ: A Journal of Lesbian and Gay Studies* 17, no. 1: 135–43.

Vargas, Jose Antonio. 2011. "My Life as an Undocumented Immigrant." *New York Times*, June 22.

———. 2012. "Not Legal Not Leaving." *New York Times*, June 25.

Vaught, Sabina. 2011. *Racism, Public Schooling, and the Entrenchment of White Supremacy: A Critical Race Ethnography.* Albany, N.Y.: SUNY Press.

Vevea, Becky. 2012. "The Proportion of Privately Run Chicago Public Schools to Increase." WBEZ, December 11. http://www.wbez.org/news/proportion -privately-run-chicago-public-schools-increase-104303.

Viguerie, Richard. 2013. "A Conservative Case for Prison Reform." *New York Times*, June 9.

Voices of Youth in Chicago Education [VOYCE]. 2011. "Failed Policies, Broken Futures: The True Cost of Zero Tolerance in Chicago." http://www.voyce project.org/voyce-demands-end-harsh-discipline-chicago-public-schools.

Wacquant, Loïc. 2009. *Punishing the Poor: The Neoliberal Government of Social Insecurity.* Durham, N.C.: Duke University Press.

Wallace, Lewis. 2007. "Restoring Classroom Justice." *In These Times,* September 4. http://inthesetimes.com/article/3304/restoring_classroom_justice.

———. 2012. "Fast Food and Retail Workers March on the Magnificent Mile." WBEZ, September 13. http://www.wbez.org/news/fast-food-and-retail-workers -march-magnificent-mile-104377.

Wallace, Michelle. 1979. *Black Macho and the Myth of the Superwoman.* New York: Dial Press.

Waller, Mark S., Shannon M. Carey, Erin J. Farley, and Michael Rempel. 2013. "Testing the Cost Savings of Judicial Diversion." Center for Court Innovation, March. http://www.courtinnovation.org/sites/default/files/documents/NY _Judicial%20Diversion_Cost%20Study.pdf.

Ward, Edward. 2012. "Testimony of Edward Ward for the Senate Committee Hearing on 'Ending the School-to-Prison Pipeline.'" *Dignity in Schools,* December 12. http://www.dignityinschools.org/document/testimony-edward-ward-senate-committee-hearing-%E2%80%9Cending-school-prison -pipeline%E2%80%9D.

Ward, Geoff K. 2012. *The Black Child-Savers: Racial Democracy and Juvenile Justice.* Chicago: University of Chicago Press.

Watkins, William H. 2001. *The White Architects of Black Education: Ideology and Power in America, 1865–1954.* New York: Teachers College Press.

Wells, Carrie. 2013. "Towson Officials Try to Reassure Community about Student Patrols." *Baltimore Sun,* March 27.

Wells-Barnett, Ida B. 2002. *On Lynching.* Amherst: Humanity Books.

Westheimer, Joel, and Joseph Kahane. 2004. "What Kind of Citizen? The Politics of Education for Democracy." *American Educational Research Journal* 41, no. 2: 237–69.

"What Is the PIC? What Is Abolition?" (n.d.). *Critical Resistance.* http://critical resistance.org/about/not-so-common-language.

Wildeboer, Rob. 2014. "Cook County Paying Costs When CPD Fails to Register Sex Offenders." WBEZ, June 12. http://www.chicagopublicradio .org/news/cook-county-paying-costs-when-cpd-fails-register-sex-offenders -110262.

Wilderson, Frank. 2003. "The Prison Slave as Hegemony's (Silent) Scandal." *Social Justice* 30, no. 2: 18–27.

Willrich, Michael. 2003. *City of Courts: Socializing Justice in Progressive Era Chicago.* Cambridge: Cambridge University Press.

Winerip, Michael. 2013. "Revisiting the 'Crack Babies' Epidemic That Was Not." *New York Times,* May 20.

Winfield, Ann Gibson. 2007. *Eugenics and Education in America: Institutionalized Racism and the Implications of History, Ideology, and Memory.* New York: Peter Lang.

Winn, Maisha. 2010. *Girl Time: Literacy, Justice, and the School-to-Prison Pipeline*. New York: Teachers College Press.

WistTV10. 2012. "Quinn Confirms Plan to Close 14 IL Facilities." WisTV, February 23. http://www.wistv.com/story/16989115/quinn-confirms-plan-to-close-14-il-facilities.

Wolch, Jennifer R. 1990. *The Shadow State: Government and Voluntary Sector in Transition*. New York: Foundation Center.

Wolcott, David. 2005. *Cops and Kids: Policing Juvenile Delinquency in Urban America, 1890–1940*. Columbus: Ohio State University Press.

Wright, Richard. 2003. "Sex Offender Registration and Notification: Public Attention, Political Emphasis, and Fear." *Criminology and Public Policy* 3: 97–104.

Wun, Connie. 2016. "Against Captivity: Black Girls and School Discipline Policies in the Afterlife of Slavery." *Educational Policy* 30: 171–96.

Young, Iris Marion. 2003. "The Logic of Masculinist Protection: Reflections on the Current Security State." *Signs: Journal of Women in Culture and Society* 29, no. 1: 1–25.

Younge, Gary. 2013. "Arrests at Chicago Schools Protest." *The Guardian,* March 27. http://www.theguardian.com/world/2013/mar/28/arrests-chicago-schools-protest.

Young Women's Empowerment Project [YWEP]. 2009. "Girls Do What They Have to Do to Survive: Illuminating Methods Used by Girls in the Sex Trade and Street Economy to Fight Back and Heal." https://ywepchicago.files.wordpress.com/2011/06/girls-do-what-they-have-to-do-to-survive-a-study-of-resilience-and-resistance.pdf.

———. 2012. "Bad Encounter Line." https://ywepchicago.files.wordpress.com/2012/09/bad-encounter-line-report-2012.pdf.

———. n.d. "Street Youth Bill of Rights." http://ywepchicago.wordpress.com/our-work/our-campaign.

"Youth in the Adult System." 2015. Juvenile Law Center. http://www.jlc.org/current-initiatives/youth-criminal-justice-system/reducing-transfers-adult-system.

Zenovia, Dagny. 2014. "Changing Directions: Community Based Programs Aim to Redirect the 'School-to-Prison Pipeline.'" *Austin Chronicle*, June 6.

Zgoba, Kristen M., Michael Miner, Raymond Knight, Elizabeth Letourneau, Jill Levenson, and David Thornton. 2012. "A Multi-state Recidivism Study Using Static-99R and Static-2002 Risk Scores and Tier Guidelines from the Adam Walsh Act." *National Criminal Justice Reference Service*, November. https://www.ncjrs.gov/pdffiles1/nij/grants/240099.pdf.

Zimmer, Carl. 2011. "The Brain: The Trouble with Teens." *Discover Magazine*, March 24.

Zook, Jim. 1994. "Ban on Pell Grants to Inmates Crushes Prison-Education Efforts." *Chronicle of Higher Education*, November 9.

Index

Erica R. Meiners is Bernard J. Brommel Distinguished Research Professor at Northeastern Illinois University. She is the author of *Right to Be Hostile: Schools, Prisons, and the Making of Public Enemies* (2007) and of articles in *Meridians, Social Justice, Women's Studies Quarterly, In These Times,* and *Radical Teacher.* She teaches women's and gender studies, justice studies, and educational studies and is a member of the labor union University Professionals of Illinois.